STUDIES ON THE CHINESE ECONOMY

General Editors: Peter Nolan, Lecturer in Economics and Politics, University of Cambridge, and Fellow and Director of Studies in Economics, Jesus College, Cambridge, England; and Dong Fureng, Professor, Chinese Academy of Social Sciences, Beijing, China

This series analyses issues in China's current economic development, and sheds light upon that process by examining China's economic history. It contains a wide range of books on the Chinese economy past and present, and includes not only studies written by leading Western authorities, but also translations of the most important works on the Chinese economy produced within China. It intends to make a major contribution towards understanding this immensely important part of the world economy.

Published titles include:

Derong Chen
CHINESE FIRMS BETWEEN HIERARCHY AND MARKET

Dong Fureng
INDUSTRIALIZATION AND CHINA'S RURAL MODERNIZATION

Du Runsheng (*edited by Thomas R. Gottschang*)
REFORM AND DEVELOPMENT IN RURAL CHINA

Qimiao Fan and Peter Nolan (*editors*)
CHINA'S ECONOMIC REFORMS

Christopher Findlay, Andrew Watson and Harry X. Wu (*editors*)
RURAL ENTERPRISES IN CHINA

Michael Korzec
LABOUR AND THE FAILURE OF REFORM IN CHINA

Nicholas K. Menzies
FOREST AND LAND MANAGEMENT IN IMPERIAL CHINA

Ryōshin Minami
THE ECONOMIC DEVELOPMENT OF CHINA

Yuming Shen
INTERSECTORAL RESOURCE FLOWS AND CHINA'S ECONOMIC DEVELOPMENT

Hong Wang
CHINA'S EXPORTS SINCE 1979

Tim Wright (*editor*)
THE CHINESE ECONOMY IN THE EARLY TWENTIETH CENTURY

Yanrui Wu
PRODUCTIVE PERFORMANCE OF CHINESE ENTERPRISES

Haiquin Yang
BANKING AND FINANCIAL CONTROL OF REFORMING PLANNED ECONOMIES

Market and Institutional Regulation in Chinese Industrialization, 1978–94

Dic Lo
Lecturer in Economics
School of Oriental and African Studies
University of London

First published in Great Britain 1997 by
MACMILLAN PRESS LTD
Houndmills, Basingstoke, Hampshire RG21 6XS and London
Companies and representatives throughout the world

A catalogue record for this book is available from the British Library.

ISBN 0–333–66546–5

First published in the United States of America 1997 by
ST. MARTIN'S PRESS, INC.,
Scholarly and Reference Division,
175 Fifth Avenue, New York, N.Y. 10010

ISBN 0–312–16422–X

Library of Congress Cataloging-in-Publication Data
Lo, Dic, 1963–
Market and institutional regulation in Chinese industrialization, 1978–94 / Dic Lo.
p. cm.
Originally presented as the author's thesis (Ph.D.)—University of Leeds, 1994.
Includes bibliographical references and index.
ISBN 0–312–16422–X (cloth)
1. Industrialization—China. 2. China—Economic conditions—1976– 3. China—Economic policy—1976– I. Title.
HC427.92.L599 1996
338.951—dc20 96–27846
CIP

This book is printed on paper suitable for recycling and made from fully managed and sustained forest sources.

10 9 8 7 6 5 4 3 2 1
06 05 04 03 02 01 00 99 98 97

Printed in Great Britain by
The Ipswich Book Company Ltd
Ipswich, Suffolk

Contents

List of Tables

List of Figures

Preface and Acknowledgements

The objective of this book is both to construct an analytically enlightening account of China's experience of economic development and reform over the period 1978–94, and to engage with the policy debate over the transformation of the Soviet-type economic system. My starting point is that a study of this kind must be based on empirical investigations rather than *a priori* conceptions. Throughout the book, the reasoning has been derived from observed (stylized) facts rather than 'first principles' of economics.

This approach of course runs the risk of lacking theoretical sophistication. However, in view of the literature that is flooded with unrefined applications of established theoretical concepts/models and where too many empirically ill-founded policies have been prescribed, the approach adopted here is a necessary correction. I also attempt to remedy the shortcoming by means of synthesizing a range of relevant, alternative theoretical perspectives. This leaves open the possibility of drawing alternative inferences and conclusions from the study. Indeed, precisely because I do not work from the notion of the 'pure' market – that is, the possibility of a perfectly functioning market system – the overall conclusion I arrive at is far more open than most available studies. The conclusion states that both market and (non-market) institutional regulations have been indispensable in accounting for the successful facets of the Chinese experience.

In this connection, a word of moral matter is in order. My critical attitude towards the market-centred approaches that are predominant in the relevant literature, to be sure, involves a personal reason: as a socialist (in a moral if not political sense), I believe that public ownership – where workers are not subject to the full rigour of the impersonal market – is potentially more humane than private ownership. Yet this moral concern does not interfere in the analytics of the book. It does prompt me, in the course of writing, to view with vigilance those writings which adopt the market-centred approaches on the ground of faith, not their analytics. Indeed, throughout the book, I use the term systemic transformation instead of the widely-used term transition. The term transition implies the presumption of the possibility and desirability of something called the market economy. In contrast, the term transformation implies an open-ended process leading to the formation of a systemic/institutional framework that might incorporate the market mechanism but is not itself on the whole reducible to the market economy.

This book is a development of my PhD thesis which was submitted to the University of Leeds in 1994. The bulk of the research was done in 1991–94. But the evolution of the main concerns (if not the actual ideas) of the book can be traced back to several years earlier, when, as a journalist, I began to seriously watch the political and economic developments in China. During this process of evolution, I have incurred an intellectual debt to my teachers, friends and colleagues.

I wish especially to thank Malcolm Sawyer who supervised the thesis. Hugo Radice, Adrian Wood, Mahmood Messkoub and Paul Dunne, among others, have given useful comments and suggestions, for which I am grateful. Simon Peck and Graham Sykes have helped me to use the computers. Chris Edwards' sympathetic yet critical comment on my MA dissertation, which was submitted to the University of East Anglia in 1991 and has subsequently become Chapter 3 of this book, has been very helpful. Encouragement from Peter Nolan and Ajit Singh has helped to strengthen my confidence in conducting the research. Chapters 3 and 4 of the book have been presented at seminars in SOAS, and I have benefited from the comments of a number of colleagues, particularly Ben Fine and Christopher Howe.

A number of friends in Hong Kong have always been a source of inspiration. I would like to thank Cheng Yuk-shing, Thomas M.H. Chan, Tsang Shu-ki and Wang Xiaoqiang for their support and friendship.

Finally, I wish to express my gratitude to the publishers concerned for permission to reproduce or draw on my previously published work. Chapter 2 of the book is an abridged version of three articles, two of which being Lo (1995a) and Lo (1995b). Chapter 7 draws substantially on Lo (1995c).

This book is dedicated to my parents, my wife and my son.

1 Overview

INTRODUCTION: THE CHINA QUESTION

The performance of China's economy over the period 1978–94 has been spectacular. Amid most parts of the developing world experiencing a 'lost decade', and countries of the former Soviet bloc struggling to cope with a great depression, the Chinese economy continues to grow at a breath-taking pace (Table 1.1). Between 1978 and 1994, the country's gross national product (GNP), on average, grew by 9.8 per cent in real terms per annum, and GNP per capita by 8.4 per cent per annum.

Along with the growth of GNP there has also been a trend of marked progress in the industrial transformation of the Chinese economy, as well as improvement in its performance in the world market. During this same period, 1978–94, the average annual growth rate of gross industrial output value (in real terms) reached 15 per cent. In the meantime, the country's exports value increased from US$10bn to US$121bn, meaning an average annual growth rate of 17 per cent in nominal terms or 12 per cent in real terms (deflated by US consumer price index) during this 16-year period. By 1994, around 84 per cent of the exports value were accounted for by manufactured products and 26 per cent by mechanical and electronic goods. This increasing export competitiveness distinguishes China from both the Latin American import substitution regimes of the 1950s–60s and the East European reforming economies of the 1960s–70s, where the experiences of rapid growth associated with the initial phases of policy-institutional changes were not sustained for long. On the whole, it appears that the Chinese economy is converging towards the typical pattern of East Asian industrialization that is characterized by rapid growth of exports and the economy as a whole.

The Chinese economic performance depicted above, naturally gives rise to two issues for intellectual exploration: namely, (a) the impetus behind the past growth and the prospects for future growth; and (b) the nature of the institutional framework which has governed this process of growth. The second issue, which has far-reaching implications for the on-going transformation of the Soviet-type economic system, rests ultimately on the explanation to the first. This book thus attempts to identify the conducive and detrimental factors that have shaped the

Table 1.1 China's Economic Growth in International Comparison, 1978–94 (percentages)

	China	*Industrial Countries*	*Developing Countries*	*(former) USSR*	*Eastern Europe*
1978–88	9.7	2.6	3.4	3.5	2.6
1988–94	9.0	2.0	4.2	−9.6	−3.9

Sources: Figures after 1985 are from UN, *World Economic and Social Survey 1995: Current Trends and Policies in the World Economy*, pp. 300–1. Before 1985, figures of industrial countries and developing countries are from IMF, *International Financial Statistics Yearbook* 1993, pp. 100–1, 148–9, 278–9. Chinese figures from ZTN 1993, p. 31; Figures of USSR and Eastern Europe from (1) UN, *National Accounts Statistics: Main Aggregates and Detailed Tables* 1987, p. 1644, and 1990, p. 2061; (2) UN Economic Commission for Europe, *Economic Bulletin for Europe*, vol. 44 (1992), p. 26, vol. 43 (1991), p. 25, and vol. 41 (1989), p. 9; and (3) IMF *World Economic Outlook*, October 1993, p. 131.

Note: All figures are GDP average annual growth rates, except those of the USSR and Eastern Europe before 1985 which are growth rates of net material products. All 1994 figures are partly estimated. The former GDR is included in Eastern Europe until 1990 and in Industrial Countries after that. Developing countries include China.

Chinese industrialization process, and based on which to clarify the actual forms and effects of market and non-market regulation thereof. This forms the basis upon which we can embark on drawing lessons from Chinese economic development and reform for wider issues concerning the transformation of the Soviet-type economic system.

THE INTELLECTUAL CONTEXT

The literature of studies on China's economic reform and development has undergone a significant change in recent years. Conspicuously, in contrast to the previously predominated approach of assessing the reality from the standpoint of purely *a priori* conceptions, there have emerged a number of breakthroughs heading towards the kind of appraisal that is based on empirical investigations.

One major factor which accounts for the shift of intellectual orientation is the sharp contrast between China and countries of the former Soviet bloc under transformation, both in terms of reform strategy and actual economic development. From the standpoint of orthodox Western economics, this contrast has given rise to a paradox: 'according to almost any version of standard mainstream property rights theory, what has been described as the "East European model" basically represents the correct approach to transformation, while what we are calling the "Chinese model" should represent a far-out recipe for economic disaster . . . The central paradox is the enormous success of the Chinese model in practice, contrasted with the sputtering, tentative, comparatively unsuccessful experience with the East European model.' (Weitzman 1993, p. 549) It is this intellectual paradox which has prompted previous sceptics or critics of China's reform to think twice.

Given the contradiction between theory and practice, a common feature of the studies which I consider to be embodying breakthroughs is the adoption of an evolutionary approach which, in effect, abandons the pursuit of optimalities and simple dismissal of imperfections.[1] The focus shifts to investigate the actual evolution of China's economic system and the working of this conceptually deficient system in the achievement of the spectacular economic development. Substantively, the following propositions have been raised:

(a) that China's economic reform and actual development have been, by and large, interrelated
(b) that the reform has successfully brought into operation genuine product market competition, both in terms of price determination and enterprise behaviour, which has been an impetus behind the economic development
(c) many significant market imperfections, especially in the labour and capital markets, continue to exist and have led to outcomes which, while complex, are not clearly detrimental
(d) whilst reform was indispensable in generating the growth, the latter has also been a pre-condition for the success of the former
(e) both of the market-oriented and less market-oriented sectors of the Chinese economy have exhibited substantial improvement in productivity, with the former somewhat leading.

The propositions listed above are not accepted generally, but rather with varied degrees of contention. People sticking to a fundamentalist vision of orthodox theory are likely to accuse the propositions of undermining the universal applicability of the principles of the market, and of overstating the ability of the Soviet-type economic system to be reformed (Fischer 1993). Indeed, for fundamentalist writers, these propositions imply an unacceptable concession to the view that the Chinese

Table 1.2 Shares of Gross Value of Industrial Output by Ownership Sectors, 1965–94 (percentages)

	SOEs	*COEs*	*IOEs*	*OOEs*
1965	90.07	9.93		
1970	87.61	12.39		
1975	81.09	18.91		
1978	77.63	22.37		
1980	75.97	23.54	0.02	0.48
1985	64.86	32.08	1.85	1.21
1986	62.27	33.51	2.76	1.46
1987	59.73	34.62	3.64	2.02
1988	56.80	36.15	4.34	2.72
1989	56.06	35.69	4.80	3.44
1990	54.60	35.62	5.39	4.38
1991	52.94	35.70	5.70	5.66
1992	48.09	38.04	6.76	7.11
1993	43.13	38.36	8.35	10.16
1994	34.07	40.87	11.51	13.55
1980–94 change	−41.90	+17.33	+11.49	+13.07

Sources: ZTN 1990, p. 416; ZTN 1995, p. 377.

Note: SOEs = state-owned enterprises; COEs = collectively-owned enterprises; IOEs = individually-owned enterprises; OOEs = enterprises of other ownership systems. Figures cover the national total, including village-and-below enterprises. Sectoral shares are calculated at current prices. The 1994 figure for SOEs will be 40.05 per cent if the output share of OOEs where SOEs have majority shareholding is included.

experience is anomalous to the intellectual paradigm which they uphold. It is because of such a challenge that some 'big bang' protagonists have attempted to argue that China's economic growth is unrelated to the institutional reform: the growth has been purely based on transfer of labour from the rural-agricultural sector – a structural feature which countries of the former Soviet bloc do not possess. They also argue that China's state industry has performed badly, while the good performance of the economy has been purely accounted for by the 'non-state' sector which grows out of a type of 'big bang' policy. The figures in Table 1.2, which show the massive shrinkage of the output share of SOEs in Chinese industry, are often cited as hard evidence supporting the above argument. The Chinese experience, in short, just does not represent an anomaly but rather validates the 'big bang' approach (Sachs and Woo 1994; Woo 1994).

In this connection, a major issue under debate concerns the measurement of total factor productivity (TFP). Until recently, relevant studies have consistently found that TFP growth has been substantial for both state-owned enterprises (SOEs) and collectively-owned enterprises, or township-and-village enterprises (TVEs). This provides support to the evolutionary propositions, particularly (a) and (e). The consensus is now broken down by 'big bang' protagonists who argue that SOEs in fact have experienced negative TFP growth (Woo *et al.* 1994). The crux rests on some data issues, especially the scope of coverage of input statistics and the construction of appropriate deflators. The TFP estimates are sensitive to these. Given the disagreement over the appropriate measurements of data, there is unlikely to be objective criteria for resolving the issue.

The division over measuring TFP, of course, need not determine the settlement of the entire debate between the 'big bang' protagonists and the evolutionary writers, as the debate encompasses not only micro-level efficiency but also macroeconomic and developmental concerns. Nor does it really split the difference between the two. The concept of TFP is based on the neoclassical model of the production function and, in the literature, there are well-known conceptual problems with its estimation and interpretation. The fact that both of the two groups pay heavy attention to it indicates their common ground. Even within the evolutionary writers, while some being stimulated by the Chinese experience have begun to ponder what is meant by a market economy (Rawski 1994), others continue to assert that 'for comparative purposes, the profit motive and market influence are sufficiently strong to characterize firms in industrial market economies broadly in terms of the neoclassical paradigm' (Jefferson and Xu 1994, p. 613). Occasionally, these writers have gone so far as to claim: 'eventually, probably sooner rather than later, extensive privatization and more complete marketization will be required for China to join the club of newly industrialized economies' (Chen *et al.* 1992, p. 221).[2]

We need not infer from the above quotations that the evolutionary writers are the same breed as 'big bang' protagonists, except for disagreement over the pace of transformation. But it is clear that, on the whole, their intellectual orientation is basically market-centred. This conditions their development of alternative conceptual framework and research strategy for the study of Chinese economic development and reform. It is against this intellectual background that this book attempts to develop a true alternative.

TOWARDS A TRUE ALTERNATIVE

The 'big bang' protagonists' comparison of SOEs and TVEs, even if it is correct, does not really give support to what they have prescribed for countries of the former Soviet bloc and for China. After all, Chinese TVEs are by no means reducible to the canonical capitalist firm – they are collectives, not private. In making the assertion quoted in the beginning of this overview, what Weitzman (1993) has in mind is precisely the anomalous nature of Chinese TVEs. This, that the theory of individualistic property rights has not been applicable to China, is virtually a consensus among the evolutionary writers.

But it is still my contention that the evolutionary propositions listed above tend to overstate the role of the market. In this book, I attempt to raise three propositions:

(a) that large- and medium-scale enterprises (LMEs), mostly state-owned, have contributed no less than market-oriented TVEs to overall economic growth
(b) that the good performance of LMEs has been related to a series of institutional reforms – inter-firm agglomeration, intra-firm restructuring, the long-term nature of employment and external financing relationships, for example – which appear to be combining both market and non-market features
(c) the reforms of LMEs have been related to the dynamics of the overall economic reform, and have emerged from China's specific political economy.

Following the thesis that the development of the Chinese economy is increasingly hinged upon the improvement of international competitiveness of LMEs, which I develop in this book, the reforms of LMEs should represent the core of China's overall systemic transformation.

A crucial link between the anomalous institutional arrangements of LMEs and their good performance is collective learning, which has been a major impetus behind the observed rapid productivity change. It is especially at this point that China's economic development converges to other comparable experiences. According to the late industrialization literature, collective learning is the key to successfully adopting, adapting and improving upon imported technology, and hence to sustained economic growth (Amsden 1989; Aoki 1990; Best 1990; Lazonick 1991). It is observed that technology imports, and with them rapid structural change which generates increasing returns, have been a central feature of Chinese industrialization over the past 16 years.

Table 1.3 Trends in China's Exports and Imports, 1987–94 (US$bn)

	(a) Total		*(b) Mechanical and electronics products in (a)*		*(c) Electronics products in (b)*		*(d) Computer products in (c)*	
	Exports	*Imports*	*Exports*	*Imports*	*Exports*	*Imports*	*Exports*	*Imports*
1987	39.4	43.2	3.9	17.4	0.745	. . .	0.045	0.416
1994	121.0	115.7	31.9	58.8	12.360	134.80	2.800	1.980
1987–94 average annual growth (%)	17.4	15.1	35.0	19.0	49.4	...	80.4	25.0

Sources: ZJN, various years; ZJDGN-J, various years; RMRB 4 March 1994, p. 1; ZTN 1994, p. 506; ZXB, 28 February 1995, p. 2. ZJDGN-D, various years; ZDB, 3 February 1992, p. 1; XXSB, 5 May 1994, p. 3; CD, 2 March 1994, p. 2; CD, 8 March 1995, p. 5; CD-BW,19–25 March 1995, p. 8.

This has propelled overall technical change and economic growth in general, and has realized the potential of collective learning of LMEs in particular.

A second theme of the book is thus to study the Chinese industrialization pattern under reform, which carries far-reaching implications for the prospects for future growth and reform. What I focus on is not only productivity change and output growth, but also intrinsic problems with the pattern. Specifically, I argue that economic growth based on technology imports and related structural change is difficult to sustain, unless the constraints arising from foreign exchange gap and demand insufficiency are overcome. The crux for breaking these constraints is the export competitiveness of dynamic, high value-added industries, which however is extremely difficult for developing countries to achieve.[3]

The Chinese experience is not entirely successful in this respect, and there is still enormous uncertainty in the prospects for its future economic growth. Nevertheless, as noted, the achievement of competitiveness is a distinctive feature of Chinese industrialization during this period. Moreover, while it is true that China's rapidly expanding exports have been significantly accounted for by labour-intensive manufactured goods, the figures in Table 1.3 indicate that the achievement as a whole is unlikely to be purely based on the principle of comparative advantage: the exports expansion of products that are generally considered to be with higher capital-intensity and technological contents tends to be faster. It is particularly worth noting that these trends have coincided with the state drive to promote the export competitiveness of high technology, high value-added industries, and that the transformation of China from an exporter of primary products to one of manufactured products took place basically during these years of 1987–94.

Thus, arguably, what has been accomplished so far with respect to the performance in the world market is, again, the outcome of a complex mix of market and non-market regulation.

On the whole, the central character of the study is to base the analysis and appraisal of Chinese economic reform on its industrialization pattern during this period. The field of vision is therefore much broader than the TFP approach, and the subject under study is far more complicated. It is because of this that the conclusion I arrive at concerning the lessons from, and future evolution of, China's economic development and reform is far more open than the mainstream writers, whose adhesion to the notion of the 'pure' market strictly limits their acceptance of anything anomalous.

THE STRUCTURE OF THE BOOK

This book is organized in three parts. Part I, comprising Chapter 2, aims to address some theoretical issues which are often taken for granted in mainstream empirical studies. These include theories of economic development, institutions, and the conceptualization of the market, all being placed under critical scrutiny.

Recent resurgence of interest in late industrialization has been stimulated by the emergence of a wealth of empirical evidence which constitutes a reinterpretation of the East Asian experience, and the rise in mainstream academic work of the so-called 'new' theories of trade and growth. Both of the two bodies of writing point to the necessity of placing technological development at the centre of industrialization. There are, however, conceptual ambiguities concerning the nature of technological development which need to be clarified. The chapter aims to undertake this task, and to argue that the imperative of development normally far outstrips the capacity of the regulation of the market.

Chapter 2 also reviews the theory of firm-level innovation, which is considered to be the key to successful late industrialization. Neoclassical theory treats the production system as essentially a black box. In contrast, a number of alternative approaches both inside and outside the mainstream hold the view that the market would often fail in the regulation of innovation activity. What remains controversial is whether the market can remedy its own failures by producing the best possible institutions. In this connection, I draw on the production-oriented literature to argue that the evolution of economic institutions including the organization of the firm is history-specific and is not reducible to any all-embracing notion like the market. If there are general conclusions on firm-level innovation which can be drawn from historical experiences, they run counter to the logic of the market – both the Walrasian vision and the theory of individualistic property rights.

Finally, the theoretical chapter addresses the question of the transformation of the Soviet-type economic system. The 'big bang'-evolutionary debate is conceptualized as an extension of the competition between two different strands in economics: namely, the standard neoclassical framework, and the evolutionary perspective which embraces various post-Walrasian theories, especially the information–economic analysis of the market and the transaction cost approach to business organization. With their emphasis on the system-specificity of information and the widespread existence of linkages, and by placing the focus on growth rather than allocative efficiency, the evolutionary writers have not only developed a forceful explanation for the dismal economic performance in countries of the former Soviet bloc under 'big bang', but also promised a better way towards development. In the chapter, however, I argue that the evolutionary challenge to 'big bang' is incomplete. My proposition concerns the need to push further the evolutionary exposition on institution, innovation and development, placing it in historical perspective. Based on this I draw on the late industrialization literature to formulate an alternative, production-oriented framework for the transformation of the Soviet-type economic system.

Part II, labelled 'explaining China', is composed of three chapters. They form the core of the book.

Chapter 3 aims to explain the experience of Chinese industrialization over the past 16 years. Recent studies in this area have broken new grounds in the depiction of the dynamics of the experience. The benchmark is a departure from simply applying the criteria of the 'pure' market on the assessment of the experience and on the prescription for reform policy. While being sympathetic with the new approaches, in this chapter I argue that the studies are deficient in one crucial respect which prevents them from breaking with the orthodox paradigm *in toto*. This, namely, is their insufficient recognition of the intrinsic contradictions of the past growth pattern. Specifically, I argue that the tremendous growth of the market-oriented sector has produced a number of problems which tend to undermine the sustainability of the growth of the economy as a whole. It is in this connection that the intervention of the state, mainly through its industrial policy, and the planned sector have been crucial in sustaining the growth and hence the success of the reform.

Chapter 4 attempts an appraisal of Chinese economic reform. Recent studies tend to focus on the working of the conceptually deficient economic system in the achievement of the spectacular economic development. This approach, which can be dubbed evolutionary, represents a break with the previously dominated approach of ascribing everything good to the notional 'pure' market and everything bad to the observed imperfections. Nevertheless, in this chapter, I argue that the break is incomplete because of the ambiguity held by the evolutionary writers concerning the economic implications of the imperfections especially the three oft-cited issues: soft budget constraint, government intervention and labour employment rigidity. Drawing on the theory of the 'learning paradigm', and based on a series of hitherto unexplained stylized facts, I submit that the imperfections have the virtue of promoting productivity improvement which, in relation to the growth pattern of the Chinese economy, has more than compensated for the possible loss of allocative efficiency and thus has propelled the economic development.

Chapter 5, which comprises some simple regression analyses, aims to provide a relatively more formal treatment of the propositions put forth in the previous two chapters. In a way to trace the sources of output growth and productivity change in Chinese industry, I test the applicability of Nicholas Kaldor's theory of demand-driven growth and dynamic increasing returns, and compare the results with the production function approach. I also test the thesis of structural change as engine of growth, which is central to my analysis in Chapter 3. On the whole, the regression analyses are preliminary yet a number of suggestive results have still been obtained.

Part III, entitled 'Sector Studies', consists of two chapters. The aim of doing sector-level studies is to examine, in a closer way, the experience of Chinese industrialization. The selection of the two industries, electronics and automobiles, is based on the recognition that they are prominent engines of overall industrial growth in the 1980s and 1990s, respectively.

Chapter 6 studies the development experience of the electronics industry. This is representative of the group of so-called 'new industries' which formed the major impetus behind the spectacular growth of the economy. It thus embodies the specificity of China's economic institutions under reform. The chapter aims to clarify the actual forms and effects of the regulatory mechanisms in the course of development of the industry. It concludes that the development is the outcome of a complicated mix of market and non-market regulation, not collapsible to the Walrasian 'pure' market which, even if it exists, is likely to have been detrimental rather than conducive.

Chapter 7 studies the motor industry. Recent changes in China's industrialization pattern have given rise to the strategic importance of the industry. However, because of the need to improve dramatically its international competitiveness, it is also likely to confront an especially heavy task of institutional reform. The chapter aims to unravel the significance of the reforms which have taken place in the industry over the past decade. In line with the logic of rationalization and flexibility, which lies at the heart of competitiveness in the world motor industry, it focuses on issues such as state industrial policy, the formation of industrial concerns, the restructuring of firm organization and the adoption of new work practices at the operational level. The chapter concludes that a series of institutional features widely evident in the industry which can be considered as market imperfections are arguably conducive for the productive efficiency and hence competitiveness of the industry.

Finally, I draw some conclusions for the book as a whole. My overall objective is both to construct an analytically enlightening account of the Chinese experience of economic development and reform, and to engage with the policy debate concerning the transformation of the Soviet-type economic system which affects the livelihood of a significant proportion of humankind today.

SOME EXPLANATORY NOTES

This book is intended to be an analytical, instead of historical or narrative, account of China's experience of economic development and systemic transformation. This means the strength and weakness of the book can be best judged by putting it in the context of the literature, that is, by explicitly contrasting the findings and insights provided here with other writings in the field. At another level, however, this also means that a number of issues that are of significance to our analysis have been either neglected or have been dealt with insufficiently. Three of these need some explanation.

First, this book devotes little space to the phenomenal structural change of China's economy from agriculture to industry. It thus cannot claim to be a comprehensive study of Chinese industrialization under reform. Instead, it focuses on the structural change within the industrial sector, particularly the rise of a range of 'new industries' which are characterized by increasing returns and heavy import dependence. The justification is that our central concern is the reform of state-owned enterprises, whose performance has been especially affected by this intra-industry structure change. However, without analysing the structural change on a broader scale, little can be said about the performance and reform of collectively-owned enterprises, particularly township-and-village enterprises.

Second, this book does not analyze the role of enterprises that involve foreign capital. This is regrettable, especially because the two industries of our case studies in Part III – electronics and automobile – are sectors where the presence of foreign capital is prominent. Nevertheless, it is noted that, at least until the massive influx of foreign direct investment in 1992–4, the role of foreign-invested firms in the process of Chinese industrialization as a whole was still rather limited. The figures in Table 1.2 show that, by 1992, the output share of OOEs (which encompass foreign-invested firms) in Chinese industry was only 7 per cent. Thus, the omission of these firms would not seriously affect the analysis.

Third, this book does not deal with the spatial aspect of Chinese industrialization. But it is well known that the growth pattern during 1978–94 was characterized by spatial unevenness, with coastal provinces outstripping inland provinces and market-oriented regions, for example, Special Economic Zones, outstripping the rest of the country. A study of Chinese industrialization without systematically examining the spatial aspect, especially the role of rents and quasi-rents in explaining the disparity in regional economic growth, is incomplete. Moreover, the role of local authorities of various levels in both the growth process and the systemic transformation has been prominent. A study of the circumstances under which these authorities would be prone to short-termism, or would behave in an entrepreneurial way, will certainly generate a lot of insights for our topic.

In this connection, yet one more neglected issue is the political economy of Chinese economic growth and reform. It is not that the author is unconcerned with the issue. It is rather that the issue is too complex to be dealt with in this book. I have long felt uneasy about the application by Western economists and journalists of such naïve notions as 'liberals' and 'hardliners' to the Chinese political economy and misguided references to the idea of a 'cold war'. But to develop a credible alternative would be an enormous task.

Part I

Theoretical Issues

2 Towards an Alternative Perspective on Systemic Transformation

This chapter explores a number of theoretical issues that have arisen from the literature on the transformation of the Soviet-type economic system. All too often, in doing empirical research and especially in making policy prescriptions, most of the relevant writings tend to hold some specific views on the nature of, and the institutional prerequisites for, economic development – views which are rarely made explicit but are in fact not at all non-debatable. This is tantamount to ignoring the rich contribution of the development literature, and the lessons from the actual experiences of development altogether. In what follows, I attempt to integrate the exposition on systemic transformation with a synthesis of recent theories of late industrialization, in the belief that this will generate important insights on the former topic as well as for understanding China's economic reform and development.

THE REGULATION OF LATE INDUSTRIALIZATION

'Trade Regime Neutrality' and its Criticism

In the literature on industrialization, the doctrine that has gained an orthodox position since the mid-1980s is what the World Bank (1987) dubbed 'trade regime neutrality'. This doctrine, in the same logic as neoclassical microeconomics of subsuming production under exchange, subsumes industrialization under trade. Specifically, as Pack and Westphal (1986, p. 88) note, '"neutral" meaning that policies should not selectively discriminate – that is, for tradeables, *vis-à-vis* world prices, and for non-tradeables, *vis-à-vis* relative scarcities – among industries'. The doctrine, therefore, means the international specialization of an economy should follow strictly its given comparative advantage. In the formulation of the so-called 'stages approach to comparative advantage', it further implies that the path of structural change would be optimal if the economy follows its shifting comparative advantage over time (Balassa 1977; Little 1982). As Balassa (1981, p. 22) asserts: 'this process is exemplified by Japan that shifted from unskilled-labor intensive exports to skill-intensive and to physical-capital intensive exports and is increasingly expanding its technology-intensive exports'.[1]

It is clear that the 'stages approach' is dynamic only in the sense that it takes into account changes over time. This is in fact well accommodated by neoclassical theory, as Bliss (1989, p. 1209) puts it: 'a fundamental insight of modern general equilibrium theory is that goods delivered at different dates can be treated as different goods and that this leaves largely unaffected the formal structure of general equilibrium theory . . . There is no formal difficulty in imagining that a less developed country (LDC) might have a comparative advantage in *two* goods: a primary product today and a manufactured good tomorrow'. But what determines the changes? Clearly, emphasizing trade regime neutrality implies leaving the changes to be determined by the world market. Focusing on relative scarcity of factor inputs further implies that the doctrine is based on the neoclassical theory of production. This makes it prone to two shortcomings: first, it assumes away the consideration of increasing returns, and, second, it does not consider the question as to why firms exist in the first place.

The assumption of constant returns to scale is necessary for the competitive equilibrium of the market, and hence is essential to standard neoclassical theory. The attempt in 'new' growth theory to relax the assumption is at most tentative, because it still has to assume that any increasing returns can only exist at the industry (or economy) level, that is, they are external to individual firms (Romer 1986; Lucas 1988).[2] But, even in this limited case, the existence of increasing returns still implies that it makes sense to treat different sectors – for example, primary or manufacturing, low or high skill/technology – differently from the outset. The idea is to develop industries that are especially dynamic yet do not necessarily accord with the existing comparative advantage. This, however, implies selective discrimination by government among industries.

But, increasing returns or endogenous technical change are not necessarily confined to the industry or economy-wide levels. In the Schumpeterian tradition, the competitiveness of firms normally rests on their ability of generating continuous innovations which place them at a favourable position in market competition (Best 1990). In the context of late industrialization, this argument is often raised in conjunction with the emphasis on the character of 'constantly improving best practice' in the world market (Pack and Westphal 1986). In contrast, the idea that structural change follows automatically the shift in (factor cost-determined) comparative advantage presumes that technology is fully tradable. It overlooks the difficulties for developing nations to attain the world competitive level of technical efficiency in entering new industries. Likewise, the orthodox doctrine overlooks the fact that adopting and improving upon new technology takes time. This is particularly the case for technically sophisticated industries.

Once the production function approach of the neutrality doctrine is deemed flawed, it becomes necessary to consider the institutional or organizational aspect of industry. This, in a sense, is associated with the question as to why firms exist. In the tradition of transaction cost economics, firms exist because the market fails. It is instructive to see how this theory can apply in the context of late industrialization. A rare attempt by Mody (1990) focuses on entry into technically sophisticated industries. The crux is capital market failure. Because the entry involves high risk and heavy sunk-investment, it is not to be achieved by the market but rather by firms having an 'internal capital market' – that is, internalizing the capital market. This provides an insightful explanation to the role of Japanese and South Korean big firms in the industrialization process, especially in the entry into industries which do not accord with the countries' international comparative advantage.

The same reasoning can be applied more generally. Aoki's (1990) model of the Japanese firm extends it to cover not only the bank-orientated financial system, which in some conceptualization is considered to resemble the internal capital market, but also long-term relationships between different firms of the same production chain (the *kanban* or just-in-time system) and horizontal information-sharing of intra-firm units. More specifically, placing continuous, incremental innovations at the centre of competitiveness, Best (1990) emphasizes the organization of the firm in a way that is conducive for collective learning. In the context of late industrialization, where the competitive edge of latecomers rests on adopting and improving upon imported technology, Amsden (1989) arrives at the same conclusion that collective learning is the key to success.

The above reasoning does not specify the condition within which the 'right' kind of firms would emerge. It does not necessarily hinge on the central thesis of 'transaction cost' economics which states that the competitive market would ensure the optimal combination of market and non-market arrangements. Indeed, Bowles' (1985) influential work on variable productivity and labour extraction contends that the market would inevitably fail in producing the most efficient firms, and firms having more participation of insider members would tend to be superior. Drawing on this, Evans (1989) argues that the institutions and organizations of industry are significant in shaping the comparative advantage of a nation.

'New International Division of Labour' and its Criticism

Normative aspect apart, the analytics of the thesis of the 'new international division of labour' (NIDL) bear a striking resemblance to the doctrine of trade regime neutrality at one point: namely, the focus on factor cost-determined comparative advantage. What marks the distinctiveness of the thesis, as opposed to the orthodox doctrine, is the conception of the nature of the world market. First, it holds the Lewisian assumption of unlimited supply of labour. Second, contrary to Adam Smith's notion of specialization as the impetus for skill improvement, the NIDL thesis holds the de-skilling notion of Charles Babbage.

The 'new' international division of labour signifies a contrast with the 'old' whereby developing nations specialize in the primary sector and depend on the advanced capitalist world for the supply of manufactured goods. The NIDL thesis, formally raised by Fröbel *et al.* (1980), is thus intended to explain the observation that starting from the 1960s there has been considerable expansion of industrial production in a range of developing nations. Three conditions are identified as the contributing factors. First, the penetration of commodity relations into Third World agriculture has given rise to a world-wide reservoir of potential labour power. Second, the development of the labour process in manufacturing activities has led to the decomposition of the production process into elementary units and the de-skilling of workers. This, in turn, ensures labour productivity in 'world factories' of the underdeveloped world being equal to or in excess of that in advanced capitalist economies. Third, the development of the means of transportation and communication has made industry less tied to specific locations. Taken together, these conditions explain the trend of growing relocation of manufacturing activities, in the form of subcontracting or foreign direct investment, to the underdeveloped world. Consequently, there is the phenomenal expansion of industry in some developing regions, under the rubric of 'export-oriented industrialization'.

At the normative level, the new international division of labour is seen by the exponents as nothing better than the 'old' (Fröbel *et al.* 1980; Frank 1981; Landsberg 1979). In line with Arthur Lewis' renowned model, the utilization of the unlimited supply of labour from developing nations implies transfer of surplus to the advanced capitalist world. The low level of skill/technology of the relocated manufacturing activities further implies the enclave nature of the world factories, that is weak linkages with the rest of the local economies, as well as low wages for the workers involved. The latter aspect also results in a demand-side problem for local industrial development: 'the purchasing power of the mass of the local population is too low to constitute an effective demand on the local market.' (Fröbel *et al.* 1980, p. 5) All these imply that underdeveloped nations are induced to specialize in the least dynamic industries, strictly following their given comparative advantage.

The NIDL thesis has been subject to various lines of criticism. Critics have pointed out that most of the involvement of transnational corporations (TNCs) in the developing world has been either directly related to production for the domestic market, or for the exploitation of raw materials, rather than for the relocation of the labour-intensive process (Amsden 1990; Evans 1989; Gordon 1988). Two factors have also been raised as having a countervailing effect on the factor cost-induced industrial relocation. The first is the potential for increasing labour productivity by technological and organizational innovations. In many cases, as is evident in the adoption of the *kanban* or just-in-time practice, these innovations may require spatial proximity of intra- or inter-firm units and some forms of re-skilling (Aoki 1990). The second counter-tendency to industrial relocation is the requirement of flexibility, that is the ability of quick response to changes in market demand structure and product quality. This is related to the flexible specialization literature which posits a fundamental shift of the nature of market competition in advanced capitalist economies (Piore and Sabel 1984). It also has a link with the neo-Schumpeterian notion of the 'entrepreneurial firm' which seeks to maintain a competitive position by means of continuous innovations (Best 1990). In either case, the logic of flexibility requires strong linkages among intra-firm divisions of production, marketing and research and development (R&D).

What remains of the NIDL thesis? It is noted, that the thesis is not simply an emphasis on 'cheap labour'. It rather focuses on the pattern of international specialization which involves various forms of optimal combination of capital and labour under the profit-maximization pursuit of capital. The emphasis on factor-cost-determined industrial relocation is based on Hymer's (1971) application of the Babbage principle on the intra-firm division of labour of TNCs, instead of the notion of the production function. Following Taylorization, the division of labour within TNCs becomes a tripartite hierarchy consisting of knowledge-intensive control and R&D functions at the top, an intermediate level of high-skilled activities, and low-skilled standardized production operations at the bottom. The implication is that: 'these three levels can be de-linked geographically, with each one seeking its appropriate supply of labour in different areas' (Schoenberger 1989, p. 93).

Thus the analytics of the NIDL thesis seems to survive the criticisms reported above. What seems untenable is its deterministic overtone. Sceptics that are otherwise sympathetic point out that, in cases where the process of internationalization of capital involves mainly production for a local market, a model of indigenous accumulation based on relative surplus value production – productivity growth – is possible (Jenkins 1984, 1987; Bina and Yaghmaian 1990). In other words, there is still the possibility for particular developing nations to enter a virtuous circle of productivity growth coupled with local market formation. The mechanism runs from industrial relocation or technology transfer (producing for the local market) to productivity improvement, growth of income, and further expansion of the local market. So market formation stands at both the start and finish points. It is the existence of the domestic market which attracts technology transfer. It is also the domestic market which sustains indigenous industrial expansion.

But what accounts for the existence of a sizeable local market in the first instance? Lipietz (1987 p. 78) puts it this way: 'in some cases, its origin lay in an earlier import-substitution policy or in a peripheral form of merchant capitalism (Chinese in Eastern Asia). In other cases, it emerged from the "miraculous" promotion of exports of raw materials such as oil or from an earlier stage of primitive Taylorization'. The second part of the answer implies at least a partial relaxation of the dependency/NIDL judgement on the impossibility of indigenous accumulation. Bina and Yaghmaian (1990) emphasize the first part, that is import substitution industrialization, as the necessary pre-condition of indigenous accumulation. It enables the growth of local autonomous capital, a sizeable urban middle class and significant elements of an experienced working class.

Thus the literature of radical political economy subsequent to the NIDL thesis tends to view world capitalism as being composed of three layers: in addition to the 'core' and 'periphery', there is a middle layer which embodies the circularity of productivity growth *cum* local market formation. Lipietz labels the first two 'Fordism' and 'primitive Taylorism', and the middle layer 'peripheral Fordism'. 'Primitive Taylorism' corresponds to that depicted by the NIDL thesis. As for the second layer, 'it is an authentic Fordism, based on the coupling of intensive accumulation and the growth of markets. But it remains peripheral in the sense that in the global circuits of productive sectors, qualified employment positions (above all in engineering) remain largely external to these countries', (Lipietz 1986, p. 32). The dynamics and contradictions of 'peripheral Fordism', therefore, can be understood only in relation with 'Fordism', that is the conception of the world techno-economic paradigm.

Techno-Economic Paradigm and Institutions

The notion of 'techno-economic paradigm' centres around the area where neoclassical economics stops and where new growth and trade theories begin to explore: namely, the sources of increasing returns. However, unlike the mainstream writings which often posit it as possible for developing countries to draw freely upon the 'world stock of knowledge', the notion of 'techno-economic paradigm' rather emphasizes the non-linearity and discontinuity of technological development.

In the flexible specialization literature, a central proposition is that a transition – from a techno-economic paradigm that is based on mass production to one based on craft production – has taken place in the world economy since the 1970s. The former paradigm is dubbed 'Fordism', and the latter flexible specialization (Piore and Sabel 1984). Each of the two paradigms is associated with a distinct principle of organization of production. Mass production involves economies of scale within the firm, increasing returns for the economy as a whole, the specialization of productive resources and the divorce between conception and execution in production. In short, it involves the search for innovations through the process of detailed division of labour as described by Adam Smith. The flexible specialization paradigm, in contrast, follows the Marxian notion of social division of labour. Here, conception and execution are integrated, and innovations are achieved 'through the tension between a deepening of understanding within a given cognitive frame and the pull to reintegrate back into a different frame in order to produce a sellable commodity'. (Piore 1992, p. 169). While the chief organization form of mass production is 'hierarchies', that of flexible specialization is 'networks' – in either case, the Walrasian market is not the chief regulatory mechanism because of the predominance of increasing returns at the firm level.[3]

In a similar formulation, the French regulationist writers see the techno-economic paradigm of Fordism as being composed of an intensive 'regime of accumulation' and a collective 'mode of regulation'. The regime of accumulation, or production system, is intensive in the sense that it is based on relative surplus value production. With economies of scale and mass production as the organizational principles, it involves heavy sunk investment aiming at rapid increase of labour productivity. As in the flexible specialization literature, the chief organization form of Fordism is hierarchies within big firms which have considerable oligopolistic power. But the regulation school also has an under-consumptionist/stagnationist emphasis. Following the Babbage principle, the detailed division of labour (Taylorization) and with it the de-skilling of workers exert downward pressure on wages, such that the mass consumption necessary to sustain mass production is jeopardized. This intrinsic contradiction of Fordism can be resolved only in a wider context, by an appropriate mode of regulation. Thus, crucial to this development pattern is the balance between productivity increase and the growth of workers' wages (Boyer 1988; Harvey 1989; Lipietz 1986, 1987). It is precisely the breakdown of the balance which has accounted for the exhaustion of Fordism, that is, the economic crisis in world capitalism since the 1970s.

The flexible specialization and regulationist stories converge at the point that the interplay between technical change and institutions is the driving force of change. This, as Boyer (1988) notes, is also in line with neo-Schumpeterian writings (Freeman and Perez 1988; Kaplinsky 1985; Tylecote 1992) in interpreting the crisis as a structural one caused by a mis-match between existing institutions and the emerging techno-economic paradigm. The transition involves crisis, for while the dynamism of the prevailing paradigm is exhausting, that of the new is yet to be realized. As Freeman and Perez (1988, p. 60) put it: 'with cheap microelectronics widely available, with prices expected to fall still further and with related new developments in computers and telecommunications, it is no longer "common sense" to continue along the (now expensive) path of energy and materials-intensive inflexible mass production'. The nature of the transition is such that it requires a transformation of the skill profile, the profile of capital equipment, consumption pattern, the financial system, etc. It involves enormous uncertainty whose unfavourable effect on business confidence and hence investment is enormous.

What characterizes the new paradigm? Because of their conceptualizing the transition as one of relative decline and rise, the flexible specialization theorists are especially willing to answer this question. The answer is social division of labour as the engine of growth. Significantly, in later writings, the actual organization form regarded as embodying this paradigm is not confined to the prototype of flexible specialization, that is the industrial districts in central Italy. For Piore (1992 p. 160), the organizational form of networks 'is often appropriate not only to organize relationships among small firms but also to structure the relationship among the internal units of large corporate enterprises and between the corporation and its suppliers, customers, and even its external competitors'. This sounds close to Aoki (1990) and Best (1990).

What are the implications of the preceding discussion for late industrialization? It implies, in the first place, a reshaping of international comparative advantage: 'newcomers are sometimes more able to make the necessary social and institutional innovations than the more arthritic social structures of established leaders . . . On the other hand, countries lacking the necessary minimal educational, managerial, R&D and design capability may be even more seriously disadvantaged in international competition', (Freeman and Perez 1988, p. 64). But there can be more specific implications arising from the diagnosis of the dynamics of change depicted in this section.[4] From the standpoint of developing nations, their integration with the world market under the changing techno-economic paradigm in the world economy is likely to result in a number of problems. First, the nature of the industries relocated from the advanced capitalist world tends to be what is depicted by the NIDL thesis as the second layer of the hierarchy: relatively high skill activities, but with R&D functions being retained in core economies. This leads to technological dependence.

Second, as the chief pursuit of international capital is market outlets, the technology tends to embody the specificity of the consumption pattern of the advanced capitalist world, that is mass production and consumption. This often compounds with the outright transposition of the consumption pattern to the developing world. Yet developing nations often do not have the right economic conditions – the level and distribution of income and the underlying social institutions – to sustain the consumption and hence the growth. Third, since this development pattern would not automatically lead to the formation of indigenous technological capabilities, developing nations would find it difficult to improve upon imported technology for promoting the export competitiveness of their industries, which however are essential for the continuous imports of technology and hence growth.

Thus, nations developing along the line of peripheral Fordism, may be constantly under the threat of under-consumption on the domestic front and of balance of payment deficits on the international front.

Under-consumption in this context is less a problem of insufficient aggregate demand than one of insufficient demand by sector, the dynamic sectors of the economy. As for external constraints, in line with the regulationist story, the contraction of demand in the advanced capitalist world, in the forms of limiting market access for exports from and capital flows to the developing world, can only make it more severe.

On the whole, what we can conclude from the literature of radical political economy is that, owing to the dynamics of change in the advanced capitalist world, there is a tendency for developing nations to be trapped in the predicament of primitive Taylorism (the NIDL thesis) or peripheral Fordism. This tendency can be viewed in a non-deterministic way, for there often remains the possibility of breaking the under-consumption and balance of payments constraints by means of modifying and improving upon imported technology. The difficulty is that this depends on the existence of indigenous technological capabilities which would not be automatically brought about under the regulation of the world market.

Rethinking Industrialization Strategy

I have argued for the centrality of technological development, and the need to transcend market regulation, in late industrialization through two routes. In the first part of this section, my argument draws on various market failure approaches. In the second and third parts, I turn to the radical literature which discards the notion of the 'pure' market altogether. It is ultimately an empirical question as to which of these strands, as well as the market-centred orthodoxy of the World Bank, has more explanatory power. Nevertheless, in the light of the preceding reviews, it is possible by now to clarify the underlying assumptions of the different lines of reasoning. This forms the basis for assessing alternative industrialization strategies.

The orthodox formulation of import substitution industrialization (ISI) and export oriented industrialization (EOI) as two mutually contradictory strategies rests precisely on the doctrine of trade regime neutrality. EOI is defined as embodying the neutrality principle. Hence ISI, which necessarily involves trade protection, is by definition not neutral.[5] It is thus subject to a number of criticisms:

(a) sacrifice of gains from trade
(b) overly high capital intensity of industries which hinders the generation of employment

(c) inefficiency of domestic industries because of being sheltered from world market competition
(d) under-utilization of installed capacity because of small domestic market, or sacrifice of economies of scale that could have been realized through cxports
(e) a tendency to generate balance of payments problem because of anti-export bias and needing to import machinery and industrial inputs
(f) the behaviour of rent-seeking resulting from bureaucratic intervention (Balassa 1981; Krueger 1984, 1985; Little 1982).

These criticisms are of a varied nature. To assess them we need first to turn to the conventional arguments for ISI. The essence of ISI, as originally raised by Latin American writers and as a received wisdom of structuralism, is to build up a domestic industrial base that encompasses technological capabilities and a skilful workforce.

The rationale rests on three points: first, that manufacturing activities are particularly associated with various kinds of dynamic efficiency, including technical change and learning; second, that a domestic integrated industrial system, through linkage effects and by promoting wage growth as the source of effective demand, can foster the development of high skill/technology industries; and, third, that structural change towards industrial production is instrumental for developing economies to alleviate the adverse effects of the trend of deteriorating terms of trade against primary products in the world market – the Prebisch-Singer thesis (Kay 1989; Schmitz 1984; Weiss 1988). Trade protection enters ISI because the strategy involves promoting industries not according with the given comparative advantage. But protection then must be selective, not across-the-board. Likewise, the effective-demand argument, which emphasizes wage growth, hinges on an appropriate pattern of income distribution.

Given these two qualifications, it is arguable that the balance-of-payment criticism, point (e), is not endemic to ISI. Structuralist writers attribute the problem to a caricature of ISI, so-called 'market-oriented ISI'. Historically, the extension of protection to all industries arose mainly from social-political pressure. And the fact that nations which adopted ISI have often been blocked at the assembly stages, and hence needed imports of intermediate inputs to sustain growth, is a reflection of uneven income distribution, because the assembled goods were often luxury consumer durables. It is based on this reasoning that the writers argue not for less state intervention but for more and of a more fundamental kind (Jenkins 1991; Wade 1990). Similarly, the rent-seeking criticism, point (f), is not regarded as endemic to state intervention *per se*, but rather resulting from specific political conditions.

Points (a) and (b) of orthodox criticism of ISI are based on the theory of comparative advantage, and are raised in contrast to the notional state of market equilibrium. But it is an established view in economics that sacrifice of gains from trade due to market 'distortions' is usually trivial in magnitude (it accounts for a fraction of trade which in turn accounts for a fraction of national income), and cannot explain much of the observed divergence of economic growth among nations (Taylor and Arida 1988). More importantly, these criticisms are partial in nature, for the focus is being placed on loss of static efficiency alone, instead of weighing it against the possible gain of dynamic efficiency from industrialization, the conventional argument for ISI.

There remain points (c) and (d) that seem to be strong enough to affect significantly long-term economic growth. This rests on the recognition that sheltered inefficiency and small market size are detrimental to learning and technical change, both in terms of incentive and capability. It thus establishes the case for industries to be export-oriented, that is to compete in the world market. However, even so, it is still difficult to see the logical link between export-orientation and trade regime neutrality. The former does not invalidate the ISI arguments on dynamic efficiency, whereas the latter tends to rule out trade protection and state intervention. But where industries are to become export-oriented, even at their infant stages, what is required is not just trade regime neutrality (no anti-export bias) but rather export-promotion policies. Thus the criticisms of ISI raised by orthodox writers are inadequate for justifying the replacement of ISI by EOI. It is only when EOI, defined as trade regime neutrality in the orthodox sense, is capable of fulfilling the stated targets of ISI that the replacement is justified. But this is unlikely, if not impossible.[6]

The above discussion finally pushes to the fore the idea of combining ISI and EOI in late industrialization. The orthodox prescription is deemed unsatisfactory because it is partial: it focuses on market-driven incentives, while disregarding the building up of capabilities. But it does not follow that incentive considerations are not important; rather, it seems that points (c) and (d) of orthodox criticism of ISI remains valid. What is untenable is the doctrine of trade regime neutrality. To combine ISI with EOI, the meaning of the latter strategy needs to be redefined: it is not imports-exports incentive neutral, but is to foster domestic industries participating in world market competition. The polarization between the two then disappears. They are not antithetical to each other, but can be complementary. In terms of sequencing, the adoption of ISI builds up beforehand an indigenous industrial base for subsequent EOI. In terms of selectivity, the efficient performance stemming from EOI and the dynamic industries built up through ISI can be mutually perpetuating under appropriate state and institutional mediation (see Lall 1992, for a schematic exposition of this capability–incentive–institution three-pronged strategy).

What about the exposition by radical writers who treat ISI and EOI not as two policy options, but rather two facets of peripheral Fordism? Or, how can the global-level dynamics be taken into account in industrialization strategy? Storper (1991), among others, proposes the strategy of flexible production. This is based on the recognition of the centrality of institutions and organizations in shaping the competitiveness of dynamic industries and hence the pattern of comparative advantage. Two kinds of flexibility, static and dynamic, are identified. Static flexibility refers to the ability to quickly adjust output quantities over the short-run without any strongly deleterious effects on the input-output efficiency, while dynamic flexibility means the ability to shift promptly from one process and/or product configuration to another. Both are crucial in Post-Fordist market competition, which is dominated by both economies of scale and scope. It follows that flexible production requires a skilful or even multi-skilled workforce, strong intra- and inter-firm co-operations that imply respectively participatory work organization and cooperative business culture, and a conducive sectoral and policy environment. All these are not simply a matter of policy choice. Yet it is not surprising that the driving force of economic development ultimately rests on the dimension of institutions and institutional change.

INSTITUTION, ORGANIZATION, AND INNOVATION

The Regulation of Innovation: Market or Institutions?

Having concluded from the discussion above that successful late industrialization rests on the capability of flexible production, we now turn to examine the organizations and institutions of industry that constitute such a capability. Again, it is convenient to begin with the orthodox position. Standard neoclassical economics assumes the existence of well-defined production functions and readily available technology through market transactions. In a perfectly competitive setting, an industry is posited to be a collection of technologically identical firms. This is because, under market competition, firms are forced to adopt the economically optimal set of technologies. By optimal, it refers to simultaneously achieving technical and allocative efficiencies, which are defined by exogenously-given technology and market competition, respectively.

Three features of innovation have often been raised to question the validity of the neoclassical vision. The first is innovation as a public good. Stoneman and Vickers (1988) contend that market regulation of innovation activities would typically result in 'double inefficiencies': under-investment by individual firms due to the problem of appropriability, and over-investment by the industry because of the problem of duplication. The second feature is that investment in innovation (R&D) is in general a long-term endeavour involving risk and uncertainty. This gives rise to the problem of imperfect information. The third feature is that innovation often brings about (static and dynamic) increasing returns. Taken together, these three features imply that the possibility of spill-over would either lead to underproduction or entail some oligopolistic market structures. In analyzing innovation activities, the assumption of perfect competition therefore cannot be taken seriously and the market structure should be treated as endogenous.

The series of game-theoretical models developed by industrial organization theorists, sometimes labelled 'neo-Schumpterian' (Romer 1994), represent attempts along this line. The 'patent race' model, for instance, says that, because of the endogeneity of the market structure, investment in innovation often involves strategic behaviours of economic agents. With the additional feature that investment would be 'forfeited' due to irreversibility and lagging behind in the race for patent registration, there is the possibility of a mixed 'racing and waiting' game: the small number of investors would calculate individually their costs and benefits of being an innovator or an imitator. This would result in multiple equilibria, or indeterminacy of outcome, with the welfare implications difficult to predict (Dasgupta 1988; Tirole 1988). Thus the market can fail – with respect to Pareto optimality and/or the logic of late industrialization – in the regulation of innovation activities.

From a different perspective, transaction cost economics considers it inevitable for the market to fail in the regulation of innovation. This stems from the following features of innovation activities:

(a) incomplete specifications of contracts, due to uncertainty about the research outcomes
(b) lack of adequate protection of proprietary information
(c) possibilities of 'lock in' phenomena with research suppliers, who can subsequently earn rents from that asymmetric advantage
(d) weak incentives to least cost performance
(e) high monitoring costs, again due to information asymmetry (Teece 1988).

These features fall into the three categories of factors which Williamson (1989) identifies as accounting for the cost of market transactions: bounded rationality, opportunism and information asymmetry. In this connection, transaction cost economics says that, if economic agents are cost-minimizing, they would normally internalize innovation activities in various forms, for example the establishment of in-house specialized R&D divisions.

It can be seen that, with respect to the regulation of innovation, both of the above two strands tend to emphasize the primacy of the market over the firm. Although adopting a market failure approach, their treatment of innovation is exchange-oriented. The concern of the game-theoretical model is to trade or not to trade, while that of the internalization theory is to trade or to internalize. These concerns make themselves imperative to equate innovation with some kind of information that is available from market transactions. This runs counter to the view that innovation, because of its tacit and idiosyncratic nature, is specific to the production system. In the distinction made by Best (1990), innovation is a kind of knowledge, not information – the former being actively generated by participants of the production system, whereas the latter is something well defined *ex ante*. This view is central to the production-oriented approach. In the context of late industrialization, the 'learning paradigm' developed by Amsden (1989) follows this line.[7]

The emphasis on the firm-specificity of innovation is very significant for considering the efficacy of market regulation. It implies denying the ubiquitous existence of the market, and the predominance of market regulation in both innovation and the evolution of the production system. The firm is not passively regulated by the market, but rather has some discretion in shaping the economic environment (Teece 1993). This is especially true for a firm which seeks to generate continuous innovations, a 'strategic firm' in the terms of Best (1990) who furthers the Schumpeterian thesis on entrepreneurship as a (if not the) shaper of the regulatory mechanism.

Nevertheless, the thesis cannot be pushed too far. The production-oriented approach does not deny the role of the market altogether. What is crucial is to appropriately integrate market regulation and the initiatives of the production system. In this regard, the notion of 'technological paradigm' appears to be relevant. It combines both incentives and constraints from the standpoint of the development of the production system. On the one hand, economic opportunities arising from the possibility of technological progress are continuously generated by breakthroughs in scientific exploration and 'localized' or in-house learning. These, called technological opportunities, act as an inducement mechanism for innovation. On the other hand, the possibility for a particular firm to reap the opportunities depends on its accumulated human and organizational resources. Moreover, the availability of technological opportunities is not indefinite but rather is limited to the domain defined by the technological paradigm of the industry involved: 'the multiplicity of potential approaches which may exist at the beginning of the evolution of a technology is gradually replaced by a convergence on a common approach' (Coombs *et al.* 1987, p. 16). This convergence is in a sense akin to the neoclassical vision of the production function, but not with its static connotation.

The significance of the notion of technological paradigm thus can be seen as twofold. First, it strikes a balance between market regulation and the initiatives of the production system. Dosi (1988b, p. 1142) puts it this way: 'on a generally broader time horizon, market conditions exert a powerful influence on the conduct of technological search, but they do so primarily by stimulating, hindering, and focusing the search for new technological paradigms. When established, however, each paradigm . . . remains quite "sticky" in its basic technical imperatives, rules of search, and input combinations.' Second, it strikes a balance between the firm-specific features and the economy- or industry-wide features (for example codifiability and transmittability) of an innovation. It provides common constraints for the technological behaviour of a large number of firms. From this, it is possible to analyze in general terms the relationship between organization and innovation, despite the varied firm-specific features.

Firm Organization and Innovation Capacity

As is often raised in the literature, the nature of technological change is generally depicted as one of two types: incremental and abrupt. This, in part, is because of difference in the degree of firm-specificity and information-like features embodied in a technology, with the former characterized by more gradual change. The significance of such a distinction is wide, but there is a historical dimension involved. According to the literature on Fordism and flexible production, which we have reviewed above, it is continuous, incremental innovation which has acquired central importance over the past two decades in accounting for the source of competitive advantage in the world market. At another level, incremental technical change is normally related to the tacitness of innovation, whereas abrupt change is akin to the production of codifiable and transmittable information. Moreover, the former is normally associated with the process of learning-by-doing/using, while the latter is probably associated with specialized research. With respect to firm organization, the implication then is that incremental change needs more integrated co-ordination among different links of the same production chain (the notion of 'networks'), or different divisions within the firm, whilst abrupt change requires the division of labour to be structured in a more specialized manner.

This implication is captured by Aoki's (1990) model of the Japanese firm. The model emphasizes horizontal co-ordination, as opposed to the vertical co-ordination that characterized the (stylized) American firm. In a situation where innovations are incremental, the sharing of the knowledge from on-site learning would require close co-ordination between different units of the production chain and different functional divisions within the firm. The benefits arising from the sharing would more than compensate for the loss due to a lower degree of specialized division of labour.

This situation is evident in industries where product innovation is prominent and where the production process is continuous and integrated, such as automobile and steel-making. In the case of Japanese automobile firms, Aoki (1990) finds that horizontal co-ordination takes the following forms: in the production chain (parts suppliers and assemblers) it uses the *kanban* (just-in-time) system, while the interdivisional relationship within the firm is characterized by successive and gradual adjustments in line with continuous inflows of information from the marketing division, and the involvement of the central planning office in the daily adjustment process is minimized. In the case of steel-making plants where integrated production across related workshops is prioritized, horizontal co-ordination takes the form of an 'integrated engineering control room' which exists side-by-side with engineering offices for each workshop, and this spatial proximity fosters locating and solving 'cross-workshop' problems through discussion and bargaining between the offices in charge of individual workshops.

How is this exposition related to the exchange- and production-oriented approaches to firm organization, particularly innovation? Take the example of the emergence of in-house specialized R&D centres, which according to the studies reviewed in Coombs *et al.* (1987) has historically overlapped with the transition of firm organization from unitary (U-form) to multidivisional (M-form) structure. Transaction cost economics says that this overlapping indicates an attempt of the top-level management to cope with 'control loss' due to the growth of firm size and subsequently the need to decompose firm structure. That is to say, the creation of a specialized R&D division in the centre represents the top management's move to control a strategic unit of the firm; and this is undertaken in a context of leaving routine operations at the discretion of the spatially- or product-differentiated divisions which are quasi-autonomous in the M-form structure.

The R&D division is considered to be strategic for two reasons. First, as mentioned in referring to Teece (1988), the peculiar features of R&D activities imply high transaction costs of buying through the market. It is thus rational to replace in-house research for outsourcing. Second, and for the same reasons, in-house R&D divisions are generally centralized in the headquarters of the M-form organization. Because of the incentive of divisions being oriented to short-term profits, 'the problems of long-time horizon, non-specificity and high uncertainty are more appropriate to levels in the firm responsible for strategic overviews rather than short-term, specific responsibilities as in divisions' (Kay 1988, p.290). More generally, the centralization of R&D activities is in line with Williamson's notion of promoting 'synergy' – that is the principle of curtailing 'weak interactions' and encouraging 'rich interactions' between different divisions of the M-form structure. On the whole, the structuring of an R&D division in the centre is seen as an organizational design by the top management for minimizing the cost of the firm as a whole. So cost-minimization, which is implicitly assumed to be emanating from the pressure (and incentive) of market competition, is the ultimate driving force.

From a production-oriented perspective, cost-minimization might be neither the ultimate driving force nor always desirable for the firm. The centralization of R&D activities (or rich interactions) and further the structuring of different divisions in an M-form manner (weak interactions) do not necessarily foster synergy. If the direction of innovation is at least partly driven by firm-specific accumulated human and organizational resources, there is no guarantee for cost-minimization (Coombs *et al.* 1987). In this circumstance, the respective scopes of rich and weak interactions have been misspecified under the M-form structure. Meanwhile, cost-minimization is not necessarily superior to other directions of innovation such as continuous, incremental improvement in products. Everything depends on the nature of competition in the market, especially the stability of demand or the factors that determine capacity utilization. The centralization of R&D activities, then, might hinder the interaction between specialized research and knowledge obtained from learning-by-doing/using. More generally, in line with Aoki's (1990) reasoning, the M-form structure might result in spatial hindrance to the sharing of learned knowledge across divisions and, in the incentive aspect, might give rise to unfavourable sectionalism.

Thus, what is crucial in determining the innovation capacity of the M-form organization is the environment which the firm confronts, or more precisely the 'openness' of the organization in adapting to the environment. This goes back to the specific technological paradigm of the industry in question – the sources of innovation. If the sources are mainly incremental on-site learning, it is unlikely that the M-form structure must be the most efficient (whether or not cost-minimizing is another matter). If, by contrast, the innovation is characterized by abrupt change, the importance of learning would then give way to specialized R&D; and the benefits gained from structuring divisions in a horizontally-co-ordinated manner would be insufficient to compensate for the loss due to the hindrance to specialization. Under these circumstances the M-form structure would appear to be more conducive to the innovation capacity of the firm.

Finally, in a situation where the concern of the firm is to drive down production cost rather than to develop ever new products, specialized R&D would be more capable than the horizontally-integrated production units in generating innovations, while the loss of learning effects would not be vital with respect to the overall competitive advantage of the firm. This seems to conform to the notion of the Fordist regime of mass production.

Ownership and Organization

The emphasis on the production system as a continuously, collectively learning entity is an effective way of tracing the sources of incremental innovations. In Best's (1990) notion of the 'strategic firm', learning effects are generated by all levels of work within the firm. In the flexible specialization literature, the sharing of information/knowledge is further extended to independent firms of the same production system. Finally, Aoki's (1990) model of the Japanese firm incorporates both. But this extension of the sources of innovation capacity raises the corresponding requirement for a more delicate incentive structure. Even within the firm, there is the question as to how the overall community (firm) interest can be promoted, or, how to cope with the possibility that information-sharing might be blocked by individual and/or sectional self-interests. All these writings tend to pick up a history-specific element of one form or another deemed prominent in shaping the evolution of the production system, particularly the emergence of relations of trust among the concerned agents.

In contrast, most exchange-oriented writings, with the assumption of the ubiquitous existence of the market, tend to deduce the evolution of the production system from market regulation. Alchian and Demsetz's (1972) model of the 'classical capitalist firm' is antithetical to the learning firm. Essentially, it says that to provide the necessary incentive for the team-work the creation of a 'residual claimant', that is conceding the disciplinary power and reward of residual benefits to specialized monitors, is indispensable. Thus, to be efficient, the reward system must be based on assessing accurately the performance of individual employees, so as to avoid free-riding in the team-work. For the same reason and especially for enabling the functioning of the monitors, the creation of an authority hierarchy is also imperative. By definition, the model rules out the organization of the firm in some forms of horizontal co-ordination. With the prevalence of a 'calculative atmosphere', it also rules out relations of trust both among workers and between workers and managers. On the whole, the model emphasizes the control by the residual claimant over every level inside the firm.

The exchange-oriented approach of course need not go to this extreme. In fact, in the tradition there are arguments which dispute the claimed efficiency-imperative of the strict hierarchy and/or individualistic assessment, the idea of 'idiosyncratic exchange' developed by Williamson *et al.* (1975) being an example. The premise of the idea is familiar: incumbent workers from learning-by-doing possess idiosyncratic knowledge of their work environment, which can be a significant source of productivity for the firm. It is thus beneficial for the firm to encourage workers establishing long-term commitment, rather than to emphasize linking short-run reward and performance for individual workers. It follows that the reward system is better structured in such a way as to tie pay to well-defined jobs, rather than to individuals, and filling higher slots through internal promotion. Also, an atmosphere of goodwill and co-operation would be more beneficial for the firm than a calculative atmosphere that is likely to cause frequent disputes and a perfunctory working ethos.

In transaction cost economics, the idea of 'idiosyncratic exchange' has another, more renowned implication: the possible dilemma of bilateral monopoly between workers and the management. By acquiring the idiosyncratic knowledge, workers might have monopolistic power to exploit. That the knowledge is firm-specific implies the management is also in a monopolistic position *vis-à-vis* workers, based on the threat of refusing to renew employment contracts. Hence, Williamson *et al.* (1975) propose that it is rational for the firm to maintain the power hierarchy and the vertical information flow channels, while at the same time creating a collective bargaining mechanism which integrates the interests of all workers into a single 'voice'. The combined functioning of these two mechanisms would minimize the opportunism of both the management and workers.

The claim by Williamson *et al.* that their check-and-balance model represents the most efficient form of firm organization (compared with the 'classical capitalist firm' and the 'peer group' democratic firm) is a matter of debate. Radical writers often criticize it for disregarding power and control relations which are prominent in the reality of capitalism. Bowles' (1985) thesis of labour extraction, which takes into account workers' preference over alternative forms of work organization, is a forceful argument against the claimed efficiency-superiority of the power hierarchy. From this perspective, the Alchian–Demsetz model is clearly untenable. But the attempt by Williamson *et al.* to formulate a model that is uniquely efficient is also put in question – there might rather be multiple organization forms that have comparable incentive effects on the learning firm.

The above debate over the employment relationship can be generalized to cover other aspects of firm organization. Regarding the incentive of intra-firm divisions, Williamson's (1985) 'M-form hypothesis' says that in modern corporations the M-form structure is superior to the unitary (U-form) and holding company (H-form) structures. This is based on the idea that the M-form structure incorporates some internal markets, which save transaction costs when compared with arm's-length exchanges, and administrative cost when compared with hierarchy. Divisions have to exhibit good performance in the 'internal capital market' when competing for financial resources. This is in turn linked to the internal promotion of middle management, thus solving its incentive problem. The M-form structure, in short, combines both the internalization of information flows – the general office is in a better position than external share-holders in monitoring the divisions – with the benefits of competitive allocation. A problem with the 'M-form hypothesis', however, is that its assumption of market competition as the ultimate source of incentive can be simplistic. It assumes the behaviour of the 'general office' being representative of the community interests. Yet it is possible to have collusion between the general office and divisions, or, between the management of the two levels. This stems from the difficulty of splitting strategic and routine decision-making, that is the appropriate balance between divisional autonomy and the general office's strategic roles (Stephen and Thompson 1988).

A final aspect of the institutional dimension concerns the capital structure of the firm, or, more generally, the problem of ownership. Neoclassical economics postulates that it makes no difference for the capital structure of the firm to be debt- or equity-dominated. But property rights theorists, who consider the operation of the stock market as particularly conforming to the principle of the market, tend to place higher regard for equity financing (see for example, Borensztein and Kumar 1991). In contrast, in the literature there is another tradition which contends that the debt-dominated structure is characterized by investors (the bank) having more long-term commitments to the firm (Berglof 1990). The commitments are expressed in bearing risk of, and exerting control over, the performance of the firm. But these two functions are often asymmetric. While providing the management of the firm a relatively stable environment, that is insulating them from frequent takeover raids through the open market, the control of the bank would only be a potential threat so long as the firm is making profit of a satisfactory level. It follows that the on-site management would have long-term commitments as well. This can be a strong incentive as the internal promotion ladder for employees would then extend to as high as the top executive position. It is for this reason that Aoki (1990) claims that the bank-oriented financial system is conducive to the incremental innovations of the Japanese firm.

If, however, there is an asymmetry between the risk-bearing and control functions of the bank, the firm would then enjoy some degree of 'soft budget constraint' – *ex ante*, it need not be fully responsible for the risk to which its decisions give rise. Thus the debt-dominated capital structure, or bank-oriented financial system, whilst being conducive to the learning firm, can violate the principle of allocative efficiency.[8]

To summarize, the incentive problem in the context of a learning firm appears to be more delicate than that envisaged by those working from an exchange-oriented perspective. Mainstream economics has much to say about competition, but little about co-operation. In contrast, the various production-oriented approaches reviewed here turn to history. To develop an analytical framework that accounts for experiences as diverse as American big business, Japanese strategic firms and the workshop industries of Italy, Best (1990) suggests that the focus can be placed at the interaction between the specific forms of technical change and class conflicts, that is techno-economic paradigms. Notions like regime of accumulation, flexible specialization and social structure of accumulation can be seen as attempts along this line (for a more economistic synthesis, see Piore 1992).

TRANSFORMATION OF THE SOVIET-TYPE ECONOMIC SYSTEM

Big Bang as a Walrasian Endeavour

The debate on 'big bang' versus gradualist approaches to the transformation of the Soviet-type economic system, as some protagonists have argued (Murrell 1991, 1992a, 1992b, 1993), can be seen in the context of the competition between two different strands in economics: namely, the standard neoclassical (Walrasian) theory and the evolutionary perspective.[9] The difference involves both spheres of focus and the underlying assumptions about economic development. In contrast to the neoclassical view of the market as an allocative mechanism, the evolutionary approach focuses on its role in generating innovations. Instead of assuming substitutability of productive inputs, it emphasizes the system-specificity of information and the widespread existence of linkages, and hence the need for forming specific institutions and expectations for the proper functioning of any economic system. The latter aspect, in particular, provides a forceful explanation for the dismal economic performance of countries of the former Soviet bloc under 'big bang': the programmes, while destroying old institutions and expectations, cannot bring into place new ones because the formation of the new is inevitably a time-consuming process.

But, it is far from definitive that the evolutionary approach must be a hostile rival of the central arguments of 'big bang'. One ambiguity concerns its vision of the end-state of transformation. So far the evolutionary writings have not made much attempt to unravel the interplay among the three aspects of their focus: institutions, innovations and economic development. They simply leave the end-state to be determined by the market, assuming that the most efficient institutions would thereby emerge. As a result, apart from the division over the pace of transformation, the evolutionary propositions appear very close to the market-mania of 'big bang' protagonists, who often contend that, whatever the initial arrangements, the optimal end-state will emerge over time through the regulation of the market. Their break with 'big bang' becomes far less complete than it appears to be.

But what is 'big bang'? In his comment on Lipton and Sachs (1990a, p. 139), Kornai states: 'the comprehensive policy discussed in Lipton and Sachs's paper and known variously as "one stroke", "big bang" or – as in my own book, *The Road to a Free Economy* – "surgery", a major operation on a patient involving a whole package of measures. If the Government is committed, strong, and enjoys a solid national backing, there is a good chance that such comprehensive reforms and measures, painful but needed, will come to pass.' To be worthwhile of the title, five major measures are typically identified (Kornai 1990; Lipton and Sachs 1990a, 1990b, 1992): stabilization, price liberalization, privatization of state-owned enterprises, promotion of the private sector, and trade liberalization. The idea is to mould every aspect of the economy as close as possible to the free market model. But there is also an internal logic for comprehensiveness. As Lipton and Sachs (1990a, p. 99) put it,

> the transition process is a seamless web. Structural reforms cannot work without a working price system; a working price system cannot be put in place without ending excess demand and creating a convertible currency; and a credit squeeze and tight macroeconomic policy cannot be sustained unless prices are realistic, so that there is a rational basis for deciding which firms should be allowed to close. At the same time, for real structural adjustment to take place under the pressure of tight demand, the macroeconomic shock must be accompanied by other measures, including selling off state assets, freeing up the private sector . . .

The premise of 'big bang', therefore, is that these different aspects can change at more or less the same speed, or at least that the lagging behind of any particular aspect would not be so serious as to the extent of disrupting the whole package. Essentially, as Tsang (1992) argues, 'big bang' proponents only look at two sets of variables, that is the 'stabilization' variables (prices, the money supply, the fiscal deficit, the exchange rate, etc.) and 'systemic' variables (ownership and management) and merely treat the latter as constraints for the former, while discounting to a negligible place all the intermediate 'medium-speed movers' in the economic system (the formation of legal-institutional frameworks, efficient information flows, and so on). The proponents assume that once liberalized, together with the easing of the systemic constraints, the economy would soon restore its internal coherence and achieve proper functioning. At its extreme, the systemic constraints are regarded as purely political in nature, artificially imposed by the privileged social strata (the bureaucracy) of the old system. Their breaking up, therefore, is considered to be both feasible and desirable.[10]

It is noted that 'big bang' proponents tend to treat price (and trade) liberalization as tantamount to market formation. In an exercise typical of the writings, Boycko (1991) attempts to prove that rapid price decontrol would lead to welfare improvement for consumers. The starting point is the phenomena of shortages, and hence queues, under the old system. It follows that if, instead of in queues, this time and effort were used at the workplace or just consumed as leisure, output and welfare could be substantially higher. An empirical calculation runs in the following way: treating the prices in the non-government stores as the market-clearing prices, the differences between them and the government prices therefore represent the welfare dissipated in queues. In the case of foodstuffs, Boycko (1991 p. 38) claims: 'if food had been sold at equilibrium prices in the Soviet Union in 1990, and the time free from queuing spent consuming leisure, the welfare gain would have amounted to 75 per cent of income!' It follows the justification for big bang-type price liberalization:

> we think that this constitutes a most important case for rapid price decontrol, at least in the consumer goods sector. The huge inefficiencies in the distribution system can be eliminated very quickly, bringing about a tremendous welfare gain even without a (positive) output response: any given output would be allocated among consumers in a much more rational way, without the wasteful expenditures of time and effort. Surprisingly, with the prominent exception of Lipton and Sachs [1990a], this point received little attention in the literature on reform in socialist economies.

Surprising? The 'big bang' protagonists should have been told that, even within the neoclassical paradigm, a comparative statics exercise of this kind is not sophisticated enough to be a policy prescription. Here, the link between price liberalization and the formation of market-clearing prices is missing. Yet with the time dimension being taken into account, the price adjustment is not instantaneous but must be a consecutive process. During this process economic agents, with varied degrees of inflation expectations, would modify their demand and supply behaviours (notably panic purchasing and hoarding), thus exacerbating inflation and disrupting the proper functioning of the economy (Hua *et al.* 1988). Moreover, for the achievement of general equilibrium, the introduction of the time dimension into the process implies enormous uncertainty. To quote Sawyer (1991, p. 28), 'when prices adjust in real time, then prices differ over time and it follows that the commodity at time *t* is to be considered as different from the commodity at time *t+1* (since there is non-uniformity of price). This indicates that the analysis of disequilibrium processes in real time in market situations is not just difficult – it is impossible'.

A further issue ignored in the above exercise, or indeed the proposal for rapid price liberalization in general, is the necessary institutional framework within which prices can adjust. In general equilibrium analysis there is the Walrasian auctioneer who not only makes the time dimension disappear but also informs the numerous economic agents when and where equilibria are reached. But in real world practice, the absence of such an auctioneer means the problem of co-ordination must be taken into account. As Wang (1993) points out, in a Soviet-type economy there is, typically, a whole distribution network which, based on planned prices, co-ordinates demand and supply. The big bang-type price liberalization, while destroying the old network, does not correspond with the formation of a new network and thus can only lead to disruption of commodity circulation.

'Big bang' writers like Kornai (1990) are confident that, following price liberalization, the private sector would be able to fill the gap left by the killed state-owned sector. Boycko (1991, p. 39) goes even further to claim that, even for the state-owned sector, 'there are few reasons to believe that the performance of a labour-managed firm or a managerial firm will be worse with flexible prices than with fixed prices unless these firms enjoy substantial monopoly power'. However, the existence of institutional and technical constraints casts the claim in serious doubt. If price elasticity of supply is low, price liberalization is likely to result in inflation only. Institutionally, whatever the speed of privatization, the prevalence of the state-owned sector will be a fact for the foreseeable future. This is because, in Kornai's words, 'it is impossible to privatize in a "big bang"'. Even for Lipton and Sachs who propose privatization at the fastest speed, disregarding Kornai's concern for equity and efficiency, a number of technical problems still bring it significant obstacles. In addition to problems of creating the legal framework and efficient information flows, there are also limitations on resources mobility and inter-sectoral substitutability.

On the whole, the significance of the existing enterprise system and industrial structure is not just a matter of 'deadweight loss' as envisaged by Boycko's static analysis. They rather make the target of price liberalization, that is the formation of 'realistic' relative prices, unattainable. After all, 'the term "market" is a reification of a set of behavioural relations which exist between participants – a market is not a thing but a behavioural relation' (Auerbach 1988, p. 122). It does not make sense to treat price adjustment as something occurring outside the participation of enterprises.

The Evolutionary Criticism and Beyond

Thus one can infer the end-state of transformation as envisaged by 'big bang' protagonists. First of all, it is on solid ground to say that they are aiming at the Walrasian 'pure' market – that is a collection of arm's-length exchanges based on parametric prices. We have shown that in 'big bang' writings there is such an implicit vision of the market which renders it possible to talk about price formation while not taking into consideration the institutional framework and the behavioural patterns of economic agents. A further feature of the writings, as Tsang (1992) notes, is the ignorance of 'the theorem of the second best'. By proposing comprehensive measures, simultaneously, to remove all 'distortions', as quickly as possible, it presumes that the economy can fulfil the major optimum conditions. To put it another way, in excluding any 'second best' solutions that are based on the recognition that some 'distortions' would inevitably remain, the 'big bang' approach presumes that the 'pure' market can be sustainable. It is true that the writers have varied degrees of faith for the 'pure' market, with Eastern bloc protagonists exhibiting far stronger enthusiasm. By proposing comprehensive and rapid transformation, however, they share the same vision of the end-state.

It is relatively easy to point out numerous economic features in the real world which deviate vastly from the 'pure' market. But what is more crucial is to argue that the features are necessary for the viability of an economy. One argument concerns incomplete information. This is endemic to the economy, and even more so for production because of ever-changing technology, behavioural patterns and market conditions. It follows the requirement of flexibility on the part of the firm. This, however, is difficult to satisfy due to bounded rationality, especially limited knowledge about the future. It is costly as well, because of enormous fixed investment. Thus, in the labour sector, it is reasonable for firms to adopt long-term and flexible employment contracts in order to achieve flexibility in supply (Best 1990). The labour sector is also characterized by enormous uncertainty because of variable productivity – the commodities (labour services) are not well-defined, arising from variable work intensity (Bowles 1985). This means employment contracts are difficult to specify. It thus reinforces the need for adopting flexible and long-term contracts. From this setting, there exists scope for bargaining and negotiation in the settlement of efforts and rewards. The criterion of pure arm's-length exchanges is thus broken down.

The above point can be generalized to cover many economic relations which involve close technical links on the one hand and uncertain environment on the other hand. These include the relationship between different firms of the same production chain. The Japanese just-in-time (*kanban*) system is a case illustrating the need to adopt flexible and long-term supplying contracts (explicit or implicit) between parts-producers and assemblers. The point is that it would be too costly to rely on purely arm's-length exchanges (Sayer and Walker 1992). The legal enforcement of contracts is also costly. For the proper functioning of the economy, there are a number of arrangements adopted to facilitate exchanges: price norms, routines of behaviours, a minimum level of trust sustained by specific business culture, etc. (Sawyer 1991). All these are 'imperfections' or 'rigidities' from the standpoint of the free market paradigm. But they are indispensable for the viability of any economy.

A further step of generalization can be made by drawing on information economics. A number of studies in this strand (Stiglitz and Weiss 1981; Shapiro and Stiglitz 1984) have showed that, for economic arrangements involving principal-agent problems, the price would affect the quality of the commodity through two effects: that of adverse selection, and that of the agent's incentive to affect the quality. The adverse selection effect stems from the general fact that the quality of the commodity is not well-defined. Hence, the principal has to rely on the price instruments as devices for screening potential agents. This however means a price–quantity relationship contradicting the law of demand and supply. Meanwhile, the incentive effect is related to the problem of information asymmetry: 'when private information affects both allocation and distribution, that information can be used to improve a person's welfare, possibly at the expense of efficiency' (Murrell 1991). It can be further argued that, even without the asymmetry, information imperfection arising from the absence of the Walrasian auctioneer would still lead to a certain extent to the same effect: 'the function of being an "auctioneer" is generally combined with some other function such as being a producer or distributor. Having the role of price setter conveys some power, and which economic agents are the effective auctioneers will influence how the economy operates'. (Sawyer 1991).

The criticism made above, which also forms the core arguments of the evolutionary writings, does not undermine the free market paradigm *in toto*. Focusing on dynamic change, which they regard as the major impetus behind economic development, the evolutionary writers argue that the free market economy is, in fact, the most efficient system. The reasons, according to Murrell (1992b, p. 39), are: 'first, there is the automatic way in which markets reallocate the control over resources from inefficient organizations to efficient ones. Second, bankruptcy and, to some extent, takeovers and mergers remove inefficient organizations. Third, there is the process of entry – the creation of a variety of new organizations, some of which will find an effective organizational structure in the new circumstances.' In short, the free market economy is flexible enough to accommodate the required innovations, whereas the Soviet-type system is not. These arguments amount to Ronald Coase's notion that a competitive market would ensure the optimal combination of market and hierarchy. In the remaining part of the chapter, I address these arguments.

To engage with the debate over market regulation of innovation, in the context of our discussion where the focus is not just market failure as such (for example the fact that innovation often exhibits the character of a public goods) but rather the failure of the market in regulating the innovation activity of non-market institutions, we can begin with a claim made by Lazonick (1991, pp. 64–5),

> the theory of the market economy fails to address the central problem of economic development: the growth of value-creating capabilities that result in higher-quality products at lower unit costs . . . In defining the economic problem as the allocation of scarce resources, neoclassical economics ignores the analysis of how individuals, firms, and economies create more value with the same amount of human and physical resources, and thereby overcome scarcity. In short, neoclassical economics has a theory of value *allocation*, but it lacks a theory of value *creation*.

In essence, the thesis of 'allocation versus creation' concerns who makes the critical decisions that determine economic development: the market or the firm? The answer from orthodox theory is unambiguously the former. In line with the models of optimal saving and overlapping generations, growth results from saving generated by forces of productivity and thrift, plus exogenous technical change. For the evolutionary writers, despite their emphasis on entrepreneurship, the subscription to the centrality of the market implies their sharing the same message with neoclassical theory: that the invisible hand will ensure resources being allocated to their most productive uses, just like any other aspect of market allocation occurring in line with the principle of consumer choice and utility maximization.[11]

This message is subject to various criticisms. In the Keynesian tradition, investment injections might not equal saving leakages. It is usually firms which make the decisions that involve the demand for investment. In the decision-making process, the market interest rate is not the sole determining factor; of equal importance is, as Lazonick (1991, p. 65) argues, 'the expected net value of an investment – an outcome that may be determined more by the organizational capability of the investing firm to develop technology and enhance productivity than by the configuration of market prices that the firm takes as given'. This highlights that firms are more crucial than the market, and production is more crucial than exchange, in determining economic development (see also Taylor 1992).

A further point concerns the sources of productive efficiency, or the factors which firms can actively generate to determine the expected returns to investment. Three factors are prominent. First, in line with Alfred Marshall's notion of 'internal economies of scale', firms can spread their fixed costs over more output thus lowering unit costs. Second, firms can enhance their productive capabilities through continuous organizational innovations. Third, firms through continuous technological innovations can have the power to shape the market and to enhance their competitive positions, a notion of entrepreneurial activity made famous by Joseph Schumpeter (Best 1990; Lazonick 1991; Taylor 1992; Teece 1993). Essentially, all these factors are in the nature of value creation rather than resources allocation. The argument that they play a dominant role in economic development contradicts the neoclassical exchange-oriented vision. It is also difficult to incorporate into the evolutionary view the concept that it is the market which regulates the firm, not the reverse.

Against Privatization

The belief on the universal applicability of the market would not be complete if it does not extend into the realm of institution creation. In a summary of the position of many big bang protagonists, Lipton and Sachs (1990b, p. 296) so aptly describe:

> advocates of rapid privatization are typically confident that even if quick privatization initially leads to an inappropriate distribution of ownership with, for example, too diffuse ownership, or firms in the wrong hands, then the capital markets will encourage a reshuffling of ownership through takeovers, mergers, and buyouts so that there is a proper matching of owners and firms. For these analysts, privatization should be undertaken as rapidly as possible, to reap the full benefits of private ownership.

It follows various privatization proposals which rely typically on some distributive schemes. Shares of ownership in state enterprises are transferred for free, or for a nominal charge, to private hands. In contrast, Western advisers like Lipton and Sachs are less concerned with the fair distribution of the supposedly all-people's assets. A free distribution scheme, in their view, would face the problem that the public at large is unlikely to be able to bid in a rational manner in the auctions for individual enterprises. And the required auction process is also of vast scale: it would include bidding by literally millions of individuals for each and every enterprise. Thus, ironically, it appears that Lipton and Sachs (1990b, p. 316) have more confidence in the institution-creating capability of the state than the market: 'it would be useful to match firms with appropriate owners in the privatization process itself, rather than relying on subsequent trading to establish the "right" owners for a firm'. They design a privatization package involving free distribution of shares to financial intermediaries (mutual funds, pension funds, commercial banks, etc.), together with the creation of a non-financial 'core investor' in each firm to oversee the management. This helps to sidestep the process of enterprise valuation. The creation of a 'stable core' in the ownership structure also helps to establish an effective corporate governance.

It should be clear that Lipton and Sachs in fact say nothing about the economic rationale of their proposed end-state. Their concern is to have owners' control over the firms as strict as possible. But even within the neoclassical paradigm, there is still the problem of market failure. The atomistic ownership structure might be inefficient due to information asymmetry and the free-rider problem. Yet the 'stable core' arrangement, just like the deficiency of equity finance, is by definition a market imperfection. It follows the need to prove that, on efficiency grounds, the balance is in favour of one kind of imperfection over another. But this proof is absent in virtually all the big bang privatization proposals.

In contrast, the idea of 'letting the market select' seems at least to have a consistent theoretical underpinning. It is in line with the property rights theory, regarding the optimal corporate governance as (as it can only be) purely an outcome of competitive market selection. This line of thinking inspires writers such as Borensztein and Kumar (1991, p. 302) to defend the superiority of private ownership. 'What is the basic case for privatization?' they ask, and give the answer: 'private ownership leads to the achievement of the conditions of a competitive environment in which market prices reflect relative scarcities, and enterprises and individuals make decisions mainly in response to undistorted market signals'. The causation rests on the incentives for the private owners, as the 'residual claimants', to ensure profit maximization as well as to monitor and control the performance of the managers effectively running the firm.

A number of questions arise. The first concerns the property rights theorists' criticism of the proposition about the separation of ownership and control. Demsetz (1983) argues that production is part and parcel of the utility-maximizing behaviour of the agents inside the firm (owners, managers and workers), and markets always exist to discipline these agents in ways consistent to profit-maximization of the firm. Thus, any 'known on-the-job consumption' is just a trade-off with lower pecuniary returns for the agents involved. Even in the case where monitoring costs are positive, the existence of competitive pressure outside the firm and the benefit of voluntary exchange would reduce shirking down to its optimal level where the marginal monitoring cost equals to the marginal value of the resources consumed in shirking, thus again leaving profit-maximization unaffected.

A counter argument, following the discussion on the conceptualization of the market, is that Demsetz's presumption that the market always exists and exists ubiquitously is flawed. Labour services, including the management, do not have well-defined qualities. This means that the market, especially in the sense of uniform and parametric prices, hardly exists. Labour productivity is variable, depending on the power relations within the firm (Bowles 1985). Moreover, the existence of enormous fixed capital in modern production makes the throughput dependent on the efforts of workers, thus capital 'productivity' (utilization) is variable as well. Capital owners are thus inclined to adopt long-term employment contracts, for the sake of ensuring management co-ordination of work to achieve high throughput (Lazonick 1991). The firm is not often a profit-maximizing entity, despite the capital owner's intention for it to do so.

A second counter argument follows our discussion on production, that is the thesis of 'allocation versus creation'. The non-existence of an ubiquitous market (which is supposedly determining the input-output prices) implies that the production function of the firm, even if it exists, is not fully specified. The endogeneity of organizational and technical innovations brings further discretion to the hands of the management. All these imply that the principal-agent relationship between external portfolio investors (the natural-personal owners) and the management is prone to break down altogether. Thus, empirically, it is observed that firms in advanced capitalist economies tend to avoid external borrowing through the stock market, a channel that is supposedly operating closest to the principle of the market. As Lazonick (1991, p. 191) argues, 'entrepreneurs avoid reliance on impersonal capital markets until they have transformed their firms from new ventures into going concerns – that is, firms that are generating sufficient value to finance *internally* their current operations'.

There is also the application of the property rights theory to the criticism of the Soviet-type system, resulting in a number of 'negative arguments' which also constitutes the proposed superiority of private ownership. Kornai (1990) claims repeatedly that the hope that the system may be reformable has gone once and for all. His argument starts with a dichotomous definition of ownership: 'entities belonging to the state sector are not in private ownership. Or, as the economic theory of property rights would put it: the residual income that emerges as the difference between receipts and expenses does not pass into the pockets of natural persons, and the losses are not covered by the same natural party' (p. 57). This embraces the central thesis of the property rights approach: that it is only the natural-personal owners who control and direct production, and that it is only based on this condition that modern capitalist economies have developed. Kornai's second argument concerns the conceptualization of the state, equally peculiar: 'the state-owned firms belong to the sphere of "government" rather than "business" . . . In fact, each organization of the governmental sphere tends to spend the money of the citizen in an unbridled manner . . . the manager of a state-owned firm is not an entrepreneur. There is no getting away from the fact that he, like the heads of other state institutions, is out to expand his spending limits as far as possible' (p. 60–2).[12] Taken together, the two arguments imply that 'it is time to abandon hope that the budget constraint can be hardened', (p. 62).

It should be noted that the term 'soft budget constraint' is not an unambiguous one. In his early work, Kornai (1980) uses it to summarize a set of enterprise behaviours observed in Soviet-type economies. These include the fact that the survival of the enterprise is guaranteed by the state, and that its expansion involves an asymmetry between rewards and punishment. In short, it can count on bargaining with the state, rather than on its own good performance in market competition, for financial well-being. At a structural level, however, as Hua *et al.* (1986) and Zhang (1987) point out, the notion of soft budget constraint is simplistic. While recognizing the existence of varied degrees of softness and hardness of budget constraint in both capitalist and Soviet-type firms, Kornai's summary collapses into simply a *spectrum* between two extremes. He disregards the possibility of multiple forms of state-firm (and market-firm) relationship which carry the same degree of softness or hardness.

Moreover, the term soft budget constraint is used by Kornai in a purely negative sense, implying that to be hard-budgeted is always better than to be soft-budgeted. It says nothing about the relative merits and deficiencies of different degrees and forms of softness and hardness. Instead, in a counter-criticism of critics who cite the fact that even in advanced capitalist world many firms are soft-budgeted if measured by the criterion of the property rights theory, Kornai (1990, p. 76), while admitting the fact, refutes the argument: 'in the West the impersonalization of property is criticized as well, and in my view these criticisms are often accurate. Ironically, the germs of socialism are already present in today's capitalism'. This, however, is not a credible way of arguing. A more reasonable approach is to unravel the economic meaning of the seemingly sub-optimal institutional arrangements. This involves investigating the causal link between ownership and organization, and adopting a criterion that is more comprehensive than allocative efficiency alone.

Take the example of Japan and consider the following (stylized) facts: of the biggest 960 firms the share ownership is so diffused that only 31 have individual shareholding exceeding 10 per cent; inter-firm (often bilateral) shareholding accounts for about one-third of these firms, with each firm possessing only a small share in any other; most firms raise external finance through bank borrowings instead of issuing shares, and the relationship between banks (which are themselves with no individual shareholding exceeding 5 per cent) and firms is characterized by long-term transactional stability; virtually all the boards of directors of firms are composed of members internally promoted, often approved by the top management; the proportion of dividend to profit of Japanese firms is the lowest among advanced capitalist countries; takeover activity is a rare phenomenon; most management executives typically do not move from one firm to another in their careers (CESRRI 1988a; Odagiri 1992; Zhang 1987). What do all these indicate? They indicate a minimal degree of owners' control. For the property rights theorists, they imply an unacceptable erosion of the very foundation of the free market economy – the impersonalization of property rights.

Focusing on the mutual shareholding between banks and industrial firms, Odagiri (1992, p. 36) provides an explanation for its economic rationale: 'stability has its own advantages which are larger as asset specificity is higher. A good bank–customer relationship, based on accumulated knowledge of each other's management and accumulated confidence, is an asset'. This is in line with the thesis of credit rationing raised by Stiglitz and Weiss (1981), from which it can be argued that the problem of imperfect information makes it necessary for creating some long-term (rigid) institutional arrangements in the capital market. The same applies to the mutual shareholding between different firms of the same production chain (CESRRI 1988a). It also applies to the practice of long-term employment relationship, for labour service is characterized by asset specificity as well, as is explained by the thesis of 'idiosyncratic exchange' raised by Williamson *et al.* (1975).

It can be argued, however, that the concept of asset specificity, and with it the various exchange-oriented theories that are incorporated into the evolutionary approach, is too static to capture the essence of the Japanese firm. Best (1990) makes a distinction between information and knowledge: information is something marketable whereas knowledge is actively generated by the participating agents – that is, collective learning. For the firm as a whole to become a learning entity, however, it requires the integration of thinking and doing in the labour process, horizontal information flows across functional boundaries as well as relations of trust between the management and the on-site workers. The same applies to the relationship between different firms of the same production chain, for example a sub-contracting relationship. As a whole, it needs the relations of 'consultative co-ordination/co-operation' among major participants of the production system.

Viewed this way, the implication of the debt-dominated financing of

Japanese firms becomes clear: it fosters long-term commitment of the participants of the production system. As Aoki (1990, p. 14) puts it, because a major proportion of external financing is from an extremely stable source, 'the managements of Japanese firms are insulated from takeover raids through the open market'. The long-term commitment of investors, in turn, encourages the long-term commitment of the on-site management. This contradicts the principle of the property rights theory where it is required that the management must be under constant pressure of the capital and managerial markets. The debt-dominated external financing of firms, therefore, must imply allocative sub-optimality. From the standpoint of production rather than allocation, however, the stable environment is a prerequisite for the long-term commitment and hence active participation of the employees.

For the property rights theory, its exclusive focus on owners' control implies a principle of business organization that is detrimental to productive efficiency. This is illustrated by Alchian and Demsetz's (1972) model of the 'classical capitalist firm', which is a logical expression of the principle. Emphasizing the prevention of shirking as an essential feature of the firm, the model proposes an employment relationship that is based on linking the short-term rewards and performance of individual employees. By placing the residual claimant at a central position, it also proposes a strict power hierarchy to facilitate the functioning of the monitors. Obviously, this model stems from a purely exchange-orientated vision of production. It presumes that the production function of the firm and the labour services of individual employees are well-defined, and that the residual claimant would ensure the attainment of the production function as well as the optimal allocation of labour in line with the market-determined factor prices. For promoting the firm to be a collective learning entity, the detrimental effect of the model is apparent. The 'calculative atmosphere' and the strict power hierarchy are antithetical to the long-term commitment and active participation of employees.

Ownership, Organization and Development: An Alternative Formulation

Lazonick (1991) contends that the Japanese experience is not an enigma but rather represents an enhancement of what has accounted for the competitive advantage of American capitalism *vis-à-vis* British capitalism: the transition of the firm organization based on owners' control to one based on commitment of the whole managerial layer, and further to one based on commitment of the entire staff down to the shopfloor level. This is a thesis related to the prominence of continuous innovations. It is particularly relevant to late industrialization, as is made clear by the 'learning paradigm' or the proposition for flexible production. As for the transformation of the Soviet-type economic system, the logical question to ask then is, how can its conducive potentials be preserved and its detrimental features be curtailed? In the light of the discussion above, and based on a number of Chinese studies (CESRRI 1987a, 1987b, 1988a; Hua *et al.* 1986, 1988; Wang 1988; Zhang 1987, 1988) and the exposition by Japanese writers like Aoki (1990) and Odagiri (1992), the following points should basically clarify the necessary conditions based on which Soviet-type enterprises can develop into collective learning entities.

The first point, which is the most fundamental, is the institutionalization of the distinctive interests of firms. This is the prerequisite for employees to identify their interests, and long-term commitment, with the firm. It is crucial for not only solving the problem of 'eating up' state assets (that is unrestricted wage expansion), but also for promoting active participation. The institutionalization does not necessarily involve individualistic natural-personal owners. Conceivably, just like Japanese firms, there can be various impersonal institutions which hold the stakes of the firm.[13]

The second point, as made by Aoki, is the dual control by financial and employees' interests over corporate decision-making. For Japanese firms, the accountability to financial interests is expressed as the threat of takeover. This is only a threat in case of firm failure, and has rarely taken place. What is crucial is that, under the lifetime employment system and the practice of internal promotion (hence midcareer mobility is low), the threat of firm failure is sufficiently large to discipline the management. For accountability to employees, the fact that firm failure would result in the same hardship for lower-level employees as that for the management necessitates it. Equally important is the need to mobilize the active participation of individual employees for the sake of incremental and collective learning.

The third point concerns the forms of external financing. Based on the fact that in Japanese firms the proportion of dividend to profit is lower than other capitalist countries, Zhang (1987) makes a distinction between the rule of 'making profits' (performance in market competition) and that of 'distributing profits' or getting external finance: the latter is not necessarily related to the former in one particular way. As long as the external financing does not blur the cost-revenue structure of the firm, it would not leave room for the firm to become soft-budgeted. Thus, while centralized physical planning is a major source of soft budget constraint in Soviet-type firms, the Japanese state's (and the banks') soft financing of firms through credit provision has not led to the same effect. In the context of late industrialization, moreover, the state can make use of redistributional financing to promote structural change in transcendence of the given comparative advantage: to get the financial benefits, firms have to compete in line with the state developmental goals.

The fourth point is competition in the product market. This is important for exerting pressure on the enterprise for good performance. Whenever possible, firms should be subject to competition, including that of the world market. The comparative disadvantage of certain domestic industries can be offset by means of state promotion measures. In our context, there is no reason to posit that product market competition cannot be established in a reformed Soviet-type economic system.

The above points, certainly, are neither complete nor conclusive. They are derived from the experience of a relatively successful example of late industrialization, which from the standpoint of Eastern Europe should be more relevant than the basically ideology-oriented transformation packages proposed by 'big bang' protagonists and their gradualist counterparts. There is no guarantee that this experience can be transposed to a vastly different structural and institutional context. But there are also no convincing theories which prove the contrary. More importantly, it is certain that no better transformation packages could afford not to take this experience into consideration.

Part II

Explaining China

3 Chinese Industrialization in Structuralist Perspective

This chapter attempts to explain China's rapid economic growth during the period of 1978–94 by applying two recurring theses of structuralist development economics: namely, structural change as engine of growth and demand constraint on growth.

It is widely recognized that the classic thesis of structural change as a major source of output and productivity growth – where, pioneered by influential theoretical works ranging from Lewis (1954) to Kaldor (1966) and Chenery and Syrquin (1986), the emphasis is on the transition from agriculture to industry – can well be applied in China. The explosive growth of rural industries seems to be a development especially in line with this thesis. Nevertheless, in line with our discussion on techno-economic paradigm in the previous chapter, our focus is rather on structural change within industry. Succinctly, our thesis is as follows. The structural change associated with the rise of a range of 'new' industries, characterized by strong increasing returns, has propelled overall output and productivity growth. But this growth pattern has also produced problems, notably the foreign exchange gap and hence the danger of debt trap. The slowdown of the expansion of consumption demand since 1989 casts further doubt on the compatibility between the growth of these 'new' consumer durable industries and the pattern of income distribution in China. In this connection, the mediation of the state and the reforming institutions has been crucial in sustaining the growth.

On the whole, my explanation of the Chinese growth experience differs from most mainstream writings which tend to reduce the sources of growth to micro-level efficiency. The focus on structural change within industry is also directly relevant to the interpretation of China's enterprise reform, which will be dealt with in the next chapter.

STRUCTURAL CHANGE AS ENGINE OF GROWTH: 1978–88

The Structural and Institutional Conditions

By the late 1970s, Chinese industry was characterized by a high degree of technological dualism. Technological gaps existed widely at the inter- and intra-industry levels. This was a legacy of the specific form of 'original accumulation' that had taken place over the previous decades since 1949. Especially, it resulted from the industrialization strategy of 'walking on two legs' – that is, centralized and decentralized industrialization proceeding hand-in-hand. Thus, institutionally, the line of dualism can also be drawn between the centrally-managed sector and the locally-managed sector. The former was characterized by relatively higher technology and capital-intensity, established under strategic considerations.

The systemic reform of the 1980s has transformed the technological dualism into a planning-market economic dualism. There has emerged a pattern of division of labour where the centrally-managed sector has been largely confined to materials and capital goods industries (the planning track) while the locally-managed sector has expanded downstream processing industries (the market track). This has resulted in the massive expansion of both downstream industries and the locally-managed sector.

A number of factors have made development along this path possible, one of which being the growth of purchasing power (Table 3.1). Between 1979 and 1988, the average annual growth rate of social monetary income registered 19 per cent in nominal terms and 13 per cent in real terms, far exceeding the growth rates of national income (9 per cent real). The bulk of social monetary income was accounted for by wage-bonus incomes, and the revenues for rural households arising from the sales of their produce to the state. The increase in monetary income in excess of economic growth reflects a pattern of income distribution that is unrelated to market regulation. It also reflects the relaxation of state control over wage-bonus expansion. Meanwhile, during the same period of 1979–88, social monetary expenditure grew at a comparable rate of 18 per cent in nominal terms. This further indicates that the consumption expansion was sustained by the specific pattern of income distribution.

China's state development strategy in the 1980s can thus be regarded as anti-Feldman in nature. Consumption expanded at the expense of accumulation. Also, the development of heavy industry was depressed

Table 3.1 Social Purchasing Power, 1979–92 (100m yuan)

	(a) Monetary income	*(b) Monetary expenditure*	*(c) Non-realized monetary income = (a) – (b)*
1979	2 094	1 976	118
1980	2 536	2 331	205
1981	2 747	2 557	190
1982	3 026	2 828	198
1983	3 441	3 169	272
1984	4 457	3 933	524
1985	5 645	5 095	550
1986 (1)	6 805	6 020	785
(2)	6 340	5 555	785
1987	7 573	6 548	1 025
1988	9 603	8 343	1 260
1989	10 818	9 327	1 491
1990	11 904	9 766	2 138
1991	13 616	11 118	2 498
1992	17 530	14 198	3 332
Average annual growth (%)			
1979–88	19.3 (12.6)	18.4 (11.7)	–
1988–92	16.2 (8.8)	14.2 (6.9)	–

Sources: ZSWTZ 1952–88, pp. 35–42; ZTN 1993, pp. 238, 602.

Notes: Figures in parentheses are real growth rates. From 1986, part of rural income and expenditure is removed from the two categories, so that figures before and after that year are not strictly comparable; the 1986 (2) figures refer to the new coverage, ie after the reduction. 'Social monetary income' includes, *inter alia*, the following two major components: total wage bills, and farmers' revenue from selling produce. 'Social monetary expenditure' is equivalent to 'gross social retail sales'. 'Non-realized purchasing power' is composed of two items: annual increases in savings and cash-in-hand.

in order to foster the expansion of light industry. This is evidenced in the differentiated treatments of the state towards different industries. In general, material incentives and the market mechanism were introduced into downstream consumer industries, whereas energy, basic raw materials and capital goods industries were restricted to operate mainly under planning. More specifically, the relative prices of upstream products were depressed in the attempts to foster the rapid growth of downstream industries.

The economic indicators in Table 3.2 show an uneven picture. In

Table 3.2 Profitability, Labour Productivity and Enterprise-Retained Profits of Selected Industrial Branches, 1980, 1985, 1988 and 1992

	(a) *AI*	*(b)* *LI*	*of (b)* *Textiles*	*(c)* *HI*	*of (c)* *Extr.*	*of Extr.* *CM*	*of (c)* *Matr.*	*of Matr.* *Chem.*	*of (c)* *Mfg*	*of Mfg* *Electronics*
1980										
G/L	3 288	3 630	4 522	3 092	2 533	1 478	6 196	3 992	2 206	2 493
P/L	2 191	2 574	3 558	1 973	1 405	381	4 777	2 881	1 196	1 328
EP/L	...	...	...	...	...	...	...	...	...	...
P/K	25.2	49.1	69.0	3.6	18.3	6.1	24.7	22.0	13.7	14.0
1985										
G/L	4 281	4 134	3 667	4 380	3 429	1 772	7 671	4 985	3 529	5 596
P/L	2 592	2 603	2 192	2 584	1 059	100	5 777	3 388	1 992	3 471
EP/L	...	...	...	...	...	...	...	...	...	...
P/K	23.8	31.8	26.5	4.3	10.4	1.2	25.3	21.7	20.0	24.9
1988										
G/L	5 883	5 973	4 756	5 819	4 427	2 352	9 751	8 148	4 766	8 561
P/L	3 130	3 334	2 263	2 985	870	–40	6 913	5 287	2 210	4 456
EP/L	588	557	481	610	209	50	1 126	960	556	989
P/K	20.5	26.9	20.0	4.5	5.9	–0.4	22.9	28.6	16.8	22.4
1992										
G/L	9 425	9 228	6 422	9 567	6 773	3 634	14 586	10 831	8 371	12 599
P/L	3 544	3 427	1 430	3 629	97	–414	8 537	4 507	2 774	3 602
EP/L	545	427	163	631	284	155	1 030	546	585	1 068
P/K	9.9	10.5	4.9	9.5	0.3	–2.1	13.5	10.5	9.1	6.3

Sources: ŹGJTN 1993, pp. 168–193.

Notes: AI = all industries; LI = light industry; HI = heavy industry; Extr. = extraction; Matr. = materials; Mfg. = manufacturing; CM = coal mining; Chem. = chemicals; Electronics = electronics and communication equipment. G/L = net industrial output value per worker (yuan); P/L = total realized profits and tax per worker (yuan); EP/L = enterprise-retained profits per worker (yuan); P/K = profit rate = total realized profits and tax / (value of fixed-asset net of depreciation + registered working capital) (%).
Figures cover all township-and-above independently accounting industrial enterprises.

1985, the second year since the implementation of the comprehensive industrial-urban reforms, all the three indicators – net industrial output value per worker, realized profit-and-tax per worker and the profit rate – show a difficult situation on the part of upstream extraction industries. In contrast, downstream industries like textiles and electronics – which are representative of the traditional and 'new' consumer industries, respectively, and have experienced rapid growth in the 1980s – exhibit far greater rates of returns. The situation worsened by 1988. Especially for coal mining, which accounted for three quarters of the country's sources of energy, the industry as a whole suffered from losses. With regard to the indicator of enterprise-retained profits per worker, which represents the material benefits conceded to enterprises, those of extraction industries were far lower than the average of all industries.

The combination of expanding consumption demand and differentiated returns to industries gave a strong inducement for the expansion of downstream processing industries. But it was the systemic reform which enabled such a development. The essence of the reform in the 1980s, on balance, is best captured by a term widely used by Chinese economists: *fangquan rangli* (decentralizing power and conceding material benefits). The state's giving up of its controls over the economy was aimed at building up a regulatory mechanism that is in line with the principles of the market. However, given the existing structural and institutional constraints, the result has been a 'market mechanism' that is far different from the textbook-type 'pure' market: it was rather based on widespread practices of negotiation, consensus, compromise, administrative intervention, etc.

Structurally, the underdevelopment of both the 'hardware' infrastructure of the market, like communication and transportation facilities, and 'software', like legal means for enforcing contracts, together with the existence of vast surplus labour and low labour mobility, contributed to the 'heterogeneous nature' of the economy. This led to the prominent role of local authorities in economic affairs. To reinforce it were various institutional peculiarities, especially the state guarantee for a wide range of welfare provisions (for studies of the regulatory mechanism of China's economy under reform, see Zhang 1988; Byrd 1991; Wu *et al.* 1988; and Hua *et al.* 1988; the latter two representing the two 'mainstreams' among Chinese economists by the late 1980s).[1] In line with *fangquan rangli*, the reform took the form of various contractual systems, with a theme of fixing the bases and dividing the incremental returns. This applied to both local authorities, in the sharing of fiscal revenues and foreign trade earnings, and state enterprises in profit-retention.

In this connection, four factors were evidently at work to shape the outcome of the reform. First, local authorities and enterprises were not purely economic agents but rather had considerable bargaining power *vis-à-vis* the state. This implies possible scope for asymmetry between benefit and responsibility arising from their economic decisions (soft-budgeted behaviour). Second, while it is arguable that a politicized economic regulatory mechanism need not inevitably produce soft-budgeted behaviour, the problem is that the Chinese reform has not been able to establish an effective system to curb it. Third, the contractual systems tended to spur the agents into behaving in a way which can be called short-termism: aiming mainly at short-term profitability, not developmental concerns. Finally, all these behavioural potentials were realized under the consumption-led booms. The result was the enhancement of the

Table 3.3 Fixed-asset Investment 1978–94: Sources of Fund (unit: 100m yuan)

	Total	*Budgetary*		*Extra-budgetary*	
		Amount	*% of total*	*Amount*	*% of total*
1978	...	...	62.2	...	37.8
1980	911	407	44.7	504	55.3
1981	961	270	28.1	691	71.9
1982	1 230	279	22.7	951	77.3
1983	1 430	240	16.8	1 190	83.2
1984	1 833	421	23.0	1 412	77.0
1985	2 543	408	16.0	2 135	84.0
1986	3 020	441	14.6	2 579	8.54
1987	3 641	476	13.1	3 165	86.9
1988	4 497	410	9.1	4 087	90.9
1989	4 138	342	8.3	3 796	91.7
1990	4 449	388	8.7	4 062	91.3
1991	5 509	373	6.7	5 136	93.2
1992	7 855	334	4.3	7 521	95.7
1993	12 458	464	3.7	11 994	96.3
1994	16 370	530	3.2	15 840	96.8
Average annual growth (%)					
1980–8	21.9	−0.1		29.7	
1988–94	24.0	4.4		25.3	

Sources: ZTN 1988, p. 559; ZTN 1990, p. 153; ZTN 1993, p. 145; ZTN 1995, p. 137.

Notes: The 'total' refers to fixed-asset investment in the economy as a whole.

power, and motivation, of these politicized economic agents to expand investment in quick- and high-return downstream consumer industries.[2]

As is indicated in Table 3.3, the 1980s saw a tremendous growth in total investment while at the same time the share of the central authorities (the budgetary portion) rapidly decreased from 62 per cent in 1978 to 9 per cent in 1988. Table 3.4 further shows that, in terms of sectoral shares of investment, the bulk of the extra-budgetary portion went to downstream industries.

Consumption-Led Industrialization

The stage was thus set for a consumption-led industrialization process. Initially in 1978–83, the upsurge of production was especially spectacular in traditional consumer durables. The annual output volume of

Table 3.4 Changes in Capital Intensity and Capital Renovation of Chinese Industry, 1980–1992

	(a) *AI*	*(b)* *LI*	*(c)* *HI*	*of (c)* *Extr.*	*of (c)* *Matr.*	*of (c)* *Mfg.*	*(d)* *SOEs*	*(e)* *COEs*	*(f)* *LMEs*
Capital intensity									
(1) K_{1980}/L_{1980}	5 655	2 748	7 381	6180	15 093	5 067	7 903	1 531	10 223
(2) K_{1988}/L_{1988}	9 870	6 793	12 109	12 420	23 867	7 166	14 194	3 947	18 016
(3) K_{1992}/L_{1992}	16 999	11 849	20 861	22 147	40 581	11 268	23 493	6 640	30 087
(2)/(1)	1.745	2.472	1.641	2.010	1.581	1.414	1.796	2.578	1.762
		(+0.727)	(−0.104)	(+0.265)	(−0.164)	(−0.331)	(+0.051)	(+0.833)	(+0.017)
(3)/(2)	1.722	1.744	1.723	1.783	1.700	1.572	1.655	1.682	1.670
		(+0.022)	(+0.001)	(+0.061)	(−0.022)	(−0.150)	(−0.067)	(−0.040)	(−0.052)
Capital renovation									
(4) K_{1980}/K'_{1980}	0.684	0.689	0.693	0.637	0.704	0.686	0.679	0.747	0.666
(5) K_{1988}/K'_{1988}	0.697	0.746	0.679	0.664	0.707	0.655	0.687	0.740	0.678
(6) K_{1992}/K'_{1992}	0.707	0.735	0.696	0.723	0.707	0.657	0.701	0.712	0.700
(5)/(4)	1.019	1.083	0.994	1.042	1.004	0.955	1.012	0.991	1.018
		(+0.064)	(−0.025)	(+0.023)	(−0.015)	(−0.064)	(−0.007)	(−0.023)	(−0.001)
(6)/(5)	1.014	0.985	1.025	1.089	1.000	1.003	1.020	0.962	1.032
		(−0.029)	(+0.011)	(+0.075)	(−0.014)	(−0.011)	(+0.006)	(−0.052)	(+0.018)

Source: ZGJTN 1992, pp. 90–3, 103–4, 170–1; ZTN 1993, p. 419.

Notes: Figures in parentheses are deviations from 'all industries'. Change in capital intensity = (K_i/L_i) / (K_j/L_j); change in capital renovation = (K_i/K'_i) / (K_j/K'_j), where K′, K and L are gross value of fixed-assets, net value of fixed-assets and number of workers, respectively, and the subscripts indicate the years. Capital intensity is expressed in yuan. SOEs = state-owned enterprises; COEs = collectively-owned enterprises; LMEs = large-and-medium scale enterprises. The definitions of AI, LI, HI, Extr., Matr. and Mfg are the same as Table 3.2.

wristwatches increased by 157 per cent, sewing machines by 123 per cent and bicycles by 223 per cent, far exceeding the respective rates of 140 per cent, 66 per cent and 72 per cent in 1974–8. During the next five-year period of 1983–8, however, the slide of the rates was as abrupt – they went down to 92 per cent, –10 per cent and 50 per cent, respectively. Their market positions were quickly taken over by a range of new consumer durables, the representative items being television sets, household refrigerators and washing machines.

From a volume of 0.5m in 1978, by 1988, China produced 25m TV sets, making itself the world's biggest producer. The output growth of colour TV sets, from 3,800 in 1978 to 10m in 1988, is even more phenomenal. As for refrigerators, the output volume increased from 28,000 in 1978 to 8m in 1988. That of washing machines increased from 400 to 11m. Thus, while in 1978 there were virtually none of these products in private households, by 1988, there were 13.2 TV sets, 6.8 washing machines and 1.8 refrigerators per 100 persons in China; and in urban areas the respective figures were 38.7, 25.1 and 6.1. Yet the output upsurge of these three products was just the tip of the iceberg. The range of 'new' consumption goods was in fact far wider.[3]

Precisely how much the 'new' consumer goods contributed to overall industrial growth is statistically difficult to measure. But it was widely agreed to be striking. CESRRI (1988b) calculates that from 1980 to 1985, while the output value of the industrial sector as a whole grew by 62 per cent and all downstream industries by 76 per cent, that of the branches producing new consumer goods grew by 108 per cent. Likewise, according to Liu and Yang (1987), of the total of incremental industrial output value during 1980–85, 31 per cent was accounted for by the 'new' industries. The contribution was likely to be far greater in the period of 1984–8, when the demonstration effects-induced consumption boom reached its peak.

Table 3.5 shows the sectoral breakdown of industrial growth during 1978–88, from which three points can be noted. The first is the uneven pattern of growth among different sectors, with the five upstream industries – metallurgy, electricity, coal and coke, petroleum and forestry – lagging far behind. Second, the unevenness became more pronounced in the second five-year period of 1984–8, as is indicated by the widening gap between the growth rates of the upstream industries and the industrial sector at large. Third, among downstream industries, the growth rate of machinery (which approximates the International Standard Industrial Classification two-digit code 38 and

Table 3.5 Major Industrial Sectors: Relative Shares in GVIO and Average Annual Growth Rates, 1978–88

	Sectoral shares (%)			*Average annual growth (%)*	
	(a) 1978	*(b) 1988*	*(b)–(a)*	*1978–88*	*1984–88*
All industries	**100**	**100**	—	**11.1**	**14.5**
Machinery	23.5	29.8	+6.3	13.8	20.2
Metallurgy	9.6	7.3	−2.3	8.1	11.1
Electricity	3.8	2.9	−0.9	8.2	10.1
Coal & coke	3.9	2.0	−1.9	4.0	6.3
Petroleum	6.4	3.9	−2.5	5.8	8.8
Forestry	2.2	1.5	−0.7	6.5	8.8
Chemicals	11.3	12.1	+0.8	11.9	14.7
Building materials	3.9	4.4	+0.5	12.4	16.8
Food manufacturing	12.1	10.9	−1.2	10.1	10.8
Textiles	12.4	14.0	+1.6	12.5	12.2
Apparel	2.1	2.4	+0.3	12.8	13.6
Leather	0.8	1.0	+0.2	13.5	16.5
Paper manufacturing	1.4	1.3	−0.1	10.7	14.6
Educational & cultural goods	2.0	2.7	+0.7	14.8	19.9
Others	3.9	3.7	−0.2	10.5	17.1

Source: ZGJTN 1989, pp. 58–61.

Notes: Sectoral shares and growth rates are calculated at 1980 constant prices. The statistics cover all township-and-above enterprises.

encompasses both producer and consumer industries) especially stands out. This indicates the rise of new consumer industries. The expansion of the educational and cultural products industry (which also encompasses many of the new consumer goods) and the gradual slowdown of growth of the textile industry (representative of traditional consumer goods) in 1984–8 further indicate it. Overall, the structural change is indicated by the changing sectoral shares in China's gross value of industrial output: the combined share of the five upstream industries in 1988 was a decrease of 8.3 percentage points from 1978, and this share was mainly taken up by the machinery sector.

In the institutional dimension, the phenomenal structural change of Chinese industry was carried out mainly by the expansion of the locally-managed sector. This was not really a natural outcome of market selection. The state's differentiated treatments towards upstream and downstream industries obliged it to take up the responsibility of developing the former group, which were non-profitable yet indispensable for the economy. The state's intention to promote rapid economic growth also resulted in the lower taxation and social burdens on the locally-managed sector than on SOEs: by the late 1980s, sales tax rates were 5 per cent for township-and-village enterprises (TVEs), 5.3 per cent for all collective enterprises and 9.3 per cent for SOEs, while the ratios of state-collected tax-and-profits out of total realized profits were respectively 25.7 per cent, 29.3 per cent and 49.6 per cent, the ratio of depreciation to fixed-asset at original value being respectively 6.8 per cent, 6.4 per cent and 4.3 per cent (ZTXB, 10 January 1991; see Chapter 4 for details). The reform also provided local authorities of various levels the power to promote and protect local industries, often through administrative means.

The locally-managed sector encompasses both local SOEs and all collectively-owned enterprises (COEs, of which TVEs account for a major share of output value). It is difficult to show the massive expansion of the sector relative to the centrally-managed sector, as well as the newly-emerged pattern of division of labour between the two. The statistical indicators available are the respective growths of SOEs and COEs; yet these alone are sufficiently striking. During 1978–88, SOEs' share of China's industrial output decreased from 78 per cent to 57 per cent, whilst that of COEs increased from 22 per cent to 36 per cent.

Regarding the pattern of division of labour, one indicator is that, in 1988, of the industrial output of TVEs 20 per cent was accounted for by the six upstream industries metallurgy, electricity, coal and coke, petroleum, chemicals and forestry, compared with the 35 per cent for all enterprises. The five industries exhibiting the greatest deviation of output shares between TVEs and all enterprises were petroleum (0.05:1), electricity (0.09:1), building materials (4.01:1), paper manufacturing (2.02:1) and leather (1.74:1). On both sides, the single most important industry was machinery, which accounted for 25 per cent of the industrial output of TVEs, and 30 per cent for all enterprises. A different source reports that, in 1987, the machinery sector accounted for 34 per cent of the output value of COEs and 27 per cent of SOEs (Jefferson *et al.*, 1992). On the whole, the faster expansion of the locally-managed sector relative to the centrally-managed sector, and the pattern of division of labour where the former was far more concentrated in downstream industries, are thus quite evident.

A consequence of the industrialization pattern – the rise of 'new' consumer industries carried by the expansion of the locally-managed sector – was the acclaimed tremendous output growth. Just like the 'golden age' of the 1950s when Chinese industry grew at an unprecedented speed under massive imports of Soviet technology, in the 1980s, the imports of Western technology at even larger scales provided a strong impetus for growth (Kang 1992). But this pattern also led to the structural problems of fragmentation of the 'new' industries and miniaturization of plant scale. These stemmed from the behaviour of the newly-empowered local authorities and enterprises, which tended to focus on short-term profitability rather than long-term development. The problems were also fuelled by the administrative promotion and protection by local authorities of various levels.

Thus, in a few years 110 colour TV production lines were imported and distributed among a similar number of plants. The number of washing machine producers jumped quickly, from two in 1978 to 300 but fell back to 147 by 1985: of which only 14 reached the minimum efficient scale by international standard, that is 200 000 sets per annum. The same applied to the production of refrigerators (more than 140 plants at its peak), air conditioners (more than 100) and other new consumer durables including various high capital-intensity products.[4] From a developmental point of view, this pattern of growth is unlikely to be sustainable. The fact that the production lines were imported from a wide range of foreign suppliers sufficed to obstruct the development of the industries moving upstream. The low technological capability and shortage of skilled workers in the locally-managed sector, especially TVEs, also resulted in slow assimilation of imported technology. The 'new' industries were thus prone to remain at the assembling stage of the production (CESRRI 1988a; Yang 1989).[5]

THE LIMITS TO GROWTH

Structural Imbalances: The 1988–89 Cyclical Crisis

The 1988–9 Chinese economic crisis, which manifested itself through rising inflation, has been explained by various approaches with varied focuses. One approach is to focus on relative prices: that the interest rate of bank loans was undervalued and the exchange rate overvalued, inducing over-consumption and over-investment. A refined version is to attribute the crisis to the over-expansion of the economic role of the state, despite the fact that the reform has eroded its revenue bases through decentralization and the profit squeeze on SOEs (Perkins 1992; Naughton 1991, 1992). This explanation, leaving aside the assertion thereby that if (and only if) a 'full market system' had been in place the crisis could have been avoided, is reasonable insomuch as economic agents did respond to relative prices.

But it is arguable that there were other factors that are far more crucial in explaining the crisis. The monetary expansion was not simply a policy mistake. In addition to the intervention by local authorities, the massive credit expansion was indispensable for sustaining the particular pattern of growth. The inability of the state to cut expenditure down to the level needed to avoid worsening deficits was ascribable to the imperative for it to curb the imbalances of the national economy under the same growth pattern. Finally, the imbalances also fuelled inflation through another channel – structural inflation.

One indicator of structural inflation was the rise of industrial product prices, which formed a cost-push effect on the general price level. In the five years 1985–9, the price index of factory-delivered industrial products increased, in percentage terms by 8.7, 3.8, 7.9, 15.0 and 18.6. These were almost in line with the social retail price index, which increased in percentage terms by 8.8, 6.0, 7.3, 18.5 and 17.8 respectively. A major force pushing up the industrial prices, in turn, was panic shortages of basic materials. According to the Centre for Development Studies under the State Council, in 1988, of the 12.3 per cent rise in the production cost of all industrial enterprises, three-quarters was accounted for by energy and raw materials price rise. The cost rose by 22.4 per cent in 1989, with around 70 per cent of it being accounted for by price rises of the two items. Because of the shortage, by 1988, one-third of the country's production capacity was forced to lie idle.

Energy shortage was especially symptomatic of the structural imbalances. By the second half of 1988, the phenomena of factories 'closing four days, opening three days (per week)' and even 'closing five days, opening two days' became widespread in industrialized yet energy-deficient coastal provinces. Entering 1989, the situation worsened. In January, the East China Electricity Network (comprising five provinces plus Shanghai municipality) faced severe coal shortages which reduced its power generation on average by 789 000 kilowatts per day. Included in the operations halted were flagship plants such as Xuzhou, Chenbi, Zhenhai and Shidongkou. The most disruptive was the threat to the two generators of Shanghai Baoshan Iron and Steel Co., China's most advanced steel giant. With one generator being forced to stop operations in January, and again in March, the Shanghai authorities had to borrow coal from Japan to ease the emergency. Meanwhile, the energy crisis was not confined to the coastal region. Even in Shaanxi

Table 3.6 Major Proportionalities in Chinese Industry, 1978–94

	Shares in GVIO (%)		Shares in HIOV (%)			Energy production
	light	heavy	extract.	materials	mfg.	elasticity
1978	43.1	56.9	12.0	35.5	52.5	0.92
1979	43.7	56.3	11.5	36.9	51.6	0.41
1980	47.2	52.8	11.3	37.8	50.9	−0.20
1981	51.5	48.5	15.2	40.6	44.2	−0.16
1982	50.2	49.8	14.3	39.3	46.4	0.69
1983	48.5	51.5	13.1	38.3	48.6	0.67
1984	47.4	52.6	12.7	36.8	50.5	0.68
1985	47.1	52.9	11.4	35.2	53.4	0.73
1986	47.6	52.4	11.3	35.8	52.9	0.39
1987	48.2	51.8	10.3	35.4	54.2	0.35
1988	49.3	50.7	9.5	33.8	56.7	0.44
1989	48.9	51.1	11.5	39.9	48.5	1.65
1990	49.4	50.6	12.1	41.6	46.3	0.43
1991	48.9	51.1	11.7	41.7	46.6	0.12
1992	47.2	52.8	10.5	41.0	48.5	0.16
1993	44.0	56.0	10.4	42.6	47.0	0.31
1994	47.1	52.9	8.5	32.9	58.6	0.56
1978–88 change	+6.2	−6.2	−2.5	−1.7	+4.2	−0.55
1988–94 change	−2.2	+2.2	−1.0	−0.9	+1.9	+0.12

Sources: RMRB 29 February 1992, p. 2; ZGJTN 1989, p. 14; ZGJTZ 1987, p. 35; ZGJTZ 1949–84, pp. 20, 26, 96; ZTN 1991, pp. 25, 34, 57, 453, 468; ZTN 1993, pp. 25, 35, 492; ZTN 1995, pp. 27, 206.

Notes: GVIO = gross value of industrial output; HIOV = gross output value of heavy industry. All sectoral shares figures are calculated from current-price data, except the 1994 figures of sectoral shares of HIOV which are calculated at 1990 constant-price value. Energy production elasticity = annual growth rate of energy production / annual growth rate of national income.

province, one of China's three coal production bases, seven power plants whose capacity accounted for 55 per cent of the whole Northwest Electricity Network experienced coal stocks falling below emergency level. Nationally, by January 1989, total coal stocks in the biggest four networks remained at 4m tons, far below the 6m tons minimum requirement set by state authorities (RMRB, 18 January and 3 February 1989; JFRB 9 April 1989; ZMTB 28 March 1989).

Nor was the energy crisis a temporary problem. As shown in Table 3.6, throughout the 1980s China's energy production elasticity (with respect to national income) had never reached unity, the level that is widely agreed to be appropriate in view of past experiences. In terms of historical comparison, for electricity alone, the average production elasticity in 1980–8 was 0.78, whereas those of the previous three decades were respectively 2.12 for the 1950s, 1.66 for the 1960s and 1.22 for the 1970s. And even the level of 0.78 was achieved through an excessive operation of the generators: by 1986, the average annual operation time reached 5974 hours (6216 hours for major plants), compared with the usual 4000 hours in industrial countries. This means that the generators were operating with inadequate security checks and maintenance. It resulted in widespread emergency situations by 1988.

The most acute bottleneck in the energy sector was coal mining, which accounts for three quarters of China's sources of energy. Two problems were prominent. First, long-term investment in coal mines had virtually been at a standstill from 1986 onwards. According to the industrial authorities, in China, it normally takes ten years to construct a medium-to-large coal mine. But in the two years 1987–8 no construction of new mines was started; and for the first four years of the Seventh Five-Year-Plan period (1986–90) the newly-started construction of medium-to-large mines was only 23 per cent of the planned target. This meant that by 1993 there would be no new mines being put into production. The reason for the severe situation was financial difficulties arising from the state strategy of discriminating against upstream industries. Specifically, under the planning-market 'double-track' system, most of China's medium-to-large coal mines were restricted to operate under mandatory planning, with outputs being mainly centrally-distributed and prices depressed to low levels. Thus for the coal mining industry, while in 1985 its realized profit-and-tax amounted to 519m yuan, in the subsequent years the figures turned negative, reaching –4b yuan by 1990. Especially for medium-to-large coal mines, in 1988, total losses amounted to 3.6b yuan (ZMTB, 26 January 1989; JJRB, 3 February 1990; ZGSB, 5 July 1990).

Second, the steady growth of coal output in the 1980s was in fact largely achieved by excessive exploitation. This arose from the fact that the bulk of the incremental output was contributed by small township-and-village mines, under the inducement of the upsurges in market prices (the other 'track' of the price system). In the Sixth Five-Year-Plan period (1981–5), of the total incremental raw coal output of 267m tons, 177m or 66 per cent were from this source. The share remained at a half in 1986–8. By 1989, there were a total of 79 000 rural mines throughout China, most of which were using low quality equipment and employing unskilled labour. Indeed, because of the extremely crude safety facilities, for each million tons of coal produced by township-and-village mines, ten human lives were lost. The resource-utilization rate was also extremely low, usually at 15–40 per cent. That is to say, for each ton of coal produced around 1.5 to 5 tons of resources were wasted. As many township-and-village mines are in fact situated near medium-to-large mines, their over-exploitative extraction often resulted in serious damages to the latter. Finally, with the exhaustion of easy-extraction resources, the need to invest for deep mining rendered township-village mines increasingly unprofitable. Thus the industry authorities predicted that in the next ten years the output growth of township-and-village mines would drop to around 2 per cent per annum, compared with the average of 19 per cent in 1981–5 (Wang *et al.* eds. 1989; see also ZXQB, 12 April 1989; JJRB, 4 January 1990; ZMTB, 16 and 23 February 1989, and 30 August 1990).

From the above description of the situation of China's coal industry, which was representative of not just the energy sector but of many of the 'bottleneck' industries during the 1980s, it is quite evident that the 1988–9 cyclical crisis was almost endemic of the unbalanced growth pattern. For Chinese industry as a whole, the general situation is indicated by the figures of major proportionalities in Table 3.6. It is noted that especially within heavy industry there was the shrinkage in relative shares of extraction and raw materials industries by 2.5 and 1.7 percentage points respectively in 1978–88, in contrast to the 4.2 points gain of manufacturing.

Theoretically, it can be argued that unbalanced growth does not necessarily result in bottlenecks and cyclical crisis. Even in a closed economy, the change of proportionality in favour of manufacturing does not necessarily lead to panic shortages of energy and raw materials, provided that it is accompanied with technical change and hence improvement in the utilization of energy and raw materials. China's economic growth after 1989 seems to be a case of this kind. During the 1980s, however, technical change was evidently insufficient to match the change in proportionality. According to surveys of the State Statistical Bureau, during 1980–9, of the total energy saved in industry, technical change accounted for 26 per cent while the remainder being contributed by the structural change towards 'industrial lightening' – that is a reduction of the relative weight of heavy industry, which is characterized by high consumption of energy and materials (*Tongji Ziliao* [Statistical Information], no.66, April 1990). This change is shown in Table 3.6: during 1978–88 the share of heavy industry in gross industrial output shrank by 6.2 percentage points. In the face of rapid economic growth and intensifying imbalances, there were limits for continuous 'industrial lightening'. The 1988–9 cyclical crisis testified to the limits.

Table 3.7 Foreign Trade Values and Trade Dependence, 1978–94

	(a) Exports (US$bn) (%)	*(b) Imports (US$bn) (%)*	*Trade balance = (a) – (b) (US$bn)*
1978	9.8 (4.6)	10.9 (5.2)	−1.1
1979	13.7 (5.3)	15.7 (6.1)	−2.0
1980	18.1 (6.1)	20.0 (6.7)	−1.9
1981	22.0 (7.7)	22.0 (7.7)	0
1982	22.3 (8.0)	19.3 (6.9)	+3.0
1983	22.2 (7.5)	21.4 (7.3)	+0.8
1984	26.1 (8.1)	27.4 (8.6)	−1.3
1985	27.4 (9.0)	42.3 (14.0)	−14.9
1986	30.9 (10.6)	42.9 (14.7)	−12.0
1987	39.4 (12.3)	43.2 (13.5)	−3.8
1988	47.5 (11.8)	55.3 (13.8)	−7.8
1989	52.5 (11.6)	59.1 (13.0)	−6.6
1990	62.1 (16.1)	53.4 (13.9)	+8.7
1991	71.9 (17.7)	63.8 (15.7)	+8.1
1992	85.0 (17.5)	80.6 (16.7)	+4.4
1993	91.8 (15.3)	104.0 (17.4)	−12.2
1994	121.0 (23.2)	115.7 (22.2)	+5.3
Average annual growth (%)			
1978–88	17.1	17.6	
1988–94	16.9	13.1	

Sources: ZTN 1990, p. 33, 641; ZTN 1995, p. 32, 537.

Notes: Figures in parentheses are imports- and exports-dependence, defined as the ratios of imports and exports value to the value of GNP, both in current-price yuan. The 1979 trade figures are statistics of the Ministry of Foreign Trade, those from 1980 onwards are customs statistics.

The Foreign Exchange Gap and the Pattern of International Specialization

A more fundamental constraint on the growth pattern of the 1980s was the foreign exchange gap. Table 3.7 shows the trade figures, from which two trends are noticeable. One is the increasing importance of trade in the economy. During 1979–88, the average annual growth rate (nominal) of exports was 17.2 per cent, while that of imports 17.6 per cent. By 1988, the export- and import-dependence ratios of the economy were 12.6 per cent and 14.7 per cent respectively. In contrast to the pre-reform era, trade was no longer marginal but was rather crucial in shaping the development of the economy. Another trend was the growth of trade deficits. In the first five-year period of 1979–83, exports and imports were basically in balance. From 1984 onwards, trade deficit expanded. The accumulated deficits over 1984–8 amounted to US$40b, which was equivalent to 11 per cent of the GNP in 1988.

The increasing trade dependence was endemic to the 'new' industries-led unbalanced growth. Of the total imports a significant share was basic materials, especially high energy-consumption products, as domestic production fell short of consumption. Throughout the 1980s, the combined share of four high energy-consumption items (steel products, chemical fertilizers, synthetic fibre and polyethylene) remained at 20 per cent. The structural imbalances of industry thus exerted pressure on the country's trade balance.[6]

From the standpoints of long-term development, a more far-reaching effect of the increase in trade dependence was the inducing of Chinese industry to specialize strictly in line with its comparative advantage, that is, its technological backwardness *vis-à-vis* the advanced capitalist world. The specific pattern of growth and trade acted against the development of dynamic industries that are not in line with the given comparative advantage. This, in the first place, was evidenced by the massive imports of foreign machinery alongside the stagnation of domestic capital goods producers.

As can be seen from Table 3.8, the expansion of imports was indeed tremendous: from US$5b in 1980, it increased four times to US$21b or three-eighths of the country's total imports value in 1988. Thus, while the utilization rate of the three million plus domestic metal-cutting machine tools remained at around 50 per cent throughout the 1980s, there were massive imports of machines tools – 44 500 sets valued at US$520m in 1988 alone. Similarly, while domestically-produced automobiles were facing sales stagnation, there was an influx of motor vehicles – 354 000 at the peak in 1985 (Yang 1989). The same happened to other industrial branches, and in general the more 'high-tech' the branch is the more acute the competition from imported products.

Conceivably, the expanding imports of machinery, if on balance not as a complement of, but rather as a substitute for, the development of the domestic machinery sector, are likely to force the country to specialize in low technology and low value-added industries. And, if the exports of low value-added goods do not expand at a pace comparable to the imports of machinery, the growth pattern cannot be sustainable. Moreover, as is explained in Chapter 2, a necessary condition for the

Table 3.8 Exports and Imports of Mechanical and Electronic Products, 1980–94 (US$b)

	Exports	*Imports*	*Balance = Exports–Imports*
1980	1.4	5.7	−4.3
1981	1.8	6.4	−4.6
1982	1.9	3.6	−1.7
1983	1.9	4.7	−2.8
1984	2.2	8.2	−6.0
1985	1.7	18.3	−16.6
1986	2.5	19.3	−16.8
1987	3.9	17.4	−13.5
1988	6.2	20.7	−14.6
1989	8.3	22.5	−14.2
1990	11.1	21.4	−10.4
1991	14.1	25.0	−10.9
1992	19.6	34.9	−15.3
1993	22.7	49.5	−26.8
1994	31.9	58.8	−26.9
Average annual growth (%)			
1980–6	10.1	22.5	—
1986–94	37.5	14.9	—

Sources: ZJDGN-J 1994, p. I-15; RMRB, 4 March 1994, p. 1; ZTN 1994, p. 506; ZXB, 28 February 1995, p. 2.

leap-frogging of a latecomer country is the building up of an indigenous technological capability which would enable itself to adopt and improve upon imported technology. But, in the case of China during the 1980s, the persistence of massive trade deficits in mechanical and electronic goods, shown in Table 3.8, indicates the development lag of the domestic capital goods sector in the face of expanding imports.

In a more clear-cut manner, along with the expanding trade dependence there was evidently a tendency towards the mutual perpetuation between the fast growing yet import-dependent 'new' industries and the technologically backward yet export expanding industries. With the specific pattern of the rise of the 'new' industries, the massive imports of parts and components (and machinery) had become indispensable for keeping the imported production lines moving. From 1981 to 1985, for instance, imports of this kind increased by 6.1 times; and in the second and third quarters of 1986 alone, because of state restrictions on imports, the volume of domestically-produced colour TVs fell by 33 per cent against the same 1985 period. In 1988, colour TV output reached a record volume of 10.4m sets, while that of colour picture tubes only 1.4m: the gap being filled by spending US$1.1b on imports, each picture tube costing more than US$100 (CESSRI 1988b; ZDB, 4 April 1989).

The same situation was widely evident in other 'new' industries. For refrigerator production, in 1987, domestic output registered 4m whereas the output volume of air compressors, a key component, was 0.5m. The result was that, for each household refrigerator turned out, it needed to import components costing US$105. The output of refrigerators increased to 7.6m sets by 1988 while the foreign exchange cost per set stood at US$100, meaning that US$760m was spent on importing parts and components for refrigerators alone (RMRB, 7 September 1989; SJXB, 30 January 1990; XXSB, 2 February 1988). Meanwhile, the low export competitiveness of the 'new' industries was evidenced by the fact that none of the explosively-growing consumer durables had an annual export value reaching US$100m before 1987. Not only were export prices generally far lower than domestic prices, but the fact that the value-added in terms of foreign exchange was very small implied heavy losses on the part of Chinese enterprises which exported 'new' consumer durables. In Shenzhen Special Economic Zone, for instance, the foreign exchange cost of domestically produced colour TVs had been equivalent to 80 per cent of the export prices even by 1991 (*Ta Kung Po*, 20 June 1991).

To sustain the growth of the import-dependent 'new' industries, it became necessary for China to expand exports at a pace comparable to imports. The low export competitiveness of the 'new' industries and the capital goods sector (both characterized by high value-added), however, means that what China could rely upon was to export primary and labour-intensive products, on which it had the international comparative advantage. This is reflected in the evolution of exports and imports commodity compositions, shown in Table 3.9.

At first sight, the evolution seems favourable: between 1980 and 1988, manufactured goods increased by 20 percentage points in the export total. But this was almost entirely accounted for by the expansion of non-classified items, which were mainly low value-added materials processing exports. For the remainder, a major proportion were labour-intensive and little-processed products. The representative items of these two categories were respectively textiles, classified under 'MM' and 'MA' in Table 3.9, and minerals. Between 1985 and 1988, manufactured exports increased by 74 per cent, while textile exports increased by 114 per cent and minerals by 249 per cent. In contrast, for the two categories representative of heavy industry, chemicals and machinery,

Table 3.9 Exports and Imports Commodity Compositions, 1980–94 (percentages)

	Exports							*Imports*						
	PP	***MP***	*CP*	*MM*	*MT*	*MA*	*NC*	***PP***	***MP***	*CP*	*MM*	*MT*	*MA*	*NC*
1980	**50.2**	**49.8**	6.2	22.1	4.7	15.7	1.1	**34.8**	**65.2**	14.5	20.8	25.6	2.7	1.6
1981	**46.6**	**53.4**	6.1	21.4	4.9	16.9	4.1	**36.5**	**63.5**	11.9	18.3	26.7	2.5	4.1
1982	**45.0**	**55.0**	5.4	19.2	5.7	16.6	8.1	**39.6**	**60.4**	15.2	20.3	16.6	2.5	5.8
1983	**43.3**	**56.7**	5.6	19.7	5.5	17.1	8.8	**27.2**	**72.8**	14.9	29.4	18.6	3.6	6.3
1984	**45.7**	**54.3**	5.2	19.3	5.7	18.0	6.1	**19.0**	**81.0**	15.5	26.7	26.4	4.3	8.1
1985	**50.6**	**49.4**	5.0	16.4	2.8	12.7	12.5	**12.5**	**87.5**	10.6	28.2	38.4	4.5	5.8
1986	**36.4**	**63.6**	5.6	19.0	3.6	16.0	19.4	**13.2**	**86.8**	8.8	26.1	39.1	4.4	8.4
1987	**33.5**	**66.5**	5.7	21.7	4.4	15.9	18.8	**16.0**	**84.0**	11.6	22.5	33.9	4.3	11.7
1988	**30.3**	**69.7**	6.1	22.1	5.8	17.4	18.3	**18.2**	**81.8**	16.6	18.8	30.2	3.6	12.6
1989	**28.7**	**71.3**	6.1	20.7	7.4	20.5	16.6	**19.9**	**80.1**	12.8	20.9	30.8	3.5	12.2
1990	**25.6**	**74.4**	6.0	20.3	9.0	20.4	18.7	**18.5**	**81.5**	12.5	16.7	31.6	3.9	16.9
1991	**22.5**	**77.5**	5.3	20.1	9.9	23.1	19.0	**17.0**	**83.0**	14.5	16.4	30.7	2.6	17.5
1992	**20.1**	**79.9**	5.1	19.0	15.6	38.9	–	**16.4**	**83.6**	13.8	23.9	38.8	6.9	–
1993	**18.2**	**81.8**	5.0	17.9	16.7	42.3	–	**13.7**	**86.3**	9.3	27.4	43.3	6.2	–
1994	**16.3**	**83.7**	5.2	19.2	18.1	41.3	–	**14.2**	**85.8**	10.5	24.3	44.6	5.8	–
Change														
1980–8	**−19.9**	**+19.9**	−0.1	0	+1.1	+1.7	+17.2	**−16.6**	**+16.6**	+2.1	−2.0	+4.6	+0.9	+11.0
1988–94	**−14.0**	**+14.0**	−0.9	−2.9	+12.3	+23.9	–	**−4.0**	**+4.0**	−6.1	+5.5	+14.4	+2.2	–

Sources: ZSWTZ 1952–88, pp. 430–431; ZTN 1991, pp. 618– 619; ZTN 1992, pp. 630–631; ZTZ 1993, pp. 102; ZTN 1995, pp. 538–539.

Note: PP = primary products; MP = manufactured products; CP = chemicals and related products; MM = manufactured goods classified chiefly by material (textiles, metals, leathers, etc.); MT = machinery and transport equipment; MA = miscellaneous manufactured articles; NC = commodities and transactions not classified. Note that the category NC has been mainly accounted for by export processing activities of foreign capital-invested firms. Thus the country's manufactured exports and imports would be better indicated by [MP–NC]. From 1992, however, trades previously classified under NC have been reclassified under other headings.

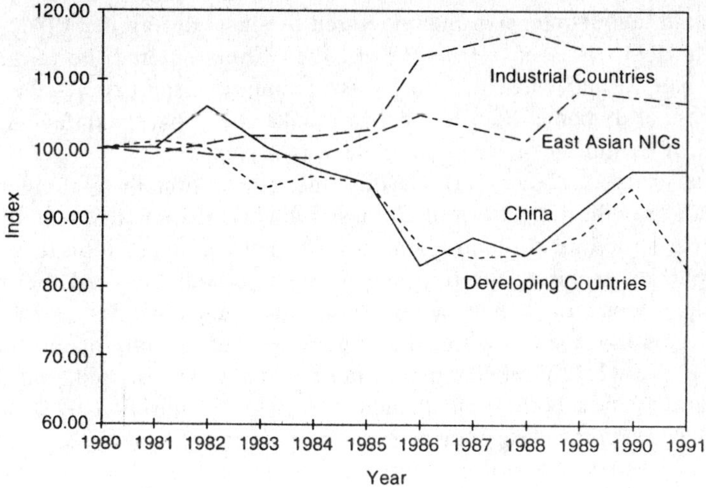

Figure 3.1 China's Terms of Trade in International Comparison, 1980–91 (1980 = 100)

Sources: Chinese figures from World Bank, *World Development Report*, various years; figures of industrial countries and developing countries from IMF, *International Financial Statistics Yearbook* 1993, p. 125; East Asian NICs figures from IMF, *World Economic Outlook*, October 1993, p. 159.

the performance was bleak: on the exports side the share increased by a mere one percentage point between 1980 and 1988, whereas on the imports side it increased by 6.7 percentage points. Finally, the growth pattern had even at times led to the shift of exports commodity composition in favour of primary products. This was evident in 1983–5 when the expansion of the 'new' industries was at its peak and China suffered the most serious trade deficits. The share of primary products in total exports increased from 43 per cent to 51 per cent, the latter being higher than the 1980 level. On the imports side, the share of manufactured products increased from 73 per cent to 88 per cent during the same period.

The evolution of the terms of trade shown in Figure 3.1 provides further evidence that, up to 1988, China basically followed an unfavourable trend of international specialization. The deterioration of the terms of trade is similar to the rest of the developing world, but is in contrast with the marked improvement of the advanced capitalist world and the East Asian newly industrializing countries. (For an analysis of the world context of deteriorating terms of trade against primary products and labour-intensive manufactured products during the 1980s, see Singh 1993.) It is only from 1989, when China entered the retrenchment period and when the state drive to improve the export competitiveness of dynamic industries began to take effect that the unfavourable trend of evolution of terms of trade was reversed.

The analysis above thus clarifies the proposition that, along with overall growth, the pattern of Chinese industrialization also resulted in adverse structural problems which were detrimental to long-term development. As far as the role played by state strategies and the institutions is concerned, two factors stand out in our analysis.

Structurally, the 'new' consumer durables were mainly mature products in the world market. Their exports demand was limited, and their technology was both sophisticated and largely controlled by a small number of world-class transnational corporations. A necessary condition for their successful development in the context of a 'late comer' country like China, therefore, was the building up of indigenous technological capabilities which would enable it to innovate in new products and process for entering the world market. However, given the oligopolistic nature of technology supply in the world market, what Chinese enterprises could import were mainly those at the fading stage of the product cycle. The 'new' industries also carried few linkages with the domestic capital goods sector which otherwise could have enhanced the innovation capacity. This was due to the differences in production technique, input specification and product standards. The capital goods sector established through pre-reform import substitution was not to serve the demonstration effects-induced consumption, and was far less competitive than its foreign counterparts in meeting the demand. These differences did not vanish over time, as there was continuous 'upgrading' in the demand structure. The most evident were the changes of demand, within a few years, from black-and-white to colour TV and further to large-screen TV and video recorders, from single-tub to double-tub washing machines, from single-door to double-door refrigerators, etc.

In the institutional respect, the fragmentation of the 'new' industries also made it very difficult for the development to move upstream and to become export competitive. This was particularly due to the fact that China had introduced production lines from the advanced capitalist world of virtually all established brand names, which were often incompatible in terms of input requirement and production technique. The miniaturization of plant scales was another source of the problem.

All these reveal that the market-oriented reform, especially the fragmentation of economic power within the administrative system and the behaviour of short-termism on the part of enterprises and local authorities, were responsible for the problem. The concern of these newly-empowered economic agents was to reap the profits from domestic consumption boom, rather than the long-term development of the economy. This sustained the fragmentation. Finally, with fragmentation moving to some upstream industries and to further high-grade products, the tendency of high import-dependence *cum* low export-competitiveness was thus continuously reproduced.

To summarize, under the industrialization pattern of the 1980s, China built up a wide range of 'new' industries which were characterized by high technical sophistication, and whose explosive expansion significantly contributed to economic growth. But the pattern also led to problems. The observable high import-dependence *cum* low export competitiveness of the industries, and subsequently their mutual perpetuation with the technologically backward industries, testified to the problems. These, together with the unfavourable effects on the building up of an indigenous technological capability, undermined the sustainability of the growth. The industrialization pattern has thus seen its limits.

DEMAND CONSTRAINT ON GROWTH: 1989–94

China's economic performance in the 1989–90 period of *zhili zhengdun* (readjustment and rectification) is a real paradox for the economics of shortage. This theory, which has been influential in the studies of Soviet-type economies, says that there are system-specific features which result in the economies being constantly under excessive demand (Kornai 1980; Perkins 1992, for application to China). However, in the case of China during 1989–90, it is clear that demand deficiency was a serious constraint on growth. What is more, the deficiency persisted in a time when the State expanded bank credits on an unprecedented scale and restored the policy of promoting rural industrial growth. The experience is thus not to be explained by the simplistic, ideology-oriented assertion that there was a conservative leadership whose anti-reformism harmed the market-oriented sector and hence the growth of the economy as a whole (Lee 1991; Lichtenstein 1991; Naughton 1995). Similarly, the rebound and subsequent hyper-growth since 1991, which has been widely publicized by the leadership and acclaimed by analysts for the fanfare on stepping up reform, need to be critically examined. There is evidence that the newly-emerged growth pattern since 1991 has produced both old problems and new tensions, putting the development prospects for the Chinese economy again in great uncertainty.

To understand the evolution from the 1989–90 demand-constrained stagnation to the 1991–2 rebound, and the future prospects, we need to place the trends and policies in a framework of structural analysis. The demand deficiency was, above all, mainly a collapse of domestic sales of the 'new' consumer durables. And the rebound was clearly investment-led. Given the existing institutional framework whereby decentralized economic agents generally incline to short-termism, the prevailing pattern of growth once again runs the risk of producing structural imbalances. But the evidently shifting focus of economic agents to capital goods industries also gives rise to new opportunities for sustainable growth. The crucial factor which would affect the prospects appears to be the mediation of State policy and the direction of further institutional reform.

The austerity measures of the *zhili zhengdun* programme, initially launched in the fourth quarter of 1988, because of the resistance by local authorities, were put into effect only by the second half of 1989. Industrial growth rate (year-on-year) fell abruptly from 10.8 per cent in the first six months to 0.9 per cent in September and –2.1 per cent in October. The stagnation persisted into 1990, with the first quarter registering zero growth. In the face of the situation, the State leadership responded by expanding bank credits. The watershed was in the last two months of 1989 within which total outstanding bank loans increased by more than 100bn yuan. This boosted the incremental amount for the year as a whole up to 186bn yuan, an increase of 22 per cent over 1988 which was supposedly a year of serious economic overheating. With stagnation persisting, the state stepped up the expansionary policy and also channelled a major proportion of the loans to township-and-village enterprises. In the first half of 1990, the incremental amount of outstanding bank loans hit an unprecedented record of 61bn yuan. During the same months the rural banking system provided 64bn yuan loans to TVEs, which was on top of the 25 per cent growth in 1989.

For 1990 as a whole, the incremental amount of outstanding bank loans registered 276bn yuan, up 48 per cent over 1989. The expansion slowed down in 1991, with the growth rate being 4 per cent (but again rising to 24 per cent in 1992, 36 per cent in 1993 and 6 per cent in 1994). This slowdown was largely due to the rebound of the economy since the second half of the year, which enabled banks to recoup previous loans. In terms of State policy, it was still expansionary, as was reflected in the 19 per cent growth in the actual amount of bank loans in 1991. Thus, overall, it is clear that during this supposedly austere period the State policy was in fact expansionary and on a massive scale. The 1989–90 demand-constrained economic stagnation is not to be explained by the *zhili zhengdun* programme itself (CASS-SSB 1992; JJCK, 18 July 1990 and 11 January 1993; JJRB, 16 July 1990; YJSB, 7 February 1993).

The co-existence of demand deficiency and State expansionary policy led to a number of problems which dominated the pattern of economic performance. The most phenomenal was the rapid increase of unsaleable stocks, which ultimately expressed itself in the increase of the amount of money tied up by inventories of finished products and that tied up by delayed payments from the commercial sector. From October 1988 to one year later, for all independently accounting industrial enterprises, the former amount increased by 61 per cent and the latter by 62 per cent. The figures further increased by 41 per cent and 65 per cent respectively by September 1990, and 17 per cent and 31 per cent respectively by September 1991. By the end of 1991, for SOEs alone, the combined total of money tied up by stockpiles and delayed payments registered a huge 332bn yuan, up 25b yuan over 1990. A further 41bn yuan was added to the total during 1992, boosting it to 373bn yuan by the year-end, which was equivalent to 34 per cent of total retail sales in the year. This resulted in 46 per cent of the incremental bank loans in 1992 being tied up by unsaleable stocks.

In addition to the financial burdens, what caused concern was the State's campaign of *xianchan yaku* (restricting production and reducing stockpiles) which fell largely on the shoulders of SOEs, while TVEs continued to pile up new stocks. The reason, again in line with the dual-track system, was that the State had more controls over the planned sector than the market-oriented sector (JJGL, August 1988, p. 25; JXDT, April 1992, p. 14; ZGJW, April 1992, p. 62; RMRB, 30 January 1992, 29 January 1993 and 9 February 1993).

A second and related problem during this period was the increase in inter-enterprise arrears, or 'triangular debts'. This, at the micro level, reflected a peculiar enterprise behaviour under crisis: that is, the tactics of shifting financial burdens onto each other and ultimately onto the State. It was also ascribable to the expansionary behaviour of State authorities of various levels, which, despite not having enough funding, sought to promote growth through debt-financed expansion of fixed-asset investment. By mid-1991, the total amount of inter-enterprise debts registered around 300bn yuan. In the one and a half years that followed, the State arranged the settlement of 219bn yuan debts by injecting 56bn yuan into the economy.

Following the latest round of investment expansion in 1992–4, however, there are signs that state authorities-promoted debt-financing is on the rise (RMRB, 31 October and 26 December 1992). This has worsened the debt problem following the slowdown of economic growth in 1994. The massive increases in stockpiles and 'triangular debts' have led to a third problem: the bleak financial performance of industrial enterprises, especially SOEs. This was particularly due to the massive outflow of funds from the industrial sector in the form of interests repayment. Compared with 1988, in 1991 realized profits of all independently accounting enterprises fell by 68 per cent, enterprise retained profits fell by 43 per cent, the (after-tax) profit rate fell from 10.2 per cent to 2.2 per cent, and total losses of loss-making enterprises rose by 3.9 times. The performance improved slightly in 1992, thanks to the acceleration of output growth. But it worsened once again under the slowdown of economic growth in 1994. In the meantime, the bleak financial performance has seriously undermined the ability of enterprises to invest in technical renovation and development. This will undermine their performance in the long-term (JJGL, August 1992, p. 12; CD, 24 December 1992).

Thus, to sum up, the sources of all these economic problems which have dominated the 1989–90 *zhili zhengdun* period can be traced to the single most crucial factor of demand deficiency. More precisely, in view of the massive credit expansion in the meantime, the deficiency was evidently structural. A further indicator was the basically positive growth of per capita real income during 1989–94: for urban dwellers, in percentage terms, –3, 9, 8, 9, 10 and 9, respectively and for the rural population, less favourably, in percentage terms, 7, 2, 2, 6, 3 and 5 respectively. This supports the judgement that the demand deficiency was structural rather than aggregate. It follows the need to identify the specific industries which were especially hard hit by the sales slump, and thus especially responsible for the demand deficiency.

A wealth of evidence indicates that it was the 'new' consumer industries built up over the 1980s which played such a role. By 1991, for instance, the production capacity of colour TV sets reached 21m per annum, and that of refrigerators 16m sets, washing machines 16m sets, and electric fans 70m sets. In contrast, the actual output volume in that year was respectively 12m, 5m, 7m and 20m, making the capacity utilization rate generally well below a half.[7]

Table 3.10 Volumes of Output, Sales and Year-end Stock of Selected Consumer Durables and Producer Goods, 1988–91 (10,000)

		1988	*1991*	*1988–91 average annual growth*
TV sets	Q	2 505	2 622	+1.5%
	S	2 364	2 658	+4.0%
	T	71	332	+67.2%
Of which: colour TV sets	Q	1 038	1 194	+4.8%
	S	1 016	1 174	+4.9%
	T	38	142	+55.2%
Household Refrigerators	Q	758	476	−14.4%
	S	724	483	−12.6%
	T	21	117	+77.3%
Washing machines	Q	1 047	683	−13.3%
	S	1 028	703	−11.9%
	T	41	85	+27.5%
Machine tools	Q	19.2	15.1	−7.7%
	S	16.6	14.4	−9.5%
	T	1.4	2.3	+18.0%
Automobiles	Q	64.5	71.3	+3.4%
	S	64.0	73.1	+4.5%
	T	2.5	2.7	+2.6%
Steel products	Q	4 689	5 547	+5.8%
	S	4 525	5 356	+5.8%
	T	78	122	+16.1%

Sources: ZTN 1989, pp. 379–80; ZTN 1992, pp. 494–5.

Note: Sales and year-end stock figures cover county-and-above level independently accounting industrial enterprises. Steel products figures in 10,000 tons.
Q = Output; S = Sales; T = Year-end stock.

Table 3.10 gives the figures of output volumes, sales and year-end stocks of the three representative items of 'new' consumer durables, and compares them with three producer goods. During 1989–91, the average growth rate of output volumes of TV sets registered 2 per cent per annum (of which colour TV 5 per cent), while that of refrigerators registered −14 per cent and washing machines −13 per cent. Perhaps more spectacular was the fluctuation in market sales. In the case of TV sets, while the average annual growth rate during 1981–8 was 28 per cent, it fell to 4 per cent during 1989–91. As a result of the sales slump, unsold stocks piled up. By November 1989, stockpiles of TV sets in the commercial sector registered 3.6m and those in producing enterprises 2.8m, up respectively by 21 per cent and 175 per cent over the previous year. In 1990, total stocks of TV sets grew by 59 per cent, of which colour TV was up 26 per cent. The situation improved somewhat in 1991. But the monthly average of colour TV stocks still registered 3–3.5m sets, far greater than the volume of 2.1m sets in 1989 year-end and 0.8m sets in 1988 year-end. As a whole, the sales slump of 'new' consumer products during 1989–91 was far unmatched by most producer goods except machine tools, which for decades has been facing over-capacity. And the rebound in 1992 was far slower on the part of the former group.

It is likely that the sales stagnation of 'new' consumer durables will persist in the long-term. For one thing, the domestic market is tending to be saturated. By 1992 year-end, the volumes of TV sets, refrigerators and washing machines owned by the population were respectively 228m, 39m and 117m. These mean that there were 113 TV sets (of which 75 colour), 53 refrigerators and 83 washing machines per 100 households in urban areas. As the per capita income of the rural population remains low and there have not been any signs of a newer 'consumption revolution' brewing, it is unlikely that the previous pattern of 'new' industries-led rapid growth will be repeated in the foreseeable future.

Overall, for the economic performance during 1989–94, the evolution from demand-constrained stagnation to investment-led rebound is indicated by the figures in Table 3.11. It is noticeable that the discrepancy between the growth rate of consumption demand and that of industrial output has widened since 1987 and reached its peak in 1989. The subsequent narrowing down in 1990–1 was the reflection of both a recovery in sales and the slower growth in industrial output. But then there followed the widening of the gap once again in 1992–4, with the combined growth rate of sales during the four-year period of 1991–4 being 40 per cent, and that of industry being 136 per cent. In contrast, the massive increase of fixed-asset investment, up 127 per cent in real terms during the same period, was clearly the demand-side factor supporting the industrial growth.

MARKET AND INSTITUTIONAL REGULATION IN THE GROWTH PROCESS

Having depicted the pattern of performance of the Chinese economy during 1989–94, we now turn to analyse the prospects for future growth,

Table 3.11 Retail Sales, Investment and Industrial Growth Rates, 1981–94 (percentages)

	(a) Social retail sales	*(b) Fixed-asset investment*	*(c) Gross value of industrial output*	*(a)−(c)*	*(b)−(c)*
1981	7.2	5.4	4.3	+2.9	+1.1
1982	7.4	27.0	7.8	−0.4	+19.2
1983	9.3	15.0	11.2	−1.9	+3.8
1984	15.3	26.2	16.3	−1.0	+9.9
1985	17.2	22.2	21.4	−4.2	+0.8
1986	8.5	9.6	11.7	−3.2	−2.1
1987	9.6	14.5	17.7	−8.1	−3.2
1988	7.8	9.7	20.8	−12.9	−11.1
1989	−7.6	−24.8	8.5	−16.1	−33.3
1990	0.4	6.2	7.8	−7.4	−1.6
1991	10.2	18.5	14.8	−4.6	+3.7
1992	10.8	30.9	27.5	−16.7	+3.4
1993	9.2	20.8	28.0	−18.8	−7.2
1994	5.2	21.0	26.1	−20.9	−5.1

Sources: Table 3.3; ZTN 1993, pp. 237, 268, 413, 611; ZTN 1994, pp. 139, 231, 246, 375, 496; ZTN 1995, pp. 137, 233, 249, 377, 523.

Notes: All growth rates are in real terms. Figures of (a) are deflated by the social retail price index. Figures of (b) are deflated by a constructed investment goods price index, which is assumed to be the average of the price indices of factory-delivered industrial products of machinery and building materials. The 1994 (a) figure is the growth rate of the sales of consumer goods, whose value normally accounts for around 90% of social retail sales, and is deflated by the consumer price index.

as well as the implications thereof concerning the roles of market and institutional regulation. To begin with, in the light of the analysis of the experience of the 1980s, it is possible to identify a number of problems that are presently brewing and are due to seriously constrain the economy.

The first concerns structural balance. The ongoing trend of industrial growth at a rate of approaching 30 per cent, and with it the growth of fixed-asset investment at a comparable rate (Table 3.11), is doomed to give rise to bottlenecks and hence will not be sustainable for long. Whereas the energy constraint has not yet come into play, that of transportation tends to be severe. Thus, if the drive for rapid growth, and with it the expansionary state policy, persists, disruptive bottlenecks are likely to emerge. A new round of painful retrenchment and readjustment will then be needed.

The second problem concerns the proliferation of small scale investment projects. Not only that fixed-asset investment has increased at a high rate of 20–39 per cent, but also that the total scale of projects under construction has increased at an even faster pace: up by 28 per cent a year from 1990 to reach the amount of 3057bn yuan by the end of 1994, which was equivalent to 1.9 times the year's actual investment. Along with the expansion of the total scale, there has been the rapid increase in the number of projects. For 50 000 yuan-and-above projects alone, the number increased by 75 000, 89 000, 78 300 and 76 500, respectively, in 1991–4 (RMRB, 29 February 1992, 19 February 1993, 1 March 1994; JJRB, 1 March 1995). A number of surveys and reports have revealed that a major proportion of the projects are of downstream processing industries and with scales below efficient levels. The pattern is in the main a repetition of that of the 1980s, induced by short-term profitability and promoted by local authorities of various levels which have the command of a major portion of investment funds. A related spectacular development is the proliferation of all kinds of 'industrial development zones' across the country: up from 117 one year ago to 2700 by 1992 year-end (JJWB, 23 February 1993). It is likely that this trend will worsen the structural imbalances of the economy and will hinder the improvement of technical efficiency.

Nevertheless, in this connection, it is noted that, in contrast to the 1980s, there has been a new development on the part of local authorities, especially those of the provincial level and in industrialized regions, which is likely to have far-reaching effects: namely, the emphasis on the development of upstream, capital goods industries. The most dramatic change is that of Guangdong, the model region of market-oriented and outward-looking reform. In its ten-year development plan for the 1990s, the provincial government shifts its focus from the 'new' consumer industries which have propelled the tremendous economic growth of the province in the 1980s to 'high-tech' heavy and chemical industries as the leading sectors in the 1990s. The same is evident in Shanghai, Jiangsu and several other coastal provinces. As a whole, the strategy is explicitly to follow the development model of South Korea and Taiwan by embarking on the track of 'secondary import substitution': the development of domestic materials and equipment industries.[8]

The third problem under the prevailing growth pattern concerns the interaction between domestic structural change and the regulation of the world market, the central issue of industrialization which we have discussed above. In 1992–4, a spectacular development in China's foreign trade was the massive expansion of the imports and exports of mechanical and electronic goods. In value terms, in 1994, exports registered US$32bn while imports registered US$59bn, resulting in an unprecedented deficit of US$27bn which far outstrips the 'import fever' of 1984–5 (see Table 3.8).

Clearly, the ongoing investment-led, large scale industrialization requires the imports of foreign technology on an unprecedented scale. As in the 1980s, this will be favourable for growth but at the same time will pose the question of sustainability. If exports of comparably high value-added goods do not increase at a similar pace, the growth pattern will again result in the mutual perpetuation between import-dependent sectors and technologically backward sectors. If, in addition, exports of low value-added goods are insufficient to maintain the flow of technology imports, the growth cannot be sustained. These points lead to the crux of the matter: whether the imports of foreign technology are, on balance, a complement of, or a substitute for, the building up of an indigenous technological capability.

It is particularly in this connection that the mediation of State policy and institutional reform will play a central role. Already in the years following the 1984–5 import upsurge, the promotion of export expansion of mechanical and electronic goods has become a crucial State policy. A package of promoting measures had been adopted since 1986. These included direct subsidies for exporting enterprises, and cheap credits for their technical renovation and development. In the Seventh Five-Year-Plan period (1986–90), a total of 1139 projects benefited from this scheme. The result was the formation of a network of exporting enterprises, around 1400 by 1990, which has accounted for more than 60 per cent of the exports of mechanical and electronic goods. Viewed in a broader angle, the exports promotion in fact has been part and parcel of the State strategy of prioritizing the capital goods sector, particularly its 'high-tech', upstream branches.

For the machinery sector, the priority is on computer numerically controlled machine tools, automatic large scale measuring instruments, high precision casting machines and so on. For electronics, the priority is on the four branches of integrated circuits production, computers, computer software development and programme-controlled telephone switching. In both cases, the promoting measures have included R&D subsidies, exemption of customs tariff for imports of key equipment and instruments, sales tax exemption and income tax reduction. The state has also adopted a range of measures to promote the assimilation of imported technology and realization of economies of scale. The indigenization of TV technology, especially the State's central role in negotiating with transnational corporations in the transfer of colour picture tube production technology, is a case in point (ZJDB, 3 March 1991, 7 January 1992, 28 February 1992 and 9 January 1993; see Chapter 6 for details).

The exports expansion of mechanical and electronic products has been tremendous under the promoting measures of the State. Over the seven-year period of 1987–94, the average annual growth rate registered 35 per cent. For electronics alone, the growth rate was around 50 per cent per annum. What is more remarkable is the expansion of the exports of a number of technologically sophisticated products, which in a sense indicates the standard the domestic production capability has attained. In 1993, China exported 9.4m TV sets of which 3.7m were colour. It also exported US$1.6bn computer products in 1993, and US$2.8m in 1994. These achievements are in sharp contrast to the very low level of development just a few years ago, as was evidenced in the virtual non-existence of exports and the widespread existence of technical and dynamic inefficiency which we describe in detail above. Indeed, without the development of the linked upstream industries, and the indigenization of the imported technology, it is unlikely that the exports expansion could have been achieved. Given that these industries are in general capital intensive, technologically advanced and hence not in line with China's comparative advantage, it is also unlikely that the development could have taken place under the unfettered regulation of the market. The crucial role of the State strategy, therefore, is quite evident.[9]

Regarding the development of an export-competitive capital goods sector, the state strategy is unlikely to achieve its targets if it is not supported by a conducive institutional framework. This, again, is underscored by recent trends in the imports and exports of mechanical and electronic products. The hefty export expansion was achieved against the background of a domestic sales slump, which provided enterprises with the incentive to export. The good performance following the 1991 foreign trade liberalization, where the practice of direct State subsidies for exports was abolished, further indicates both the incentive and ability of the exporting enterprises to meet the competition of the world market. According to the State authorities, after an initial period of difficult adjustment, by late 1991, most of the exporting enterprises have been able to deal with their own profits and losses. This helped to support the exports upsurge in 1992–4 (JJGL, August 1992; ZJDB, 2 January 1993). The performance indicates the conducive side of the reform over the 1980s, arising from the enhancement of competition in the domestic market, the institutionalization of the distinctive interests of enterprises, and the organizational restructuring of enterprises towards rationalization and flexibility (see Chapter 4).

Looking forward to the long-term, the pattern of large scale industrialization, whether in the form of 'secondary import substitution' or a newer 'consumption revolution', requires large increases in technology imports. This in turn requires marked improvement of technical and dynamic efficiency on the part of exporting enterprises, especially large scale capital goods-producing SOEs. The direction of future institutional reform will be decisive. A central factor to shape the direction will be the policy orientation of the State, which has hitherto exhibited contradictions in its attitude towards the tension between short-term growth and long-term development. This results in its ambivalence to the expansionary behaviours of local authorities. It also results in contradictions in its treatment of SOEs. In particular, following the termination of the *zhili zhengdun* programme, the leadership is facing a formidable choice between two approaches. To continue the drive for rapid growth, it can resort to the strategy of forcing large-and-medium enterprises of upstream industries to sacrifice. This is already evident in a new policy, with effect from 1993, whereby the State would maintain the controls over the output prices of key SOEs while decontrolling their input prices (ZJDB, 12 November 1992).

On the other hand, the bleak performance of SOEs during the retrenchment period has fully exposed their difficult positions after a decade of development lag and lacking investment. The severity has reached such an extent that it seriously affects the economy, especially State revenue which relies very much on SOEs. Thus, since 1991, the State leadership has been stressing that the central task of reform and development in the 1990s is to revitalize SOEs. A number of measures, including tax reduction and more enterprise autonomy, have been adopted. On balance, however, the policy environment of the SOEs is yet to be determined. We turn to study China's enterprise-level performance and the systemic reform in the next chapter.

4 (Re)interpreting Chinese Enterprise Reform

This chapter seeks to interpret China's economic reform over the period of 1978–94 in a way that differs significantly from the orthodox emphasis on marketization and privatization. Succinctly, my central thesis is that the observed good performance of Chinese industrial enterprises of all ownership types should be seen as the outcome of the combination of improved micro-level efficiency and favourable macro-level and development conditions. As far as micro-level efficiency is concerned, the improvement, in turn, has been accounted for by an appropriate combination of the market and non-market institutions. Throughout, the argument is based on a wealth of empirical evidence that appears to be contradicting the orthodox accounts, but being consistent with the late industrialization literature which I draw upon.

ASSESSING THE PERFORMANCE OF STATE-OWNED ENTERPRISES

The Significance of the SOEs–COEs Comparison

The performance of Chinese State-owned enterprises (SOEs) under economic reform is an issue of continuous debate. Nevertheless, economists generally agree that, regarding the comparison between SOEs and non-SOEs (mostly collectively-owned enterprises, or COEs), the former have been outperformed. After all, the fact that the output share of SOEs in Chinese industry has shrunk by a huge 44 percentage points, from 78 to 34 per cent, during 1978–94 seems to speak all. From these observations, is it possible to make the further claims that (a) in relative terms, the weaker performance of SOEs is accounted for by their institutional arrangements that are less conformed to market regulation, and (b) in absolute terms, Chinese SOEs, just like SOEs everywhere (and especially in countries of the former Soviet bloc), are not reformable? People known as 'shock therapy' or 'big bang' advocates categorically affirm both claims (Sachs and Woo 1994; Woo 1994).

Moderate economists, on the other hand, tend to agree with (a) while disagreeing with (b) (Jefferson and Rawski 1994, 1995; McMillan and Naughton 1992; Naughton 1994, 1995).

In contrast, it is my intention to deny both of the two claims. In the face of the observations indicated above, my strategy is to bring into the scene the performance of Chinese large-and-medium scale enterprises (LMEs for short), the vast majority of which being in fact SOEs. As will be given below, all available indicators – output growth, financial performance, and productivity change – show that the performance has been indeed comparable to COEs. Moderate economists have now begun to recognize that Chinese LMEs have been doing well (Jefferson and Xu 1994; Naughton 1994). By and large, however, they tend to posit that this performance must be mainly accounted for by the increase in market competition. They therefore claim that the future prospects for LMEs, just like the Chinese economy as a whole, rest on further marketization.

But it should be remembered that LMEs are at the heart of China's traditional Soviet-type economy. Their operations have been far less marketized (especially under the planning-market dual-track system), and their institutional arrangements far less conformed to private ownership, than the rest of Chinese industry. The fact that their performance has been comparable to COEs indicates that to attribute it to the market is not an adequate explanation. Moreover, it should be noted that the use of the comparison between SOEs and COEs as a means for making inferences on the effects of Chinese economic reform, particularly those related to ownership difference and variation in the degree of marketization, has its limits. The institutions of COEs (of which most are township-and-village enterprises, TVEs) are not reducible to the canonical capitalist firm, that is with market-determined, individualistic property rights (Bowles and Dong 1994; Weitzman and Xu 1994). The comparison, therefore, would not allow for making any claim that private ownership is superior, and that mass privatization is indispensable for economic development.

As for the SOEs–COEs comparison itself, the clear-cut picture that has been built up in the literature – with respect to output growth and change in productivity, but not financial performance (see below) – is blurred if we bring LMEs into the scene. In terms of the size of employment, LMEs form what would be classified as China's 'very large' enterprises by international standards, as virtually all of them have more than 500 employees. More important, the vast majority of LMEs are in fact SOEs: according to the 1985 Industrial Census, 97 per cent of the output value of LMEs were accounted for by SOEs. The share remained at 96 per cent in 1986 (SC-ICO 1990, pp. 70, 402; ZGJTZ 1987, p. 142).

Subsequent developments have not changed the situation much. Naughton (1994) estimates that, by 1991, SOEs still accounted for 93 per cent of the output of LMEs. It is only after the wave of corporatization, that is, the transformation of SOEs into joint-stock companies, in 1992–3 that the output share of SOEs in LMEs has seen substantial decrease, but still at 80 per cent in 1993 and 73 per cent in 1994 (in terms of the number of enterprises, the proportion of SOEs in LMEs is 76 per cent in 1993 and 71 per cent in 1994; see ZTN 1994, pp. 378, 388; ZTN 1995, pp. 388, 392).[1] Since the majority of these corporatized firms have the State as the dominant owner, and, more crucially, since the essential features of their governance structure – especially concerning the three aspects that we shall discuss in details below, that is, soft budget constraint, government intervention, and the employment relationship – have appeared to remain intact, China's LMEs are still overwhelmed by SOEs.[2]

As the core of China's traditional Soviet-type economy, the evolution of the conduct and performance of LMEs deserves a close examination. It is likely that this would generate significant insights into the country's heterodox reform experience.

Output Growth

Concerning the comparison of output growth, if we divide Chinese industry along firm size (instead of ownership sector), it is clear that LMEs have outperformed small enterprises. During 1980–92, of the industrial output of all township-and-above enterprises, the share of large scale enterprises increased by 10 percentage points. For LMEs combined, the gain is 12 percentage points, from 43 per cent to 55 per cent (Figure 4.1).[3]

How can one reconcile the expansion of LMEs with the shrinking share of SOEs as a whole in China's industrial output? Clearly, the only possibility is that the loser has been small scale SOEs. Naughton (1994) estimates that the output share of these enterprises in the national total fell from 36 per cent in 1978 to 12 per cent in 1991. In contrast, there is evidently a trend of convergence between township-and-above independently accounting COEs and other COEs: their respective output shares in the national total were 17 per cent and 7 per cent in 1980, and 22 per cent and 16 per cent in 1992.

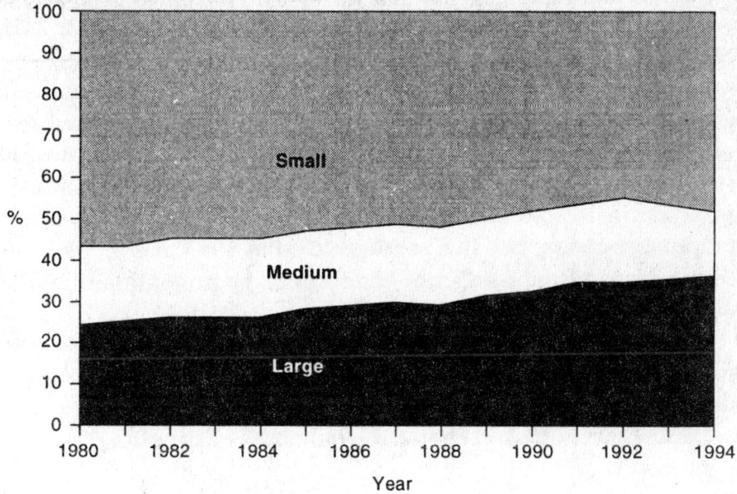

Figure 4.1 Relative Shares of Large, Medium and Small Scale Enterprises in the Gross Value of Industrial Output of Township-and-Above Enterprises

Sources: ZGJTZ 1987, p. 37; ZTZ 1988, p. 36; ZTZ 1990, p. 68; ZTZ 1993, p. 70; ZTN 1994, p. 378; ZTN 1995, pp. 382, 388.

Note: Figures of sector shares are calculated at current prices GVIO after 1985, and at 1980 constant prices GVIO before 1985.

The uneven development in State industry implies that the often-adopted approach of comparing SOEs and COEs is simplistic, and the assertion thereby that SOEs because of their less market-oriented institutions have been out performed is not being substantiated. This extreme unevenness, though, remains a major issue for future research. Perhaps the micro-level analysis of the reforms of SOEs in the sections that follow may shed some light on it.

Financial Performance

It is well known that the financial performance of Chinese SOEs has deteriorated under reform. Sachs and Woo (1994) emphasize that this should be taken as the most important indication of SOEs' performance, because the deterioration affects state budgetary revenue and expenditure and thus threatens macroeconomic stability.

It is, however, less well known that the same trend of deteriorating

Table 4.1 Profit Rate, Loss-to-Profit Ratio, and Proportion of Loss-Making Enterprises, 1980–94 (percentages)

	1980	*1985*	*1986*	*1987*	*1988*	*1989*	*1990*	*1991*	*1992*	*1993*	*1994*
AEs											
(a)	25.2	23.8	20.4	20.0	20.5	16.8	12.2	11.9	9.9	10.3	10.2
(b)		2.4	4.3	4.5	4.7	10.3	23.3	21.3	16.8	16.3	13.7
(c)		10.9	13.2	14.4	11.7	15.9	21.1	18.7	15.9	19.3	20.3
SOEs											
(a)	24.9	23.5	20.7	20.3	20.6	17.2	12.4	11.8	9.7	9.7	9.8
(b)	3.7	2.4	4.0	4.0	4.6	10.2	23.2	22.1	19.0	18.5	16.8
(c)		9.6	13.1	13.0	10.9	16.0	27.6	25.8	23.4	28.8	...
COEs											
(a)	26.6	24.6	19.4	18.2	19.8	15.4	11.5	11.9	10.1	10.9	10.7
(b)			5.3	6.4	4.8	10.5	22.4	17.2	10.7	...	...
(c)		11.7	13.2	14.7	11.7	15.7	19.4	16.7	13.7	16.5	...
LMEs											
(a)	27.4	25.6	22.3	22.0	21.9	18.1	13.6	12.9	10.6	11.1	11.3
(b)		1.5	2.7	3.0	3.9	9.2	19.3	18.6	16.3	...	...
(c)		5.3	8.8	9.1	8.2	12.4	24.6	24.6	20.4	24.9	...

Sources: ZGJTN 1993, pp. 90–3, 116–19, 129–32, 142–5, 168; *ZGJY*, 1994, no. 2, pp. 13–15; ZTN 1994, pp. 378–81, 399; ZGJTN 1994, pp. 81–6, 93–95, 120–5; ZTN 1995, pp. 388–91.

Note: AEs = all enterprises; SOEs = state-owned enterprises; COEs = collectively-owned enterprises; LMEs = large-and-medium scale enterprises. (a) = (taxes + profits) ÷ (value of fixed assets net of depreciation + working capital); (b) = total losses of loss-making enterprises ÷ (taxes + profits); (c) = number of loss-making enterprises ÷ number of enterprises. Figures cover township-and-above independently accounting industrial enterprises.

financial performance has also happened to COEs. The comparison between SOEs and COEs in this respect is also not clear-cut. The three indicators in Table 4.1 – (pre-tax) profit rate, loss-to-profit ratio, and the proportion of loss-making enterprises – rather show a mixed picture: that SOEs basically outperformed COEs during the boom period of 1985–8, but were outperformed in the recession and subsequent rebound period of 1989–92. Meanwhile, LMEs have consistently outperformed COEs except in the two loss-related indicators during 1991–2. Thus the claims that SOEs have performed worse financially than COEs, and that this indicates the inefficiency of the former, are not substantiated.

The trend of deteriorating enterprise financial performance is a real problem for the Chinese economy. In the worst year of 1991, total losses in loss-making SOEs amounted to 36.7bn yuan, which is equivalent to 22 per cent of the (pre-tax) profits generated by all SOEs. Of the 75 248 township-and-above independently accounting SOEs, 19 443 or

26 per cent were in the red (compared with the 17 per cent or 55 874 loss-making COEs). This trend indeed requires an explanation. It is noted that most mainstream studies tend to assume that enterprise financial (and measured input-output) performance is solely determined by micro-level efficiency, rather than being an outcome of various factors including the macro-level and developmental conditions. I shall analyze some of the factors when coming to examine the policy regimes of enterprises in the next section.

TFP Change

The debate over total factor productivity (TFP) change in Chinese industry has received much attention. Woo *et al.* (1994) find that, in the 1980s, the growth of TFP of township-and-village enterprises ranges between slightly and strongly positive, while that of SOEs between strongly negative and zero. These results do not agree with those of Jefferson *et al.* (1992), where SOEs and COEs both register positive TFP growth, with the latter slightly leading by two percentage points. The crux of this dispute rests on two difficult issues: the construction of appropriate deflators, especially those for intermediate inputs, and whether or not to treat 'non-productive' capital and labour as part of the inputs.

It is not my intention to participate in this seemingly unresolvable debate. What I want to focus upon is how far it can go in making inferences from the estimation results about the sources of productivity change in Chinese industry, and further about the effects of institutional reforms. Thus, in the calculation below, I concede to the approach of Woo *et al.* (1994) in making minimal adjustment of the data, but just bring into the SOEs–COEs contrast the performance of LMEs. The deflator issue is more difficult to get away, and I shall cope with it in more details in Chapter 5. Here, I adopt a simple approach of using a constant-returns, two-inputs production function, and assume the responsiveness of output to labour and capital being equal for all groups of enterprises. This might seem to be rather arbitrary, but, for the purpose of looking at the relative (rather than absolute) performance of the different enterprise sectors, it is unlikely to be seriously flawed.

Table 4.2 presents the estimation results. For the period of 1980–8, the TFP growth rates are 0.62 per cent for SOEs, 3.21 per cent for COEs and 3.04 per cent for LMEs. The difference between the former two is 2.6 percentage points, which is rather close to the widely-cited result obtained by Jefferson *et al.* (1992): 2.40 per cent for SOEs and 4.63 per cent for COEs, a difference of 2.2 percentage points. Using

Table 4.2 TFP Growth, 1978–94 (percentages)

	1980–8	*1978–92*	*1978–94*
AEs	1.44	2.32	3.69
SOEs	0.68 (1.54)	0.34 (1.72)	0.89 (2.19)
COEs	3.23 (2.23)	3.50 (1.89)	5.57 (4.01)
LMEs	2.50 (3.38)	2.34 (3.76)	2.68 (4.03)

Sources: Calculated from data appendix of Chapter 5.

Note: The responsiveness of output to labour and capital are assumed equal for all enterprises sectors, that is, $a = q - 0.5l - 0.5k$, where q, l and k are average annual growth rate of NVIO, employment and value of capital, respectively, and a the TFP growth rate. Figures in parentheses are alternative estimates based on the same output deflator of AEs. Figures cover township-and-above independently accounting industrial enterprises.

the same method of estimation, however, the TFP growth rate of LMEs is very close to that of COEs. The picture is basically unaltered if we extend the estimation to cover the 14-year period of 1978–92. Now, the average annual growth of TFP of COEs outstrips that of SOEs by 3.2 percentage points, and that of LMEs by 1.2 percentage points. The difference between COEs and LMEs, at least, is still hardly impressive.

The real difference emerges when we further extend just two more years to cover 1978–94: now, COEs outstrip SOEs by 4.7 percentage points, and LMEs by 2.9 percentage points. So the miracle took place in 1993–4 – indeed the single year of 1993, when the net output of COEs grew by 91 per cent (real), while SOEs grew by 16 per cent and LMEs by 14 per cent. But, is the miracle real? Serious doubt must be cast on it. A close look at the output deflators (which are gross-output deflators but are used here for calculating the real growth rates of net output) reveal that the movements are erratic. In 1993, the deflator rose by 21 per cent for SOEs and 5 per cent for COEs. As for the five-year period from 1990 to 1994, the deflator rose by 50 per cent for SOEs and 26 per cent for COEs. Probably for similar reasons, official statistics give a far lower conversion factor between 1990 and 1980 constant-price gross output for COEs than for SOEs, 1.274 and 1.655, respectively. The implication for the comparison of TFP growth, however, is that the difference between SOEs and COEs is suddenly widened by a large margin once we extend the period of coverage into the 1990s.

In this connection, it is noted that, regarding comparison across enterprise sectors, current-price measurements are likely to be more appropriate than constant-price ones. The reason is that the calculation of the latter is based on output *volume*, while the former is based on sales *value* and hence has taken into account product quality improvement. Moreover, because many COEs are beyond the reach of State statistical authorities, they have tended to report their current-price output figures when being asked to report constant-price figures (see Rawski 1993, for a discussion). It is reasonable, therefore, to believe that the conversion factors and price deflators indicated above tend to underestimate the relative performance of SOEs *vis-à-vis* COEs, especially in the 1990s. For comparison, the figures in parentheses of Table 4.2 are alternative estimates of TFP growth rates based on the same output deflator of AEs. Finally, the assumption of equal output responsiveness to labour and capital might also underestimate the relative performance of SOEs (and LMEs) *vis-à-vis* COEs. As SOEs in general are far 'older' than COEs, their capital should on average belong to earlier vintages of technology and their labour should be more skilful. Thus, the contribution of labour (relative to capital) to output in SOEs is likely to be higher than COEs, and, in conjunction with the fact that for all the enterprise sectors the growth rate of output is lower than that of capital but higher than that of labour, the TFP growth rates of COEs might need to be adjusted down and those of SOEs and LMEs be adjusted upwards.

In any event, the presence of LMEs makes it quite impossible to say that COEs are much more efficient than SOEs. To put the TFP growth rate of LMEs at zero or below, in addition to using the dubious deflators that are unfavourable for LMEs (and SOEs), we must also put the growth rate of COEs at 0.2 per cent in 1980–8 and 1.4 per cent in 1978–92. That is to say, the performance of Chinese industry as a whole becomes very unsatisfactory. But then one might question the value of the analysis of TFP change. In the face of China's sustained industrial growth over the past 16 years, and its contrast with the dismal situations in countries of the former Soviet bloc and most parts of the developing world, one might consider the estimation result of low TFP change as not really important.

At this point, it is indeed worthwhile to rethink the significance of TFP analysis. In a sense, this is a powerful tool because it takes into account both the input and output sides of economic units. Based on the assumption of equal returns (marginal revenue products) to equal amounts of factor inputs, the measured input-output ratios can be used for comparing the relative efficiency of different enterprise sectors.

But the inference must not be pushed too far. If competition among enterprises takes place mainly in a context of rapid structural change (the Schumpeterian notion of competition where 'new' capital/technology kills off 'old'), the assumption of converging returns to factors might not be realistic. This criticism of TFP analysis is an old theme in the literature (Nelson 1981). In the context of the discussion here, the point is that we need to take into account the pattern of China's industrial growth under reform. This, however, is a neglected topic in the literature. The few studies available indicate that the pattern is indeed characterized by rapid structural change, associated with the rise of the 'new (consumer durables) industries' (see Chapter 3). In this instance, a major determinant of measured input-output efficiency has been the capacity utilization rate which, in turn, depends on continuous investment in new technology (especially the introduction of foreign technology that is crucial for enterprises to keep up with the changing consumption demands). Thus, the measured input–output efficiency of enterprises is affected by their investment capability, and behind it the policy regimes they face. We now turn to analyze the different policy regimes faced by SOEs and COEs.

THE POLICY REGIME: GETTING THE FACTS STRAIGHT

Are SOEs Especially Favoured?

It is often alleged that Chinese SOEs are especially favoured by the State, and, in line with the discussion above, favouritism can significantly alter their measured relative performance versus COEs. In this section, I try to argue that the actual situation is rather the opposite. This judgement is not definitive because it is constrained by data availability (especially those related to the external financing of both SOEs and COEs). Nevertheless, the wealth of evidence presented below does tend to support the judgement. At the least, it gives a necessary correction to the exclusive focus on the favour received by SOEs (namely, the issue of state subsidies) that is typical of available writings.

In an attempt to argue that the continued existence of a large SOEs sector is not only unviable in the long term but also harmful with regard to short-term macroeconomic stability, Sachs and Woo (1994) emphasize the issue of state subsidies. They estimate that, by 1991, total subsidies were equivalent to 8 per cent of China's GDP. The basis upon which the estimation is made, however, is debatable. For what they call 'subsidies to SOEs' are in fact composed of three different things: enterprise loss subsidies, price subsidies, and central bank credits to banks. It is not obvious that the second item is ascribable to the existence of SOEs *per se*, and that the third item is really a subsidy. Price subsidies are seen better as arising from the implicit contract between the state and the whole urban population (and hence the historical development of Chinese political economy), where the former undertakes to guarantee a certain level of welfare provision for the latter. The issue of central bank credits is more complex, in the first place because we don't know the actual distribution among enterprise sectors. Moreover, as will be discussed below, it is not clear that the increasing reliance of SOEs on bank credits is indeed a favour – it rather tends to be a burden on them.

As for enterprise loss subsidies proper (which in 1991 amounted to 51bn yuan or 2.5 per cent of GDP), in the context of the discussion here on industry, it is necessary to include only the share for industrial SOEs. An approximate indication is the distinction in official statistics between subsidies to productive enterprises and those to non-productive enterprises. In 1992, the total of 45bn yuan subsidies (1.9 per cent of GDP) was almost equally divided between the two (ZTN 1993, pp. 31, 216). If this was also the case in 1991, the share that went to industrial SOEs would amount to 25.5bn yuan (a World Bank estimation actually puts it at a far smaller amount of 14.5bn yuan; see Jefferson and Rawski 1995). This is equivalent to 70 per cent of the total losses (37bn yuan) incurred by industrial SOEs in that year. However, as will be discussed in detail below, around 40 per cent of the losses of SOEs were incurred by the energy sector where output prices were kept artificially low under the planning-market dual-track system. In other words, the bulk of state subsidies were intended to compensate for this unfavourable effect on state industry.

The Effect of the Dual-Track System

As mentioned, in 1991, total losses incurred by loss-making SOEs amounted to 37bn yuan. It is noted, however, that the losses were concentrated in four industries: coal mining (21 per cent of the total), oil and gas mining (13 per cent), machinery (10 per cent) and textiles (10 per cent), which combined to account for 54 per cent of the total (Table 4.3). The two mining industries belonged to those upstream sectors whose relative prices were being depressed under the plan-track, and hence were either with very low (pre-tax) profit rate (2.1

Table 4.3 Top Ten Loss-Making Industries of SOEs and Non-SOEs, 1991

Sectors	*SOEs' % of sector GVIO*		*Sector % of SOEs' loss*		*Sector % of non-SOEs' loss*	
	1989	*1991*	*1989*	*1991*	*1989*	*1991*
Oil and gas mining	99.99	99.99	23.97	12.70	0.00	0.00
Tobacco	96.93	96.67	3.83	5.16	0.21	0.66
Electricity supply	96.17	93.76	7.35	4.44	0.70	0.64
Ferrous metals processing	86.52	86.43	0.53	2.71	1.34	3.65
Food manufacturing	81.12	78.06	4.44	5.42	3.36	4.30
Coal mining	79.36	81.00	27.77	20.46	0.51	1.38
Chemicals	79.30	73.73	3.30	4.13	3.08	4.82
Machinery	68.51	65.63	5.49	9.68	3.35	6.26
Electronics	68.05	56.66	1.34	1.96	1.37	4.74
Textiles	59.00	53.20	2.81	10.24	7.94	19.96
Building materials	51.55	50.67	2.58	3.16	9.11	8.54
Electrical equipment	50.59	45.20	0.49	1.58	2.25	6.96
Metal products	27.07	24.01	0.33	0.70	2.68	5.22
Plastic products	23.78	20.24	0.18	0.38	2.27	4.73

Sources: ZTN 1990, pp. 419–20, 441–8; ZTN 1992, pp. 411–32; ZGJTN 1992, pp. 132–41, 170–80.

Note: GVIO = gross value of industrial output; SOE % of GVIO = GVIO of SOEs ÷ total GVIO; Sector % of SOE loss = SOEs loss in the industry ÷ total SOEs loss. There are, in total, 40 industries at this level of breakdown. Because of overlapping of loss-making industries between SOEs and non-SOEs, the number of industries shown is 14, instead of 20. The 1989 figures, and figures of SOEs share of GVIO, are for comparison. Figures cover township-and-above independently accounting industrial enterprises.

per cent for oil and gas) or making losses across-the-board (–4.0 per cent for coal). The two processing industries, textiles and machinery, faced basically free market prices (except heavy machinery and agricultural machinery, whose planning-depressed prices have put heavy financial burdens on SOEs). However, in the same year, the two industries also accounted for large shares of losses incurred by non-SOEs, with textiles being 20 per cent and machinery 7 per cent. This indicates that the dismal financial performance of both SOEs and non-SOEs in the two industries was accounted for by the general economic condition, that is the market sales slump whereby the two industries were especially hard-hit, rather than enterprise efficiency.

Focusing on the performance in 1989, the sectoral concentration of losses incurred by SOEs is even more striking. For the three industries coal mining, oil and gas mining and electricity alone, the losses combined to account for 60 per cent of the total. Since 1989 was the year when the sales slump had not yet taken its full effect, the situation is more indicative of the effect of the dual-track system on the financial performance of SOEs. Thus it can be seen that, compared with COEs, SOEs face a less favourable environment in this respect.

Social Burdens on SOEs

Heavy social burdens on SOEs are yet another arrangement that eases the pressure on the state budget. It is well known that SOEs face many costly obligations of this kind, especially those connected with education, medical and child care, which have no parallel elsewhere. To illustrate the connection between these obligations and the state budget, here, we just look at one particular form: the payment by SOEs for retirees. For most SOEs were founded in the 1950s–70s, in the traditional system whereby they were not allowed to retain profits and thus no savings were kept as pension funds for the future. By the 1980s when, under reform, SOEs were asked to see to their own profits and losses, the payment for retirees which should have been the responsibility of the state fell on their shoulder.

Increasingly, this has become a drag on SOEs: the amount of payment increased from 9bn yuan in 1985 to 29bn in 1990, equivalent to 12 per cent and 74 per cent respectively of their after-tax profits in the two years. In the meantime, the ratio between retirees and on-the-job employment has been rising steadily, from 23 per cent in 1985 to 30 per cent in 1990. For many SOEs in traditional industrial centres like Shanghai and Liaoning, the ratio has even exceeded one (SC-EMO 1991; SC-PRU 1992; ZGJTN 1992, p. 26). By contrast, for the vast majority of COEs which emerged during the 1980s, they simply recruited young workers and thus have not confronted the same problem.

Taxation and Enterprise Retained Profits

Meanwhile, SOEs have faced far higher tax rates. Formally, until 1993, LMEs were levied 55 per cent of income tax. Small scale SOEs and all COEs have been levied at eight progressively increasing rates of income tax in the range of 10–55 per cent. In actual practice, there have been a range of tax exemption or reduction measures exclusively for non-SOEs (Wang et al., eds. 1991, p. 95). It is reported that, in 1987, the actual rate of sales-tax was 11.8 per cent for LMEs, 9.2 per cent for other SOEs, and 5.4 per cent for COEs. For the actual rate of income tax (out of realized profit and tax), in that year, the respective figures were 65.4 per cent, 60.7 per cent, and 30.7 per cent for the three categories of enterprises (SC-ICO 1990, p. 274).

Table 4.4 gives the data of enterprise total realized profits and retained

Table 4.4 Total Profits and Enterprise-Retained Profits, 1986–92 (100m yuan)

		1986	*1987*	*1988*	*1989*	*1990*	*1991*	*1992*	*86–92 change*
SOEs	(a)	1341	1514	1775	1773	1503	1661	1944	
	(b)	228	265	324	309	224	226	266	
	(b)/(a) (%)	17.0	17.5	18.2	17.4	14.9	13.6	13.7	−3.3
LMEs	(a)	1069	1232	1448	1488	1340	1543	1907	
	(b)	160	193	238	230	175	199	268	
	(b)/(a) (%)	15.0	15.7	16.4	15.5	13.1	12.9	14.0	−1.0
Non-SOEs	(a)	324	379	514	502	443	572	856	
	(b)	60	78	106	97	87	95	164	
	(b)/(a) (%)	18.6	20.7	20.7	19.3	19.6	16.5	19.2	+0.6

Sources: ZGJTN 1992, pp. 142–4; ZTN 1993, p. 419.

Note: (a) = total profits (or pre-tax profits) = realized taxes + profits; (b) = enterprise-retained profits. Figures cover township-and-above independently accounting industrial enterprises.

profits during 1986–92. It indicates that, since 1988, there has been a trend of decreasing enterprise-retained profits both in absolute terms and as a ratio of total realized profits. For LMEs, by 1992, the ratio was 14 per cent (compared with the 14 per cent of all SOEs and 19 per cent of non-SOEs), slightly lower than the rate of 15 per cent in 1986. This was partly attributable to the general decline in industrial profitability. But there is evidently a squeeze by the State, owing to its worsening fiscal position. Besides profit-and-tax remittance, in 1988–9, the state also instituted another two kinds of taxation (not indicated in the table): enterprise contributions to the energy and transportation construction fund and state budget adjustment fund. Moreover, there have been a number of extra-taxation levies instituted by local authorities of various levels. Thus, a survey of 206 LMEs in 1992 (which belonged to 22 industries and 26 provinces) finds that the ratio of enterprise-retained profit was just 10 per cent, four percentage points lower than that shown in Table 4.4 (JJCKB, 17 August 1993, p. 4).

In any event, a profit-retention rate that is persistently well below 20 per cent is unlikely to enable enterprises to pursue growth. It is evident that SOEs have confronted grave difficulties even in replenishing for the current scale. This is especially indicated by the vast deficiency in depreciation funds. In 1989, the depreciation fund of LMEs amounted to 34bn yuan. Deducting 25 per cent or 8.5bn yuan for contribution to the 'two funds', the actual amount was 25.5bn, meaning a depreciation rate of just 3 per cent. As the Chinese depreciation system is set in accordance with the original purchase prices of fixed assets, the real depreciation rate is also well below the nominal rate in the circumstances of inflation. It is estimated that the value of re-purchasing would be as high as 1.6 times the book value of China's industrial fixed assets. According to SC-EMO (1991), the depreciation funds actually used by SOEs by the late 1980s were equivalent to just one-sixth of what was needed to maintain the current production scale and technological capability.

The deficiency in internal finance has seriously affected the capability of enterprises in expanded reproduction, particularly in technological development. As early as 1985, the State authorities decided to allow SOEs to keep 1 per cent of sales revenues for R&D expenditure. However, in practice, the amount actually used for this purpose by all SOEs during 1984–8 was just 0.3 per cent of sales revenues. By 1989, the percentage for large scale SOEs was 0.5 per cent while that for medium SOEs was 0.4 per cent, far lower than the normal level of around 5 per cent in Western industrial corporations (SC-EMO 1991). Given this situation, it is no wonder that in the economic downturn of 1989–91, most SOEs were unable to upgrade their technology and restructure their output-mix to cope with the slump in market sales.[4]

External Financing

Because of insufficient internal finance, industrial SOEs have become heavily dependent on the bank, the only source of external financing up to recently. Bank credits have tended to dominate the capital structure of SOEs since the introduction of the lending-for-appropriation financial system reform in 1983, whereby bank lending replaced fiscal appropriation as the source of external financing. According to official surveys, bank borrowings have also been the major factor sustaining the growth of production of SOEs amid shrinking internal finance (SC-EMO 1991; SPC-EMB 1991).

Table 4.5 shows the growth of bank loans for production in relation to enterprise working capitals. Despite the state stipulation that SOEs must contribute to their working capitals at least 30 per cent initially and 70 per cent in the long term, the ratio of bank loans to working capital increased from 32 per cent in 1983 to 62 per cent in 1992. For all 'in-budget enterprises' (40 000-plus enterprise, basically covering all LMEs), by 1992, the ratio reached 89 per cent (400bn to 453bn yuan), while the ratio of outstanding fixed-asset loans to their total value of fixed assets net of depreciation reached 53 per cent (420bn to 788bn yuan). The result is a drain on enterprise profits in the form of

Table 4.5 Working Capital and Bank Loans for Production, 1983–92 (100m yuan)

	(a) RW	*(b) BP*	*(b)/(a)(%)*
1983	1663	597	32
1984	1831	884	49
1985	2265	1165	51
1986	2733	1650	60
1987	3143	2044	65
1988	3728	2086	56
1989	4802	2725	57
1990	5815	3559	61
1991	6784	4236	73
1992	7945	4956	62

Sources: Wang and Li eds. (1991), p. 101; ZGJTN 1993, p. 116; ZTN 1993, p. 664.

Notes: RW = annual average outstanding registered working capitals; BP = bank loans for production. Note that figures cover *all* township-and-above independently accounting industrial enterprises, not SOEs alone.

interest payment. This was especially serious by the late 1980s when the profit rate of SOEs decreased to a level below the 10 per cent-plus interest rate. By 1990, for all in-budget industrial enterprises, total interest payment exceeded their after-tax profits by 4.8bn yuan (ZTZ 1993, p. 82; JGT 1993, no. 17, pp. 3–7).

The study of 769 SOEs during 1981–9 by Tang (1992) further reveals that there has been a 'double squeeze' of profit-and-tax remittance and bank interest payment on SOEs' retained profits. Despite the lending-for-appropriation reform, the State has continued to ask SOEs to remit profits as returns to capital-owner. Thus, for the same investment funds, SOEs have simultaneously faced two separate claimants: the State and the bank. The result has been a serious drain on the capability of re-investment of SOEs.[5]

MAKING SENSE OF THE REFORM-GROWTH DYNAMICS

The Market-Centred Approaches

Having reviewed the available indicators of China's enterprise performance, I now turn to see what the literature has to offer in explaining the relationship between the performance and the institutional reform that took place in the meantime. Two decisive twists, which took place in around the turn of the decade, are discernible. The first is a transition from ideology-oriented writings to empirical investigations. The second is the adoption of an evolutionary perspective, focusing on the imperfect reality rather than the ideal model.

The first twist is represented by the emergence of a range of writings which, because of their adhesion to standard neoclassical economics, can be subsumed under the rubrics of a 'convergence-productivity approach'. The central character of this approach is summarized by Jefferson *et al.* (1992, p. 240): 'a successful program of economic reform should generate evidence of gradual convergence in the marginal revenue product of similar inputs across multiple uses'. There follow various explorations along this line, of which the study of TFP change has been especially influential. At one level, this approach is significant because it is an attempt to address explicitly the relationship between the systemic reform and the actual performance. It is conspicuous that, up to the late 1980s, the literature was still overwhelmed by writings that simply seek to examine the degree of conformity of the reformed institutions to the norms of the market, with the presumption that the market would guarantee the optimal economic outcome (see for example Balassa 1986; Kueh 1991; Lee 1991; Lichtenstein 1991; Perkins 1988; Putterman 1992; Wong 1986; Yennal 1990). At another level, however, the fact that the convergence-productivity writings follow strictly neoclassical theory implies that their explanatory power is limited. It is well known in the development literature that allocative efficiency does not normally play a major role in explaining growth. Moreover, in line with the construct of the production function, which treats the production process as a black box, the study of TFP change does not identify the sources of the change, and hence the writings have in fact little to say about the effects of China's economic reform.

There comes now, an analysis of the evolutionary approach, which focuses on examining the working of the conceptually deficient Chinese economic system in the achievement of the spectacular performance. This approach was first formulated by McMillan and Naughton (1992), and has culminated in the story of cumulative reform-growth dynamics by Jefferson and Rawski (1995). McMillan and Naughton (1992, p. 131) state: 'China's reform success can be seen with hindsight to have resulted from, first, massive entry of non-State firms; second, a dramatic increase in competition, both among State firms and between State firms and non-State firms; and, third, improvements in the performance of State-owned firms resulting from State-imposed market-like incentives.' In a dynamic sense, the high profitability of manufacturing, arising from the traditional unbalanced pattern of industrialization, induced entry of non-State firms. This increased competition for State firms and eroded the revenue base of the State. In response, the State sought to enhance the profit-orientation of State firms by both intensifying monitoring and providing material incentives. State firms responded by increasing efficiency. So went a growth-*cum*-market formation virtuous circle.

The crux in the evolutionary story is market formation. Two questions arise: first, is market formation a true depiction of China's experience, and, second, how does it contribute to the efficiency improvement and growth. Conceptually, the increase in market competition can be split into two aspects: price determination and enterprise behaviour. It is a consensus among students of the Chinese economy that, by the 1990s, State control over prices has become a minor mechanism in the economy (Naughton 1994; Perkins 1992). This, together with the observed trend of equalization of profit rates across industries, implies a successful price reform (Naughton 1992). With respect to reform strategy, and from the contrast with Eastern Europe where price decontrols often led to worsening inflation and disruption of commodity circulation, a related issue is how did China achieve successful price reform. The crux, according to the studies by Byrd (1991) and Wang (1993), lay in the co-action of growth and the planning-market dual-track system. The catchwords are 'growing out of the plan' and 'buyer's market price reform'. The dual-track system – which allowed SOEs to be involved in market transactions after fulfilling state-set quantitative quotas – implies that, at the margin, the inputs and outputs prices of enterprises were determined by the market. The buyer's market condition implies the pressure of competition on enterprises. In a dynamic sense, following growth, the share of the market track expanded and more and more commodities turned into the condition of buyer's market. Thus growth became the ultimate impetus of the success of price reform.

The increasing market-orientation of enterprises has involved two developments: the entry of vast number of new firms and the reform of existing ones. For township-and-above industrial enterprises, the number increased from 348 000 in 1978 to 463 000 in 1985 and further to 532 000 in 1994, an increase of 53 per cent during this 16-year period. Of this increase, the state sector accounted for around 10 per cent, while the remaining majority were collective enterprises. But the biggest increase was that of village-and-below enterprises. Taking this category into account, the total number of industrial enterprises in the country doubled from 5m in 1985 to 10m in 1994. This means 99 per cent of those newly-emerged during 1985–94 were village-and-below enterprises (ZGJTN 1992, pp. 23–4; ZTN 1995, p. 375). From the conventional wisdom of the structure-conduct-performance paradigm, the massive entry implies increased competition. The trend of equalization of profit rates mentioned above confirms the judgement from a dynamic perspective.

The re-orientation of enterprise behaviour is more complex and difficult to gauge. An early study by CESRRI (1987a) reports that, by 1985, the market environment was becoming competitive and enterprises had become profit-focused. Meanwhile, however, enterprises were strongly inclined to increasing employees' income while having insufficient incentive to control cost and to economize on external finance. Subsequent studies reveal basically the same situation. Ma's (1992) survey of 213 enterprises shows that, in addition to profitability, growth and market share have become major concerns of most enterprises. The survey also finds that, along with the increase in firm size, developmental orientations – profitability, growth and market share – tended to dominate while the importance of increasing employees' income diminished. In a separate survey of 769 SOEs, Zheng (1992) reports that enterprises generally sought to maximize profits in order to increase employees' income and to compete for Government approvals of investment projects and favourable bank loans.

Thus, it is largely a consensus among available field studies that profit-orientation has become predominant among SOEs. But behind the profit orientation there are deeper considerations, of which the pursuit of improving workers' living standards is a major one (Byrd 1992; Groves *et al.* 1994). Relatively weak financial discipline, expressed mainly in the form of *ad hoc* bargaining between enterprises and the State over the sharing of profits (and losses), has also persisted, although it is observed, especially during the recession period of 1989–91, that enterprises have become far more sensitive to the costs of external financing. Overall, restricting to the aspect of market competition, McMillan and Naughton's (1992, p. 134) summary appears to be the prevailing view: 'China's state-owned firms now face active product-market competition. This market-based discipline has given the state-owned firms additional incentives to improve their productivity'.

One can see that all the approaches described above focus on micro-level efficiency and market formation in explaining China's economic growth and assessing its institutional reform. This focus, while having its merit, can be flawed in two senses. First, by explaining economic growth in terms of micro-efficiency, it ignores the effects of the macro-level and developmental conditions. This can result in over-emphasizing the role of the market in the growth process. Second, by reducing micro-efficiency to allocative efficiency, it ignores the contribution from technological and organizational innovations. This, again, can exaggerate the role of the market, especially in the face of the now prevailing view in growth and trade theories on market failure in the generation of innovations.

The Evolution of Firm-Level Reform: A Depiction

A further problem with the market-centred writings reviewed above is that they tend to hold a 'black box' view of the firm. Indeed, even when trying to explain firm-level performance, their focus is on the market – and from a rather static, structure-conduct-performance perspective – instead of the firm. These writings thus neglect an important (arguably the most important) aspect of Chinese economic reform. Moreover, the approach which they adopt is inadequate in accounting for the two significant trends which we documented in the first section: that SOEs have outperformed COEs financially in boom years but have been outperformed in recession, and that LMEs have consistently outperformed COEs and small scale SOEs in basically all the indicators. To develop an alternative interpretation of the reform experience, we need first to depict the evolution of the reform inside the firm, especially looking at two major issues: the contractual management system and the formation of industrial concerns.

Evolution of Chinese Enterprise Reform

Essential to China's enterprise reform has been a process of re-defining the State–enterprise relationship. In official terms, the track of reform can be summarized as an evolution from the traditional administrative planning system to the profit-retention system, the tax-for-profit system and eventually, until recently, the contractual management system. The focus of these reform measures, as the terms themselves suggest, is on the division of the economic surplus or residual. However, with the proceeding of reform, it is revealed that behind this distribution aspect are more fundamental issues concerning the autonomy of, and ownership over, enterprises (the following depiction draws on Hua *et al.* 1988; Liu and Zhou eds. 1992; Lu *et al.* 1987; Wang *et al.*, eds. 1991; and Zhang 1987).

The profit-retention system was adopted in 1979. It allowed profit-making enterprises to retain part of their profits to set up three internal funds: production development, welfare of employees, and bonus. The magnitude of the retention was set, pro rata, to the profits actually realized, and the proportion was fixed for a three-year term. Essentially, this aimed at transforming enterprises from traditional cost centres to profit centres. The modification of the system in 1980 to become a two-tier package combining a fixed base of profit-retention plus a flexible extra-base proportion of profit-retention was further intended to enhance the incentive of enterprises to make profits.

The tax-for-profit system, which was instituted in two successive steps in 1983 and 1984, is an extension of the profit-retention system. Ideally, with this system, enterprises would be required to pay tax instead of profit-remittance, and would fully retain the after-tax profits. The various kinds of tax were paid according to some pre-determined, generally applicable rates, which would both ensure a level playing field for different enterprises to engage in market competition and would provide leverages for the State to manage the economy. Enterprises would be asked to see to their own profits and losses after paying tax. Nevertheless, in actual practice, the ideal was not realized. The state had to introduce an 'adjustment tax' which required enterprises to deliver part of their after-tax profits at negotiable ratios. The reason is that enterprises confronted very uneven conditions arising from some pre-determined factors like technological capabilities, fixed-assets under controls, Government-administered input and output prices, locations, etc. This made it impossible for them to be on a level playing field. The resentment against the unfairness was detrimental to the original design of the reform, which aimed at increasing enterprise incentive. The adjustment tax was thus set to even out inter-enterprise differences of state-enterprise profit sharing under the tax-for-profit system. This, however, means a retreat to the previous, case-by-case bargaining regime of the profit-retention system.

The contractual management system was adopted in 1987, against the background of falling enterprise realized profits and State budget revenue subsequent to the comprehensive economic reform which started in late 1984. In effect, the system abandoned the pursuit of a single rate of State–enterprise division of profits which would be applicable across-the-board. Its central idea is to fix the base of tax-and-profit remittance and to retain extra-base profits in enterprises. It requires enterprises to ensure a steady increase in tax-and-profit remittance (or decrease in subsidies and/or tax exemptions for loss-making enterprises) over the pre-contract remittance which is taken as the base. In addition to the requirement on increasing current profits, enterprises have to ensure the fulfilment of another two tasks: technical renovation investment and the linking of wage bill with total realized profits, the latter being set as a device both to enhance enterprise incentive and to avoid bonus expansion at the expense of State assets accumulation. There was also the requirement to keep separate accounts of State-owned funds and enterprise-owned funds. The former comprises fixed-assets and working capitals inherited from the pre-contract period, while the latter arise from enterprise-retained profits. This was to avoid the situation of enterprises being responsible only for profit-division, not for loss-sharing: accumulated enterprise-owned funds were to serve as a sort of mortgage or risk fund.

The above reform measures are all intended to provide incentives to enterprises. In addition, there has also been a process of increasing autonomy of enterprises. Initially, during 1979–83, along with the practice of the profit-retention system, enterprises were granted partial rights – after accomplishing state mandatory directives – to choose their output-mix, to sell products to the market, and to use retained funds. They were also allowed to appoint their own middle management staff, although top managers continued to be appointed by State supervisory authorities. The comprehensive reform started from 1984 further transferred to enterprises a range of decision-making powers. In addition to those covering production, marketing, internal funds utilization and staff appointment, enterprises gained some rights in pricing, inputs purchasing, assets utilization, inter-enterprise agglomeration and internal settlement of workers payment. All these were in line with the overall reform strategy: the planning-market dual-track system and the target model of 'State regulating the market, the market co-ordinating enterprises.' The institutional framework of State–enterprise relationship was thus set up, and in subsequent years the evolution process has been one whereby the State gradually relinquished its economic power along the above lines, that is, a general tendency towards the marketization of enterprise operations.

The institutionalization of the interests and autonomy of enterprises pushes to the fore the rationality of their behaviour and organization. These issues surfaced first as worsening soft-budgeted behaviour, and later as immobility of productive assets or rigidity of the capital stock in relation to the requirement of structural adjustment. Thus, along with the 'marketization', the State has attempted to stipulate the norms of enterprise behaviour and organization. The various kinds of 'economic responsibility system' that have been generally applied since the early 1980s can be seen as such a manifestation. Enterprises are required to be responsible for the fulfilment of a number of technical efficiency indicators, in addition to profit generation. At the intra-firm level, the 'internal responsibility system' takes the form of decomposing the various economic and technical efficiency indicators into sub-indicators which are then applied down to the shopfloors. Practices like 'intra-firm banking', whereby a system of monetary accounting is established to link rewards with the 'profits' and 'losses' of divisions and workshops, are of this nature. The adoption of various wage settlement methods (such as piece wage) forms another part of the system.

The outcome during 1984–8, immediately following the comprehensive economic reform, was unsatisfactory. There was a persistent tendency of investment and bonus 'double expansion', indicating an asymmetry between benefits and responsibility. It was observed that the investment hunger of enterprises was mainly motivated by the fact that the benefits generated by their actions far outweighed the risks which they had to bear. It was also observed that the bonus expansion was not linked to productivity improvement but rather being fuelled by the so-called 'wage emulation' phenomenon – that is to strive for an income level that would at least be on a par with workers elsewhere, disregarding inter-enterprise difference in financial performance. These investment and payment behaviours appear to be what many economists characterize as arising from soft budget constraint.

The Contractual Management System

The contractual management system, which was generally applied to Chinese enterprises by the late 1980s, aims at coping with the problem of soft-budgeted behaviour. The idea is to 'personify' enterprises amid their taking up of rights and duties. In conjunction with the manager responsibility system, which was first put into practice in 1984 and completed its replacement for the traditional party committee-dominated enterprise leadership system by 1988, managers are designated as the legal representatives of enterprises and are responsible for the fulfilment of the tasks set in the contracts.

Ideally, according to the original design of the contractual system, the selection of managers would normally undergo a competitive bidding process, that is, a simulation of the managerial market. On the part of the State, the new system would define its relationship with enterprises in clear contractual terms, thus reducing its *ad hoc* interference in the operations of the latter. The task of concluding contracts with enterprises would normally involve not only industrial bureaux (the supervisory authorities), but also other local government offices, for example those responsible for planning, finance, auditing and the bank. As for workers, because of their low mobility, the conditions set in the contracts are a matter of paramount concern. In practice, all these have resulted in the establishment of contract-issuing committees that are composed of Government offices and the bank, workers of the enterprises concerned, and experts recruited from the public. Their functions are similar to that of the board of directors of the firm in market economies: recruitment of managers, and examining and approving enterprise mid-term development plans and financial plans.

The actual outcome of the application of the contractual management system is a subject of heated debate. This is particularly complicated by the fact that the period within which the first round of contracts took effect, 1988–90, basically coincided with the cyclical downturn of the development of the economy, the period of 'rectification and readjustment'. It is thus difficult to make definitive judgements on the effect of the system, and on the very diverse practices adopted in the process of concluding the second round of contracts in 1990–1. In many cases, there has been a tendency to re-introduce some economic and technical efficiency indicators into the new contracts, a practice that is likely to increase Government interference in enterprise operations. Also, for around 80 per cent of the enterprises, the incumbent managers or management teams were retained in the second round of contracts. This, in effect, implies abandoning the practice of competitive bidding. These practices were both aimed at stabilizing the performance of enterprises, especially the managers who were generally unwilling to enter into the second round of contracts amid the economic downturn. They give rise to the argument that the contractual management system is effective only in boom periods, while being unable to cope with severe fluctuations in the market which, however, can be the norm of economic development (Du 1992). Overall, in view of the actual performance in the period 1988–91, what is generally agreed is that the system was effective in increasing State budget revenue and workers income, but not favourable for accumulation – the task of technical renovation and upgrading investment being a soft constraint.

The contractual management system has often been characterized as strengthening managerial interests while shunning the transformation of ownership. From the depiction above, it seems more appropriate to characterize the system as clarifying the boundary of the interests of enterprises while leaving out the clarification of the property rights of individuals. It thus enables the adoption of a range of measures to restructure intra- and inter-firm organizations. For the State–enterprise relationship, by specifying rights and duties over the contractual period, the system stabilizes the expectations of enterprises and hence enables them to formulate and implement their development plans. The priority of the profitability objective fosters the adoption of the internal responsibility system. In particular, it enables enterprises to choose middle management staff according to capability rather than seniority. It also motivates the tightening of work discipline. Finally, the system has given rise to the practice whereby an enterprise enters into a contract with the State to manage another enterprise, thus fostering the mobility of productive assets. Being concerned mainly with profitability, local authorities are willing to grant autonomy to enterprises and to accept their management being contracted out to entities of other affiliations, especially big industrial concerns which are capable of sharing losses in case of business failures. In practice, this paved the way for the wave of agglomerations and mergers in 1990–2.

The Formation of Industrial Concerns

The construction of industrial concerns, or business groups, is significant in two senses. First, it is intended to break the rigidity of the industrial system which, underpinned by the immobility of productive assets, has hindered the realization of economies of scale. The formation of the concerns is not simply grouping together a number of enterprises. It rather involves the experiments of shareholding system and delegation of the power of state assets management to core enterprises of the concerns. Some concerns are granted with the autonomy of doing foreign trade, issuing shares to the public, and making their own decisions on various aspects including investment. They are also designated to experiment various forms of firm organization, especially the multidivisional (M-form) model where the firm is structured in a three-tier system composed of a strategic investment centre, profit centres and cost centres. In a developmental sense, it is noted that most of the core members of the concerns are in fact those which represent, technologically, the most advanced sector of Chinese industry. The construction of industrial concerns, given top priority in the enterprise reforms in the 1990s, is clearly an attempt to enhance the international competitiveness of Chinese industry.

In terms of actual evolution, the process of the formation of industrial concerns formally started in 1987. By 1988, there were in total 1630 self-styled industrial concerns. But of these only around 280 were truly worthy of the name, that is member enterprises being bound together by property ties, the remainder being either renamed local industrial bureaux (or their sub-ordinates) or groups of enterprises bound together for co-operation in production and marketing. By 1990, the number of industrial concerns reached 2000-plus, of which around 430 were considered to be real. The vast majority were (and are) characterized by member enterprises being normally within the same ministerial or local-governmental affiliations, the same channels of tax-and-profit remittance, and the same ownership systems – so-called 'three unchanges'. Even the wave of agglomerations, mergers and take-overs in 1990–2 took place mainly within these boundaries. This underscores the complex role of local authorities in China's industrial system. To the extent that the agglomeration-and-related activities were conducive for economic development, yet would not have taken place by the initiatives of enterprises, the role can be regarded as entrepreneurial. But the segmentation of the industrial system seriously hinders the formation of industrial concerns, and with it the movement and re-grouping of productive assets, in broader scopes.

The formation of nationwide industrial concerns, initiated by the central Government, can be seen as an attempt to break the rigidity arising from the segmentation. The major measure adopted is the so-called 'separated planning', which in effect means empowering the concerns to be independent of any particular localities or ministries. In 1989, the State admitted 15 industrial concerns into the category. The number increased to 55 in 1991, and was set to reach 100 in 1995. Core members of the concerns are the country's financially most powerful and technologically most advanced enterprises. The concerns are granted the autonomous powers to adopt the various forms of firm organization mentioned above. Core members are required to centralize decision-making which covers major aspects of the activity of the concerns: formulation of mid-term and annual development plans, concluding contracts with the State, dealing with the bank in borrowing for capital construction and technical renovation investment, imports and exports, the accumulation and transaction of State assets, and the appointment of the leaders of main member enterprises.

To achieve the target of constructing nationwide industrial concerns, particularly the adoption of centralized decision-making, core members have been empowered to deal with enterprises of other affiliations in various ways. In addition to shareholding, leasing, and contracted management, some of them are entrusted to manage State-owned assets of main member enterprises of the concerns. There have also been cases where core members borrow from the bank, which they are in a good position to do because of their credit-worthiness and privileged status, and then invest in other member enterprises to become share-owners. On the whole, most of these measures are an extended application of what have been regarded as successful experiences of business groups like Dongfeng Auto (of which the Second Auto Works is the core member), Jiefang Auto (the core member being the First Auto Works) and Shoudu Iron and Steel Corp. in the course of their development during the 1980s.

TOWARDS AN ALTERNATIVE INTERPRETATION

Having constructed a picture of China's enterprise performance under reform that contradicts significantly the prevailing perceptions which focus on marketization and privatization, in this section, I attempt an alternative interpretation of the reform experience. Given the fact that the performance depicted in section one has hardly been recognized in the literature, and hence there is so far little explanation about it, my interpretation is unavoidably tentative and schematic. Nevertheless, it is hoped that the interpretation will be both consistent with the observed evidence and based on well-developed theoretical grounds.[6]

Let me summarize the major enigmatic features of the observed performance. These include: first, that Chinese LMEs have done well; second, that there has been an extreme unevenness of performance within state industry, with small scale SOEs doing badly; and, third, in terms of financial performance, the SOEs sector as a whole did better than COEs in boom period, but was outperformed under recession. How are these features related to the institutional arrangements of the respective enterprise sectors?

Below, I pick up several characterizations of Chinese enterprises, which are well documented in the literature, and I anticipate no major arguments about their validity. These include:

(a) compared with COEs, the institutional arrangements of SOEs (large scale SOEs in particular) are less conformed to market regulation

(b) as a result, the contrast between COEs and SOEs (again, LMEs in particular) can be characterized as flexibility versus rigidity in responding to the market
(c) specifically, the lower degree of responsiveness to the market of SOEs is underpinned by arrangements like soft budget constraint, government intervention, and labour immobility (Hay *et al.* 1994, is by far the most definitive study on the subject; see also Byrd 1992).

On the whole, we may say that characteristic of China's reformed enterprise system is a nexus of control infused with the active participation of, and the mutual check and balance among, local authorities, related business entities, the bank, and the workers. This seems to be especially true under the contractual management system, adopted since 1987, where all these participants are in one way or another involved in the process of contract negotiation (for details see the previous section).

To the extent that the depicted enterprise performance is indeed related to the characterized institutional arrangements, two analytical questions can then be asked: first, how does the reformed Chinese enterprise system distinguish itself from the traditional Soviet-type enterprise, and, second, what conducive effect can be generated by this system on enterprise competitiveness, amid the loss of allocative efficiency that is (theoretically) likely to be caused by the rigid arrangements?

To answer the first question, we focus on soft budget constraint, which has long been considered as the fatal weakness of Soviet-type enterprises. Conceptually, based on China's experience, Hua *et al.* (1986) argue that an essential condition for constraining soft-budgeted behaviour is the clarification of the boundary of interests of enterprises. Zhang (1987) further makes the point that, so long as the soft external financing does not blur the enterprise's cost-revenue structure, it would not leave much room for soft-budgeted behaviour. As is well recognized in the literature, the hardening of Chinese enterprises' budget constraint is achieved mainly through the increase in market competition. This, coupled with the granting of autonomy and incentive especially under the contractual management system, tends to institutionalize the distinctive interests of enterprises. In the respect of external financing, the lending-for-appropriation financial reform after 1983 also appears to have brought about the effect of hardening the budget constraint. By replacing bank lending for State allocation, it reduces the shortcoming of the previous system which blurred the cost-revenue structure of enterprises. By requiring payment for the cost of external financing, the reform also forces enterprises to economize on its uses (Wang *et al.*, eds. 1991).[7]

Similarly, regarding Government intervention, the contractual management system is also likely to have reduced its negative effects. The system implies the institutionalization of a bargaining regime, whereby local authorities are involved in enterprise decision-making, while abandoning the pursuit of an arm's-length State–enterprise relationship. Nevertheless, there is a crucial difference between the new bargaining regime and the old: namely, that the bargaining centres largely around financial performance, rather than inputs allocation and outputs delivery which are characteristic of the traditional physical planning system. This change, as discussed, curtails the room for soft-budgeted behaviour on the part of enterprises. It also implies that Government intervention is more formal, or less *ad hoc*, because it is largely carried out through the unified contract-issuing committees rather than the industrial bureaux and other offices which are not mutually coordinated. The formation of industrial concerns since the late 1980s has also seemed capable of restructuring the State–enterprise relationship in a way that reduces crucial deficiencies of Government intervention. This is related to its dealing with the immobility of productive assets across localities or ministerial affiliations. Especially in fast growing industries like automobile, electronics and steel, there are cases whereby nationwide industrial concerns take over the control of enterprises from the concerned local authorities. The latter thus become shareholders, and their intervention in enterprise operations becomes less *ad hoc*.

Finally, with respect to labour employment, it is well known that the Chinese system is characterized by both low labour mobility and rigid wage adjustment. It is also well known that the reform has fallen far short of official targets. Measures like dismissal and widening wage differentials among workers have seldom been practised, whereas workers through a collective bargaining regime can considerably influence the distribution of enterprise surplus. All these are problematic, especially from a neoclassical point of view. Nevertheless, compared with previously, it is still likely that some improvement has been made in reducing the downside effects of the system. One reform measure is the so-called 'unemployment inside the enterprise' which promotes competition among workers for formal jobs, with those outcompeted becoming 'unemployed' but continuing to stay in the enterprise. These workers thus receive only basic wage, rather than wage plus bonus, and have to face the embarrassing status of working at informal jobs (Liu, 1993). Thus, by strengthening the link between reward and performance, the reform is likely to have enhanced work incentives. The strengthening of the link between the income of the inside members as a group and that of the enterprise under broader reforms is also likely to have brought about peer group pressure on individual workers for good performance.

Turning to the second question, the conducive side of the reformed enterprise system, it is noted that the nexus of control in corporate governance appears to be in line with the concept of networks in recent theories of late industrialization. In his analysis of the Japanese firm, Aoki (1990) argues that an institutional arrangement where firms are accountable to major 'stake-holders' – including both the external financing entities and the employees – rather than shareholders alone, can be more conducive for productive efficiency. This is because of the prominence of collective learning, or continuous and incremental technical change, in productivity growth. In this connection, the long-term commitment of major participants of the production system is crucial. Thus, the rigidities characteristic of China's reformed enterprises, particularly in terms of low labour mobility and close Government–enterprise ties, though detrimental to allocative efficiency, might have been conducive for productive efficiency. This is just like the (stylized) Japanese firm, where the long-term commitment of the inside members are underpinned by a range of rigid arrangements that cushion them from the full rigour of the managerial and labour markets as well as the market for corporate control (Odagiri, 1992).

But precisely because rigidities can have both conducive and detrimental effects on enterprise efficiency, we need to investigate under what circumstances the outcome of the enterprise system, on balance, will be positive. Aoki (1990, p. 9) goes on to suggest that '[in the situation] where external environments are continually changing but not too drastically, the J-mode is superior. In this case, the information value created by learning and horizontal coordination at the operational level may more than compensate for the loss of efficiency due to the sacrifice of operational specialization'. In other words, the net outcome depends on the pattern of economic growth. This view is in line with the discussion on the techno-economic paradigm that is now at the focus of various dissident strands of economics: structuralism, neo-Schumpeterian theory, flexible specialization, the French regulation school and so on (see Chapter 2). A common theme of these strands is on the connection between the nature of technical change and demand-side conditions, the latter being, in turn, regulated by social institutions. Succinctly, an appropriate match between the two sides (for example mass production and mass consumption) can greatly promote productivity growth, whereas a mismatch would often result in crisis.

Late developing countries are more prone to mismatch because of their position as technology followers and because of possible consumption demonstration effects from developed countries.[8]

In the light of the above discussion, and in the context of late developing countries where enterprises face continually shifting demands towards new products, which in turn implies good rewards for early entrants, successful adoption and improvement upon imported technology can be crucial for the competitiveness of enterprises. This is even more so if the environment is coupled with rapidly expanding market demand, which promotes productivity growth through dynamic economies of scale. In this regard, there is ample evidence which suggests that China's economic growth pattern over the past 16 years has been, basically, of this kind. Specifically, the crucial role of technology imports and changing market demand is associated with the explosive expansion of the 'new (consumption durables) industries', the impact of which has been felt by virtually the entire Chinese population. And these industries are in general characterized by high income, elasticity of demand and rapid technical change (see Chapter 3). Thus, the capabilities of collective learning of LMEs, underpinned by their relatively more rigid institutional arrangements, are likely to have been an important source of their competitiveness.[9]

The discussion thus finally leads us to a coherent explanation of the three depicted features of Chinese enterprise performance. The crux is that rigidity (or flexibility) has both its merit and defect with respect to enterprise performance, and the outcome on balance depends on the wider context of the pattern of economic growth. As is indicated above, in the boom period of 1985–8, SOEs basically outperformed COEs in financial terms. In the recession period of 1989–91, however, SOEs were outperformed. According to Zheng (1993), during this second period, while as many as one-third of TVEs stopped operations or even went bankrupt, the same phenomenon was rare on the part of SOEs. This explains the dismal financial performance of SOEs, mainly for two reasons. First, without the exit option, SOEs have to keep on running even in times of recession when market demand for their products is weak. Second, because of the rigidity of wage adjustment, the unit cost of production goes up amid contraction of the production scale.

On the whole, the experiences seem to confirm our proposition that rigid institutional arrangements of the kinds depicted above are bad for enterprises in responding to severe market fluctuations, but good for improving productivity in the context of stable market demand.

The comparison of financial performance between the SOEs sector as a whole and COEs can be explained in this way. And the fact that small scale SOEs have been persistently outperformed by both LMEs and COEs suggests that, in their case, the gain from rigidity is not sufficient to compensate for the loss from lacking flexibility.

5 Testing Alternative Explanations of Growth

This chapter attempts a relatively more formal treatment of a number of propositions which have been put forth in the previous two chapters. It consists of a range of simple regression analyses. Section 1 briefly summarizes the propositions to be tested. Section 2 covers the estimation of total factor productivity, focusing on the relative performance of different enterprise sectors. Section 3 tests alternative theories of firm-level productivity growth. Section 4 tests the thesis of structural change as engine of growth, which is crucial for the integration of firm-level performance with the overall pattern of economic growth. A data appendix is provided to examine a number of measurement issues, to which the estimation results are sensitive.

MAIN PROPOSITIONS

In Chapter 3, focusing on the pattern of Chinese industrialization during the period of 1978–94, I raise two propositions:

(a) that the spectacular pace of economic growth was largely underpinned by two factors, namely, the rapid expansion of domestic consumption demand and the massive imports of foreign technology. The growth pattern was thus dominated by a structural change associated with the expansion of 'new' consumer durables industries which, characterized by strong increasing returns to scale, were capable of promoting productivity and output growth in Chinese industry as a whole.

(b) that this growth pattern, however, has been constrained by the foreign exchange gap and, later, by the slowdown of the growth of domestic consumption demand. These two constraints imply that it is necessary for Chinese industry – especially its dynamic sectors – to improve its international competitiveness, and this has indeed taken place under the regulation of a mix of market and non-market institutions.

In Chapter 4, where the focus is on China's enterprise reform, I propose that:

(c) Chinese industrial enterprises, regardless of the institutional setting of ownership and market orientation, have in the main improved their measured input-output efficiency. This was largely due to the favourable growth pattern mentioned in (a). The improvement has taken place despite the general trend of falling profit rate, the sources of the latter resting more on the macroeconomic condition than on enterprise efficiency

(d) a major source of the improvement of enterprise productivity has been collective learning by participants of the industrial system. This has been especially true for large-scale SOEs, whose rigid institutional arrangements, despite being criticized for not conforming to market regulation, have been conducive to collective learning. Indeed, this appears to be the most crucial factor which has accounted for their outstanding performance, comparable to the widely-acclaimed TVEs.

These propositions are contentious. Above all, they run counter to the explanation of China's experience by economists who not only adopt a market-centred approach but also a fundamentalist version of that approach. The essentials of this literature, in relation to the 'big-bang-versus-gradualism' debate over the transformation of the Soviet-type economic system, are summarized by Sachs and Woo (1994, p. 101): 'Differing performance primarily reflects different economic structures prior to reform: China was a peasant agricultural society, Eastern Europe and the Former Soviet Union (EEFSU) was urban and overindustrialized . . . China's state enterprises have not performed as well as the rest of the Chinese economy and do not explain its success; rapid growth was possible because the large agricultural sector contained vast surplus labour, and did not enjoy subsidies and soft budget constraints.'

The view that China's economic growth has been solely accounted for by transfer of surplus labour from the rural sector is not based on serious study. The assertions thereby that SOEs have been dragging on the economy, and that enterprise efficiency in general has not had substantial improvement (presumably because even TVEs are not private), are at best controversial. The series of joint studies by the China Academy of Social Sciences and several US–UK institutions, following the studies by the World Bank, have consistently found that Chinese enterprises have substantially improved their measured input-output efficiency over the past 16 years (see, for example, Groves *et al.* 1994; Jefferson *et al.* 1992; Jefferson and Rawski 1994). The real issues, therefore, are rather the sources of the efficiency improvement and the relative performance of SOEs *vis-à-vis* TVEs. Recent studies on the convergence of returns to enterprise/industry (profitability, marginal revenue factor products, and so on) represent initial attempts to formally analyze the issues from a market-oriented but evolutionary perspective (Naughton 1992; Jefferson and Xu 1994).

The propositions I list above clearly do not fit into the market-oriented approaches. Rather than focusing on micro-level efficiency alone, I posit that enterprise performance is to a significant extent determined by the macro and developmental conditions. The emphasis on increasing returns further puts the efficacy of market regulation in question. On the whole, my study entails a competing, production-oriented approach. I therefore follow an alternative research strategy, with an emphasis on examining the interaction between firm organization and the general pattern of economic growth.

TFP CHANGE: THE RELATIVE PERFORMANCE

As mentioned in Chapter 4, the recent debate over the estimation of TFP change in Chinese industry rests on two issues: namely, the construction of appropriate input deflators and the appropriate adjustment of data. My intention here is not to dwell on the issues, which affect the estimation results mainly in their absolute measurements, but rather to look at the relative performance of different enterprise sectors. Thus, in the analysis below, I adopt a 'minimalist' approach by conceding to the position of 'big bang' writers in keeping minimum adjustment of data that might produce results favouring SOEs. I also try to shun the deflators issue as far as possible. Finally, I do not dispute the unqualified application of production function analysis on Chinese industry, but the attempt to draw on alternative theories in subsequent sections indicates reservations over it.

Following the standard procedure of imposing certain restrictions on the general translog production function for value added Q, in terms of capital K and labour L (see Chen *et al.* 1988; Jefferson *et al.* 1992; Woo *et al.* 1994), one has the Cobb-Douglas production function for estimation:

$$\ln Q = \alpha_0 + \alpha_T T + \alpha_L \ln L + \alpha_K \ln K + u \qquad (1)$$

Table 5.1 Estimating TFP Growth (Original Data), 1978–94

(1) $\ln Q = \alpha_0+\alpha_T T+\alpha_L \ln L + \alpha_K \ln K + u$

	α_0	α_T	α_L	α_K	$\bar{R}^2$	N	DW
AEs	1.593	−0.020	−0.562	1.335	0.971	17	1.250
		(−0.234)	(−0.842)	(2.137)*			
SOEs	6.550	0.050	−0.133	0.1911	0.974	17	1.044
		(1.292)	(−0.367)	(0.526)			
COEs	9.284	0.107	−0.984	0.616	0.962	17	1.246
		(0.714)	(−0.969)	(0.473)			
LMEs	3.049	0.010	−0.672	1.141	0.950	17	1.351
		(0.181)	(−0.986)	(1.899)*			

(2) $\ln(Q/L) = \alpha_0 + \alpha_T T + \alpha_K \ln(K/L) + (\alpha_L + \alpha_K - 1)\ln L + v$

	α_0	α_T	α_K	$(\alpha_L + \alpha_K - 1)$	$\bar{R}^2$	N	DW
AEs	1.593	−0.020	1.335	−0.228	0.930	17	1.250
		(−0.234)	(2.137)*	(−0.199)			
SOEs	6.550	0.050	0.191	−0.941	0.935	17	1.044
		(1.292)	(0.526)	(−1.632)^			
COEs	9.284	0.107	0.616	−1.368	0.922	17	1.246
		(0.714)	(0.473)	(−2.423)*			
LMEs	3.049	0.010	1.141	−0.532	0.950	17	1.351
		(0.181)	(1.899)*	(−0.846)			

Note: Figures in parentheses are t-ratios; * and ^ are significant at 5% and 10% confidence interval, respectively. Q = net output.

where T is time trend, and α_T gives the TFP growth rate. Alternatively, to explicitly check constant returns to scale (ie $\alpha_L + \alpha_K = 1$), we can test the following intensive-form production function:

$$\ln(Q/L) = \alpha_0 + \alpha_T T + \alpha_K \ln(K/L) + (\alpha_L + \alpha_K - 1)\ln L + v \quad (2)$$

Applying the equations on the 1978–94 original data of all township-and-above independently accounting industrial enterprises (AEs), state-owned enterprises (SOEs), collectively-owned enterprises (COEs) and large and medium scale enterprises (LMEs), we obtain the results presented in Table 5.1.

These results are impressive in the sense that for all the four 'enterprise sectors' the estimated value of TFP growth rates cannot be viewed as significantly different from zero. But the results are unsatisfactory even from a purely econometric point of view. For, with the exception of α_K for AEs and LMEs, all the coefficients of $\ln L$ and $\ln K$ for all the enterprise sectors are not significantly different from zero – meaning that the growth of both inputs does not contribute to the growth of output. Conversely, as can be seen from the regression result of equation (2), in the cases of SOEs and COEs the value of $(\alpha_L + \alpha_K - 1)$

Table 5.2 Estimating TFP Growth (Adjusted Data), 1978–94

(1a) $\ln Q = \alpha_0 + \alpha_T T + \alpha_L \ln L' + \alpha_K \ln K' + u'$

	α_0	α_T	α_L	α_K	$\bar{R}^2$	N	DW
AEs	4.452	0.014	−0.672	1.083	0.960	16	1.239
		(0.130)	(−0.848)	(1.319)			
SOEs	8.464	0.073	−0.153	−0.043	0.969	16	1.071
		(1.529)^	(−0.369)	(−0.957)			
COEs	8.856	0.358	0.601	−1.576	0.961	16	1.542
		(2.046)*	(0.501)	(−1.025)			
LMEs	8.506	0.035	−1.631	1.365	0.954	16	1.437
		(0.589)	(−1.843)*	(1.920)*			

(2a) $\ln(Q/L') = \alpha_0 + \alpha_T T + \alpha_K \ln(K'/L') + (\alpha_L + \alpha_K - 1)\ln L' + v'$

	α_0	α_T	α_K	$(\alpha_L - \alpha_K - 1)$	$\bar{R}^2$	N	DW
AEs	4.452	0.014	1.083	−0.589	0.907	16	1.239
		(0.130)	(1.319)	(−0.415)			
SOEs	8.464	0.073	−0.043	−1.195	0.921	16	1.071
		(1.529)^	(−0.957)	(−1.710)^			
COEs	8.856	0.358	−1.576	−1.975	0.920	16	1.542
		(2.046)*	(−1.025)	(−3.122)*			
LMEs	8.506	0.035	1.365	−1.266	0.871	16	1.431
		(0.589)	(1.920)*	(−1.822)*			

Note: Figures in parentheses are t-ratios; * and ^ are significant at 5% and 10% confidence interval, respectively. Q = net output.

is both strongly negative and statistically significant – meaning strong decreasing returns to scale which result in the insignificant contribution of input to output growth. These results seem to be unlikely.

Two potential sources are conceivable for causing the strange results of Table 5.1: first, that there might be problems with the specification of the equations, and, second, that the original data might not be consistent with the specification. We focus on the second issue. Following Chen *et al.* (1988), we can use the mid-year figures of the labour and capital stock, that is, L' and K', which are calculated as arithmetic averages of consecutive year-end totals. Note that this adjustment is technical in nature, and is not a matter of dispute – the dispute is on whether 'non-productive' labour and capital should be excluded from the original labour and capital data. Thus the equations to be estimated become:

$$\ln Q = \alpha_0 + \alpha_T T + \alpha_L \ln L' + \alpha_K \ln K' + u' \quad \text{(1a)}$$

$$\ln(Q/L') = \alpha_0 + \alpha_T T + \alpha_K \ln(K'/L') + (\alpha_L + \alpha_K - 1)\ln L' + v' \quad \text{(2a)}$$

Table 5.2. gives the estimation results. These seem to make a little bit more sense as there are more coefficients taking a value that is significantly different from zero. But they in fact make no significant improvement over the previous ones. Now, we have the TFP growth rate of 36 per cent for COEs and 7 per cent for SOEs, both being statistically significant. But these are unlikely to be accepted by even the most optimistic observers of industrial development in China. Again, the result that all the enterprise sectors except AEs exhibit strong decreasing returns to scale, with the value of ($\alpha_L + \alpha_K - 1$) ranging from −2.0 to −1.2, is dubious. The negative contribution of labour input to output growth in all the cases except COEs is also dubious, and the negative contribution of capital input to output growth in SOEs and COEs is even harder to believe.

A further possible factor that causes these unbelievable results in Tables 5.1 and 5.2 is the deflators. It is likely that the output figures have been over-deflated, meaning that the gross-output deflator which we use here consistently exceeds the true deflator for net output. It is also likely that the capital figures have been under-deflated, as is indicated by the fact that the official price indices for fixed-asset investment during the 1990s (China's statistical authorities have never published the same indices for the 1980s) have tended to exceed our constructed ones. Given this and other problems mentioned above, it is difficult to go further in the estimation of TFP change in Chinese industry without involving the controversial issues of deflators and data adjustment.[1]

Alternatively, since our concern is on the relative (instead of absolute) performance of enterprise sectors, we can adopt an 'arbitrary' approach of simply assuming that the values of output responsiveness to labour and capital would lie within a certain reasonable range. Column (a) of Table 5.3 gives the result calculated from the equation $a = q - 0.5l - 0.5k$, where q, l and k are average annual growth rates of net output, employment and value of fixed capital (both mid-year figures), respectively, and a the TFP growth rate. It can be seen that, if we exclude the exceptional years (where the data of COEs are dubious) of 1993–4, the TFP growth rates of COEs exceed those of LMEs at most by 1.2 percentage points – hardly impressive.

It is, nevertheless, possible that the different sectors might have different values of output responsiveness to inputs. Column (b) of the table gives the result for COEs from the equation $a = q - 0.6l - 0.4k$, and column (c) from $a = q - 0.7l - 0.3k$. Now, for 1978–92, the TFP growth rate of COEs exceeds LMEs by 2.2 percentage points in (b) and 3.2 percentage points in (c). The differences are now more significant, but still far distant from the result of SOEs–COEs comparison

Table 5.3 TFP Growth (An 'Arbitrary' Approach), 1978–94 (percentages)

	1980–8			1978–92			1978–94		
	(a) ß=0.5	(b) ß=0.6	(c) ß=0.7	(a) ß=0.5	(b) ß=0.6	(c) ß=0.7	(a) ß=0.5	(b) ß=0.6	(c) ß=0.7
AEs	1.44			2.32			3.69		
SOEs	0.68			0.34			0.89		
COEs	3.23	4.27	5.32	3.50	4.52	5.55	5.57	6.61	7.65
LMEs	2.50			2.34			2.68		

Sources: Calculated from data appendix.

Note: Figures are calculated from the equation $a = q - ßl - (1-ß)k$, where q, l and k are average annual growth rate of NVIO, employment and value of capital (both mid-year figures), respectively, and a the TFP growth rate.

obtained by big bang advocates (8–10 percentage points in Woo *et al.* 1994). But the result in (a) is much more likely than those in (b) and (c). As explained in Chapter 4, there are strong reasons to believe that the contribution of labour (relative to capital) to output in SOEs is likely to be higher than that in COEs, rather than the other way round. Hence, the difference in TFP growth rate between COEs and LMEs should be smaller than 1.2 percentage points, rather than greater.

Overall, from both the formal estimation above and from our 'arbitrary' approach, there is no clear-cut result to support the judgement that the TFP growth rate of COEs is significantly higher than that of LMEs. In the case of the 'arbitrary' approach, if we take into account the possibilities that the output of COEs has tended to be under-deflated, and that its output responsiveness to labour is lower than other enterprise sectors, the TFP growth rate of LMEs is likely to be at least on a par with COEs.

LEARNING EFFECTS AND DEMAND-DRIVEN GROWTH

The applicability of production function analysis in Chinese industry is a matter of concern, not least because of its restrictive assumptions on the sources of growth. It is supply-oriented, in the sense that it treats factor inputs as exogenously given and independently determining output growth – instead of being 'pulled' into the production process in response to demand. Its assumption of equal returns to equal inputs is also based on a static view of competition, which might not be realistic. But the fact that it is essentially a 'black box' approach, and hence not capable of identifying the sources of growth, makes it difficult to check the validity of its assumptions on growth and competition. Finally, the 'black box' approach is also unsatisfactory because the identification of the sources of growth, especially efficiency improvement, is of paramount importance in interpreting China's enterprise reform.

Conceptually, measured input–output performance of enterprises can be of multiple sources, ranging from allocative efficiency, learning effects of participants of the production system, to technological and organizational innovations. Standard neoclassical theory focuses on allocative efficiency. The endogenous growth literature incorporates increasing returns into analysis, but still focusing on market competition. In contrast, structuralist development economics emphasizes the effect of macro-level conditions on micro-level efficiency (e.g. the effect of income distribution on firms' capacity utilization), while the late industrialization literature extends its field of investigation to the internal organization of the firms as well as the role of market-governing, Schumpeterian entrepreneurship.

In this and the next section, I adopt an approach that is in the spirit of the latter two theoretical traditions for analyzing the sources of growth in Chinese industry. This, namely, is the interpretation by Nicholas Kaldor of what he calls Verdoorn's law (Kaldor 1966; McCombie and Thirlwall 1994; Wulwick 1993). The central idea of this 'law' is simple: that there is often a two-way causal relationship between output growth and productivity change. This is expressed in the form of either one of the following two equations:

$$p = \alpha + \beta q + u \tag{3}$$

$$l = \alpha^* + \beta^* q + u' \tag{4}$$

where p, q, and l are exponential growth rates of labour productivity, output and employment, α and α^* are constant terms, β and β^* are coefficients, and u and u' are disturbance terms. Equation (3) is Kaldor's original formulation. But because definitionally $p = q - l$, q appears on both sides of the equation and hence some degree of spurious correlation might be present. Re-specifying the equation yields (4), where $\alpha^* = -\alpha$ and $\beta^* = 1 - \beta$. This can act as a check of whether spurious correlation is present in (3). If β^* is statistically significantly different from unity, or equivalently β differs from zero, it indicates that change in labour productivity depends on output growth.

Table 5.4 Testing Verdoorn's Law in Chinese Industry, 1979–94

(3) $p = \alpha + \beta q + u$	α	β	$\bar{R}^2$	N	DW
AEs	4.088	0.994 (7.986)*	0.807	16	1.591
SOEs	0.382	0.639 (5.375)*	0.666	15	2.130
COEs	0.278	0.836 (5.882)*	0.706	15	2.310
LMEs	−5.796	1.105 (3.279)*	0.394	16	2.075
(4) $l = \alpha^* + \beta^* q + u'$	α^*	β^*	$\bar{R}^2$	N	DW
AEs	4.236	−0.025 (10.425)*	−0.068	16	1.598
SOEs	−0.359	0.324 (5.902)*	0.334	15	2.094
COEs	−0.300	0.105 (6.400)*	−0.032	15	2.469
LMEs	6.252	−0.143 (3.818)*	−0.054	16	2.124

Note: Figures in parentheses are t-ratios; * and ^ are significant at 5% and 10% confidence interval, respectively. Q = gross output. Note that equation (4) tests against the null hypothesis Ho: $\beta^* = 1$. In the case of SOEs, instead of using the original variables which give poor results of DW-test, 0.830 for both (3) and (4), we use the first differences of the variables. The same applies to COEs, where the DW-statistics in using the original variables are 1.050 for (3) and 1.118 for (4).

Table 5.4 gives the regression result of applying both (3) and (4) on Chinese data (now we use gross output instead of net output). The coefficient β is significantly different from zero across-the-board (and β^* different from unity), and its value ranges from 0.6 to 1.1. But how can one interpret this result?

Kaldor interprets Verdoorn's law as indicating a dynamic process where expansion in the size of the market, reflected by output growth, increases the scope for specialized division of labour and generates learning effects and technical progress. This implies the existence of increasing returns. From a neoclassical perspective, Jefferson (1988) raises four points of criticism of Verdoorn's law:

(a) it omits capital and other factors which can be substituted for labour
(b) it ignores short-run productivity dynamics, including costs of adjustment and the tendency of firms to hoard labour over the business cycle

(c) it fails to distinguish whether labour productivity growth originates from classical scale economies within the firm or through channels external to the firm, such as economies of agglomeration
(d) the usual reliance on the least-squares estimator ignores the potential for simultaneity bias within the Verdoorn's equation.[2]

Point (b) need not bother us because what Verdoorn's law represents is a long-term relationship. Points (c) and (d) concern the fact that Verdoorn's equation is a reduced form. Exponents of Kaldor have attempted to remedy these shortcomings by specifying the 'demand regime' and 'productivity regime' which underpin the structural relationship between output growth and productivity change (Boyer and Petit 1991). Even in its reduced form, Verdoorn's law still might not be invalidated, if it is interpreted in a 'minimalist' way: that is it just indicates a two-way causation between output growth and productivity change over the long term. What seems the most serious criticism, therefore, is point (a), which is precisely what marks the difference between Verdoorn's law and the neoclassical production function. This, inevitably, is because of Kaldor's specific observations of the reality, that is that capital–labour ratio remains basically unchanged is one of his 'stylized facts'. Yet it is also this formulation which has especially invited criticism from neoclassical writers. For comparison, one can apply the following equation on the data of Chinese industry:

$$p = a + b\,(k - l) + v \tag{5}$$

where p, l, and v are defined as previously, k is the exponential growth rate of capital and hence $(k - l)$ the change in capital–labour ratio, a is a constant term and b a coefficient. Table 5.5 gives the regression result of equation (5). The result is significant for all but SOEs.

In a sense, equation (5) can be interpreted as a re-specified version of the Cobb-Douglas production function. This can be seen by comparing it with the intensive-form production function of equation (2) above. Substituting the identity $p = q - l$ into the equation yields $q = a + b\,k + (1 - b)\,l$, where a can be interpreted as the change in TFP.

But, equation (5) is also Kaldor's technical progress function, for which he gives a contrasting interpretation. The term a is interpreted as representing disembodied technical change, which in turn includes both autonomous technical progress (r_1) and learning-by-doing (c_1q), ie $a = r_1 + c_1q$. The change in capital–labour ratio $(k - l)$ represents embodied technical change, which is again partly autonomous (r_2) and partly induced (c_2q). Thus equation (5) becomes

$$
\begin{aligned}
p &= a + b\,(k - l) \\
&= (r_1 + c_1 q) + b\,(r_2 + c_2 q) \\
&= (r_1 + b\,r_2) + (c_1 + b\,c_2)\,q \qquad (6)
\end{aligned}
$$

Equation (6) is an expanded version of Verdoorn's law. Comparing equations (6) and (3), $\alpha = (r_1 + br_2)$, and $\beta = (c_1 + bc_2)$. Kaldor's interpretation distinguishes itself from the production function approach by emphasizing the direction of causation from output growth to both embodied and disembodied technical progress, and eventually to productivity change. Comparing our estimation result for equations (3) and (5), it can be seen that the coefficient of q in general takes a higher value than that of $(k-l)$. This implies output-induced learning effects are more significant than autonomous embodied technical change in the contribution to productivity change in Chinese industry.

Comparing the sources of productivity change between COEs and LMEs yields another result. For COEs, the Verdoorn's coefficient β in (3) is 0.836 and the coefficient of the change in capital–labour ratio b in (5) is 0.950. This is the only case where the b coefficient takes a higher value than the β coefficient. In contrast, for LMEs, the coefficients are 1.105 and 0.649, respectively, meaning that output growth is relatively more important than embodied technical progress in propelling productivity change. This, in conjunction with the fact that LMEs have been consistently among the fastest productivity-growing sector of Chinese industry, suggests that LMEs are more capable than small enterprises, particularly COEs, in generating learning effects. It also goes some way to explaining why, despite being more seriously constrained by insufficient internal financing and costly external financing, LMEs have still been able to generate productivity change at a respectable rate.

The analysis above is constrained by the small number of observations. To check the robustness of the results, we can pool the data of the four groups of enterprises (AEs, SOEs, COEs and LMEs), and run equations (3) and (5) again. In the former case, the equations for the individual enterprise sectors are

AEs: $p_1 = \alpha_1 + \beta_1 q_1 + u_1$

SOEs: $p_2 = \alpha_2 + \beta_2 q_2 + u_2$

COEs: $p_3 = \alpha_3 + \beta_3 q_3 + u_3$

LMEs: $p_4 = \alpha_4 + \beta_4 q_4 + u_4$

These can be combined into a single equation by assigning appropriate dummy variables

$$p = \alpha_4 + (\alpha_1 - \alpha_4) D_{11} + (\alpha_2 - \alpha_4) D_{21} + (\alpha_3 - \alpha_4) D_{31} + \beta_4 q + (\beta_1 - \beta_4) D_{12} + (\beta_2 - \beta_4) D_{22} + (\beta_3 - \beta_4) D_{32} + u$$

where $D_{11} = 1$ for AEs, and *0* for others; $D_{21} = 1$ for SOEs, and *0* for others; $D_{31} = 1$ for COEs, and *0* for others; $D_{12} = q_1$ for AEs, and *0* for others; $D_{22} = q_2$ for SOEs, and *0* for others; $D_{32} = q_3$ for COEs, and *0* for others. I take LMEs as the base group, because from the estimation results of equation (3) we know that LMEs take the highest β value among the four enterprise sectors (Table 5.4). If we assume $\beta_1 = \beta_2 = \beta_3 = \beta_4$, that is, the equations for the groups differ only in the intercept terms α_i but not in the slope coefficients β_i, then the combined equation can be re-written as

$$p = \alpha_4 + \beta_4 q + (\alpha_1 - \alpha_4) D_{11} + (\alpha_2 - \alpha_4) D_{21} + (\alpha_3 - \alpha_4) D_{31} + u \tag{3a}$$

Alternatively, if we assume $\alpha_1 = \alpha_2 = \alpha_3 = \alpha_4$, that is, the equations for the groups differ only in the slope coefficients β_i but not in the intercept terms α_i, then the combined equation can be re-written as

$$p = \alpha_4 + \beta_4 q + (\beta_1 - \beta_4) D_{12} + (\beta_2 - \beta_4) D_{22} + (\beta_3 - \beta_4) D_{32} + u \tag{3b}$$

The same method can be applied on equation (5). Let the combined equation for the four enterprise sectors be

$$p = a_3 + (a_1 - a_3) D_{11} + (a_2 - a_3) D_{21} + (a_4 - a_3) D_{41} + b_3 (k - l) + (b_1 - b_3) D_{13} + (b_2 - b_3) D_{23} + (b_4 - b_3) D_{43} + v$$

where D_{11}, D_{21} and D_{41} are of the same definitions as above, and $D_{13} = (k_1 - l_1)$ for AEs, and *0* for others; $D_{23} = (k_2 - l_2)$ for SOEs, and *0* for others; $D_{43} = (k_4 - l_4)$ for LMEs, and *0* for others. Again, I take COEs as the base group this time because they take the highest b value in the estimation of equation (5). If we assume, first, $b_1 = b_2 = b_3 = b_4$, and, second, $a_1 = a_2 = a_3 = a_4$, the combined equation can be re-written in the following ways, respectively

$$p = a_3 + b_3 (k - l) + (a_1 - a_3) D_{11} + (a_2 - a_3) D_{21} + (a_4 - a_3) D_{41} + v \tag{5a}$$

$$p = a_3 + b_3 (k - l) + (b_1 - b_3) D_{13} + (b_2 - b_3) D_{23} + (b_4 - b_3) D_{43} + v \tag{5b}$$

Table 5.5 Testing Alternative Sources of Labour Productivity Growth, 1979–94

(5) $p = a + b(k - l) + v$	a	b	$\bar{R}^2$	N	DW
AEs	1.978	0.656 (3.722)*	0.461	16	1.307
SOEs	3.360	0.195 (1.211)	0.301	16	1.477
COEs	4.745	0.950 (2.253)*	0.214	16	1.450
LMEs	2.220	0.649 (3.846)*	0.479	16	1.740

Note: Figures in parentheses are t-ratios; * and ^ are significant at 5% and 10% confidence interval, respectively. Q = gross output.

Table 5.6 gives the regression results of running equations (3a), (3b), (5a) and (5b). The coefficients of all but two of the dummy variables are not statistically significantly different from zero – the exceptions being D_{21} and D_{23}, which, consistent with the regression results in Table 5.5, indicate that productivity change of SOEs is not much dependent on the change in capital–labour ratio. This implies the same structural relationships basically apply to all the four enterprise sectors.

Now, it can be seen that both the β and b coefficients take high value, with the former substantially higher – 0.909 for (3a) and 0.891 for (3b), compared with 0.630 for (5a) and 0.867 for (5b). This supports the inference which I make above: that output-induced learning is more significant than autonomous embodied technical change in the contribution to productivity growth. The differences between the corresponding coefficients of LMEs and COEs in the two equations, though, are not significantly different from zero. Given the large increase in the degrees of freedom due to pooling data, the regression results in Table 5.6 should be more reliable than those in Tables 5.4 and 5.5.

STRUCTURAL CHANGE AS ENGINE OF GROWTH

If productivity change cannot be interpreted as independently determining output growth, then there must exist some other factors which are external to, yet instrumental for this growth–productivity virtuous circle. In this section, I test the thesis of structural change as an engine of growth. This thesis is again, much in the spirit of Kaldorian

Table 5.6 Testing Sources of Productivity Change by Using Pooled Data, 1979–94

(3a)

$$p = \alpha_4 + \beta_4 q + (\alpha_1 - \alpha_4) D_{11} + (\alpha_2 - \alpha_4) D_{21} + (\alpha_3 - \alpha_4) D_{31} + u$$

$$p = -3.282 + \underset{(10.080)^*}{0.909\, q} + \underset{(0.163)}{0.264\, D_{11}} + \underset{(1.136)}{1.932\, D_{21}} - \underset{(-0.598)}{1.025\, D_{31}}$$

$\bar{R}^2 = 0.557$; N = 64; DW = 1.696

(3b)

$$p = \alpha_4 + \beta_4 q + (\beta_1 - \beta_4) D_{12} + (\beta_2 - \beta_4) D_{22} + (\beta_3 - \beta_4) D_{32} + u$$

$$p = -2.692 + \underset{(7.004)^*}{0.891\, q} + \underset{(0.096)}{0.011\, D_{12}} + \underset{(0.490)}{0.086\, D_{22}} - \underset{(-0.505)}{0.054\, D_{32}}$$

$\bar{R}^2 = 0.648$; N = 64; DW = 1.703

(5a)

$$p = a_3 + b_3 (k - l) + (a_1 - a_3) D_{11} + (a_2 - a_3) D_{21} + (a_4 - a_3) D_{41} + v$$

$$p = 4.671 + \underset{(5.510)^*}{0.630\, (k - l)} - \underset{(-1.064)}{2.350\, D_{11}} - \underset{(-2.441)^*}{5.409\, D_{21}} - \underset{(-1.029)}{2.277\, D_{41}}$$

$\bar{R}^2 = 0.384$; N = 64; DW = 1.445

(5b)

$$p = a_3 + b_3 (k - l) + (b_1 - b_3) D_{13} + (b_2 - b_3) D_{23} + (b_4 - b_3) D_{43} + v$$

$$p = 2.101 + \underset{(5.800)^*}{0.867\, (k - l)} - \underset{(-1.276)}{2.154\, D_{13}} - \underset{(-3.144)^*}{0.569\, D_{23}} - \underset{(-1.279)}{0.202\, D_{43}}$$

$\bar{R}^2 = 0.418$; N = 64; DW = 1.474

Note: Figures in parentheses are t-ratios; * and ^ are significant at 5% and 10% confidence interval, respectively.

Table 5.7. Testing Structural Change as Engine of Growth, 1979–93

(7)	(8)
$q = \alpha + \beta c + u$	$q' = \alpha^* + \beta^* c + v$
$q = 5.491 + 0.509c$	$q' = 0.719 + 0.359c$
(8.971)*	(5.056)*
$\bar{R}^2 = 0.850$; N = 15;	$\bar{R}^2 = 0.637$; N = 15;
DW = 1,385	DW= 1.432

Note: Figures in parentheses are t-ratios; * and ^ are significant at 5% and 10% confidence interval, respectively. Q = gross value of industrial output of all township-and-above enterprises.

theory but in fact has a long tradition in development economics. The argument is that, in conjunction with this particular techno-economic paradigm, some industries can be especially dynamic in the sense that they embody strong increasing returns. For the Chinese case, I identify in Chapter 3 the 'new' consumer durables industries as the dynamic sector of the 1980s.

For estimation purposes, the 'new' industries are proxied by the machinery sector. This sector, in the Chinese context, approximates the International Standard Industrial Classification two-digit code 38; that is fabricated metal products, machinery and equipment. Encompassing a wide range of consumer and producer industries – as diverse as consumer electronics and mining machinery – this sector includes more than 'new' industries and also does not exhaust all 'new' industries. But it is certainly the closest proxy. Table 5.7 gives the results of regressing the output growth of all industries (q) on that of the machinery sector (c), covering all township-and-above enterprises (TAAEs) over the period of 1979–93 (see data appendix). The regression involves two separate equations:

$$q = \alpha + \beta c + u \tag{7}$$

$$q' = \alpha^* + \beta^* c + v \tag{8}$$

where q' is the growth in the gross output of all industries excluding the machinery sector. For equation (7), because q and c are definitionally related, the specification can be spurious. This can be seen in the following way. Consider the identity $Q = C + Q'$, where Q, C and Q' are the output levels of all industries, the machinery sector, and the non-machinery sectors, respectively. The growth of output is then approximately given by $q = wc + (1 - w)q'$, where w and $(1 - w)$ are the respective output shares of C and Q' in Q. Hence, any β coefficient obtained using equation (7) may just reflect the output share of the machinery sector in all industries (ie $\beta = w$). Equation (8) is used as a check on whether this is the case.

Comparing the regression results of (7) and (8), it is clear that the machinery sector has been significant in contributing to overall industrial growth not just because of its rapidly expanding output share. The β^* coefficients take a value of around 0.36, which means a one percentage point increase in the growth of the machinery sector increases the growth of output of the non-machinery sectors by 0.36 percentage point. This gives support to the thesis of structural change as engine of growth.

A question that arises concerns the determination of the structural change. In Chapter 3, I propose that this has been accounted for by two factors, namely, the expansion of domestic consumption demand and the imports of foreign technology. These are crucial for the rise of mass consumption and production industries in a late industrialization setting, where foreign technology is needed for building the production capabilities yet the industries are not sufficiently competitive in the initial stage to enter the world market. Given our broad definition of foreign technology, which encompasses not only machines and know-how but also new quality standards and design as embodied in imported industrial inputs, there is unfortunately no appropriate data to act as the proxy. So, here, I just focus on the demand side. Testing the above proposition involves the following equations:

$$c = \alpha + \beta s + u \tag{9}$$

$$\Delta c = \alpha' + \beta' \Delta s + u' \tag{9a}$$

where s is the real growth rate of social retail sales, and variables with the Δ sign indicates first differences. It can be seen from the regression result of equation (9), shown in Table 5.8, that the value of DW statistics is low, indicating the presence of some degree of serial correlation. So equation (9a) is used instead. Now, with a value of 1.178 for coefficient β', s is highly correlated with c. This indicates that a significant part of the machinery sector are mass consumption industries. To confirm this inference, we can test the following equations

$$q = \alpha^* + \beta^* s + u^* \tag{10}$$

$$\Delta q = \alpha^{*\prime} + \beta^{*\prime} \Delta s + u^{*\prime} \tag{10a}$$

$$q' = \alpha^{\wedge} + \beta^{\wedge} s + v \tag{11}$$

$$\Delta q' = \alpha^{\wedge\prime} + \beta^{\wedge\prime} \Delta s + v' \tag{11a}$$

Table 5.8 Testing Consumption Demand and Economic Growth, 1979–93

(9) $c = \alpha + \beta s + u$	(9a) $\Delta c = \alpha' + \beta'\Delta s + u'$
$c = 7.956 + 0.753s$	$\Delta c = 2.288 + 1.178\Delta s$
(1.416)^	(2.915)*
$\bar{R}^2 = 0.067$; N=15; DW = 0.683	$\bar{R}^2 = 0.366$; N = 14; DW = 2.241
(10) $q = \alpha^* + \beta^* s + u^*$	(10a) $\Delta q = \alpha^{*\prime} + \beta^{*\prime}\Delta s + u^{*\prime}$
$q = 9.769 + 0.357s$	$\Delta q = 1.680 + 0.587\Delta s$
(1.201)	(3.105)*
$\bar{R}^2 = 0.031$; N = 15; DW = 0.529	$\bar{R}^2 = 0.399$; N = 14; DW = 1.548
(11) $q' = \alpha^\wedge + \beta^\wedge s + v$	(11a) $\Delta q' = \alpha^{\wedge\prime} + \beta^{\wedge\prime}\Delta s + v'$
$q' = 10.307 + 0.241s$	$\Delta q = 1.474 + 0.411\Delta s$
(0.991)	(2.426)*
$\bar{R}^2 = -0.001$; N = 15; DW = 0.641	$\bar{R}^2 = 0.273$; N = 4; DW = 1.134

Note: Figures in parentheses are t−ratios; * and ^ are significant at 5% and 10% confidence interval, respectively. Q = gross output.

The variables are defined as previously. Again, the reason for using the first differences is that regressing the original variables (q or q') on s involves some degree of serial correlation, with both DW statistics taking a very low value. The regression results are also shown in Table 5.8. In both equations, Δs is significant in explaining Δq_t and q'_t. But coefficient $\beta^{*\prime}$ of equation (10a) takes a higher value (0.59) than coefficient $\beta^{\wedge\prime}$ (0.41) of equation (11a), indicating, again, that among all industries the growth of the machinery sector is especially sensitive to the expansion in domestic consumption demand.

Overall, we can infer from the above regression analyses that the machinery sector has been an engine of growth. A major reason is that it encompasses a range of mass consumption and production industries which, according to the depiction in Chapter 3, embody strong increasing returns. The proposition that the expansion of these industries have been driven by the expansion in domestic consumption demand is also confirmed.

CONCLUDING REMARKS

The regression analyses of this chapter are not far away from the first step of an alternative research programme on the sources of productivity and output growth in Chinese industry. Nevertheless, the results reported here are still of importance, and fit better into our production-oriented approach than the market-centred approaches. To summarize, these results include the following:

(a) It is evident that productivity and output growth have been to a significant extent mutually enhancing, thus the former cannot be assumed to be independently determining the latter.
(b) Among industrial enterprises, and particularly in comparison with COEs/TVEs, LMEs (which are mostly SOEs) have been more capable of generating learning effects, as is evident by their productivity change being more dependent on output growth than on the change of capital–labour ratio.
(c) There is evidence that the machinery sector has been a major engine of growth of Chinese industry as a whole.
(d) A major factor which enables the machinery sector to play such a role is that it encompasses a range of mass consumption/production industries, as is indicated by its strong dependence on the expansion of domestic consumption demand.

These results give broad support to the propositions which I raise in the previous two chapters and summarize at the beginning of this chapter. Results (a), (c) and (d) cannot easily be incorporated into the market-centred approaches which, in studying firm-level productivity change, typically focus on the micro-level while discounting (indeed ignoring) the effects of the macroeconomic and developmental settings. Result (b), in conjunction with the outstanding performance of LMEs among Chinese enterprises, disputes the approach of simply attributing everything good to the (notional) market and everything bad to the observed imperfections. From a production-oriented perspective, it can be argued that LMEs' learning capabilities are based on their relatively more rigid institutional and structural arrangements which promote the long-term commitment of major participants of the industrial system (see Chapter 4).

DATA APPENDIX TO CHAPTER 5

Output

As has its industry, China's statistical system has undergone significant changes over the past 16 years. As a consequence, consistent series of industrial statistics needed for analyzing productivity change and its sources are not often available and various ways of estimation need to be adopted. Table 5.9 gives the gross output data of three categories of industrial enterprises: all enterprises (AEs), township-and-above enterprises (TAAEs) and township-and-above independently accounting industrial enterprises (TAIAEs). These categories are distinguished by different levels of administrative affiliation, and each of them is broken down in two ways, either by ownership (state, collective, pri-

Table 5.9 Gross Value of Industrial Outputs, 1978–94 (100m yuan)

	Current prices			*1980 constant prices*		
	AEs	*TAAEs*	*TAIAEs*	*AEs*	*TAAEs*	*TAIAEs*
1978	4 237			4 335	4 214	4 137
1979	4 681			4 717	4 572	4 484
1980	5 154		4 703	5 154	4 972	4 879
1981	5 400			5 375	5 176	5 087
1982	5 811			5 796	5 574	5 394
1983	6 460			6 444	6 157	5 934
1984	7 617		6 818	7 493	7 015	6 903
1985	9 716	8 722	8 435	9 096	8 261	8 025
1986	11 194	9 799	9 436	10 158	8 979	9 202
1987	13 812	11 829	11 319	11 955	10 307	10 496
1988	18 225	15 291	14 586	14 440	12 127	11 905
1989	22 017	18 345	17 474	15 673	13 218	12 502 (12 295*)
1990	23 924	19 701	18 689	16 889	14 083	13 340
1991	28 248	23 136	22 089	19 384	16 041	15 163
1992	37 066	28 942	27 724	24 719	19 520	17 994
1993	52 692	41 023	39 693	31 650	25 316	23 836*
1994	76 909	53 373	51 353	39 904	28 295	27 224
Average annual growth (%)						
1980–8				13.74	11.79	11.80
1978–94				13.24	11.57	11.07

Sources: ZGJTN 1989, p.58; ZGJTN 1993, p.142; ZJN 1994, p. 788; ZTN 1990, pp. 414–15, 417; ZTN 1994, p. 378; ZTN 1995, pp. 377–8, 385; ZTZ 1988, p. 36; ZTZ 1990, p. 68; ZTZ 1993, p. 70.

Notes: *Published figure.

vate-individual, etc.) or by technical characteristics (coal mining, metallurgy, machinery, textiles, etc.).

In Table 5.9, all the current-price figures and the constant-price figures of AEs and TAAEs (1978–88, 1994) are published data. The 1989–92 constant-price figures of TAAEs are converted from current-price figures by using the implicit deflator of AEs, while the 1993 constant-price figure is calculated by multiplying that of TAIAEs by 1.0621 which is the average of the ratios between TAAEs and TAIAEs in 1992 and 1994. The 1986–92 constant-price figures of TAIAEs are calculated by multiplying labour productivity and employment data; and those of 1978–85 by summing up the GVIO of SOEs and COEs (which combined to account for 99.3 per cent in 1980 and 98.6 per cent in 1985 of the current-price GVIO of all TAIAEs). Because the employment data used are year-end (instead of year average) figures, the 1986-92 constant-price figures of TAIAEs are slightly overestimated, by 1.7 per cent in 1989, but this might not affect the calculation of the growth rates.

It is at the level of TAIAEs that consistent series of output, employment and capital assets data have been collected and published. These data are also broken down into sub-sectors. Table 5.10 gives the gross-output data of AEs, SOEs, COEs and LMEs at the level of township-and-above-independently accounting industrial enterprises. Again, the 1986–92 constant-price figures

Table 5.10 GVIO of Enterprise Sectors at the Level of TAIAEs, 1978–94 (100m yuan)

		GVIO at current prices				*GVIO at 1980 constant prices*			
		AEs	*SOEs*	*COEs*	*LMEs*	*AEs*	*SOEs*	*COEs*	*LMEs*
1978						4 137	3 385	752	1 829
1979						4 484	3 680	804	2 021
1980		4 703	3 799	871	2 627	4 879	3 924	955	2 148
1981						5 087	4 042	1 045	2 231
1982						5 394	4 250	1 144	2 480
1983						5 934	4 635	1 299	2 776
1984		6 818	5 184	1 559	3 517	6 903	5 217	1 686	3 150
1985		8 435	6 167	2 149	4 183	8 025	5 818	2 207	3 817
1986		9 436	6 759	2 536	4 700	9 202	6 004	2 494	4 288
1987		11 382	7 997	3 144	5 751	10 496	6 880	3 074	4 864
1988		14 586	9 947	4 220	7 357	11 905	7 686	3 834	5 651
1989		17 474	11 873	4 945	9 224	12 502	7 901	4 062	6 191
1990		18 689	12 570	5 247	10 203	13 340	8 183	4 409	6 644
1991	(a)	22 089	14 372	6 178	12 366	15 163	8 854	5 171	7 998
	(b)					15 163	9 716	4 371	8 776
1992	(a)	27 724	17 091	8 106	15 917	17 994	9 735	6 622	9 143
	(b)					17 994	10 682	5 597	10 033
1993	(a)	39 693	22 088	11 888	22 247	22 578	10 333	9 099	10 659
	(b)					22 578	11 340	7 687	11 698
1994	(a)	51 353	25 301	15 836	28 484	27 224	10 587	11 506	12 496
	(b)					27 224	11 619	9 721	13 714
Average annual growth (%)									
1980–8						11.80	8.77	18.98	12.85
1978–94	(a)					12.50	7.39	18.59	12.76
	(b)					12.50	8.01	17.35	13.42

Sources: ZGJTN 1993, pp. 142–5; ZTN 1993, p. 431; ZTN 1994, p. 378; ZTN 1995, p. 388; ZGJTZ 1949–84, pp. 85, 253; ZGJTZ 1987, pp. 18, 142; ZGJTZ 1986, p. 185.

are calculated by multiplying labour productivity and employment data. The 1978–84 constant-price figures of COEs are calculated from figures of all COEs, that is including non-independently accounting enterprises, assuming the ratio in 1985 (0.959) had remained the same before that year. Note that the conversion factor between 1990 constant-price and 1980 constant-price GVIO is 1.508 for AEs, 1.655 for SOEs and 1.274 for COEs. The reason remains unclear. But since constant prices GVIO is derived from physical output *volume*, whereas current prices GVIO from current sales *value*, the latter should be more accurate in reflecting the actual performance – it takes into account product quality improvement – especially for inter-sectoral comparison (see Rawski 1993). This means either the GVIO figures of SOEs after 1990 are understated or those of COEs are overstated. Hence, for 1991–4 constant-price GVIO figures, (a) are calculated on the basis of the varied conversion factors whereas (b) are based on the same conversion factor of AEs.

In production function analysis, theoretical consistency requires using either net-output data in the two-input case (labour and capital), or gross-output data in the three-input case (labour, capital and materials). The net-output data of the various enterprise sectors at the level of TAIAEs are also avail-

Table 5.11 Price Indices of GVIO (1978 = 100.00), 1978–94

	AEs	*SOEs*	*COEs*
1978	100.00	100.00	100.00
1979	101.54	102.58	97.93
1980	102.31	103.53	98.89
1981	102.77	104.11	99.39
1982	102.58	104.22	98.45
1983	102.56	104.37	98.25
1984	103.99	106.41	99.15
1985	109.27	112.83	102.92
1986	112.74	117.54	105.00
1987	118.21	124.98	108.59
1988	129.12	139.26	116.73
1989	143.72	159.88	126.03
1990	144.93	164.36	125.39
1991	149.10	173.21	125.31
1992	153.43	183.69	125.80
1993	170.37	221.48	132.63
1994	197.23	239.77	158.86

Sources: Calculated from the current-price and constant-price output figures of AEs, SOEs and COEs at the level of national total. See ZTN 1990, pp. 414–15; ZTN 1995, p. 377.

able, but only at current prices. To convert the data into constant-price figures, we need to use the price indices for gross outputs because those for net outputs are not available. Table 5.11 gives the deflators, while Table 5.12 gives the NVIO figures both at current prices and at constant prices.

Again, note the price indices of GVIO are problematic, especially that the movement in 1991–4 is erratic. Hence, (a) figures are calculated on the basis of the varied price indices whereas (b) are based on the same indices of AEs. We use the deflators of SOEs for LMEs. In Table 5.12, the 1979 and 1981–3 NVIO data are from Jefferson *et al.* (1992), which are in turn provided by the Chinese statistical authorities. We assume the data of AEs in these years are the sums of SOEs and COEs (this causes an error of around 1 per cent for 1985, as is indicated by the ratio between the sum and the true figure in that year). The Chinese authorities have ceased to publish the net output data since 1993, but have published the value-added data instead. The ratios between net output and value-added (both at current prices) in 1985 and 1992, according to ZGJTZ 1986, p.21, and ZTN 1993, p.417, are as follow: AEs (0.9009, 0.9715), SOEs (0.8935, 0.9328), COEs (0.9223, 1.0555), and LMEs (0.8903, 0.9285). We assume the ratios for 1993 and 1994 remained the same as in 1992.

Labour

There are two series of labour employment data available, but both do not cover the whole period of 1978–94 for all enterprise sectors. The first is the

Table 5.12 NVIO of Enterprise Sectors at the Level of TAIAEs, 1978–94 (100m yuan)

	NVIO at current prices				*NVIO at 1978 prices*						
	AEs	*SOEs*	*COEs*	*LMEs*	*AEs*	*SOEs*		*COEs*		*LMEs*	
						(a)	*(b)*	*(a)*	*(b)*	*(a)*	*(b)*
1978	1 358	1 109	249	710	1 358	1 109	1 109	249	249	710	710
1979	1 485	1 215	270	772	1 462	1 184	1 197	276	266	753	760
1980	1 648	1 303	285	853	1 611	1 259	1 274	288	279	824	834
1981	1 661	1 318	343	716	1 616	1 266	1 282	345	334	688	697
1982	1 742	1 373	369	775	1 698	1 317	1 338	375	360	744	756
1983	1 916	1 501	415	862	1 868	1 438	1 464	422	405	826	840
1984	2 235	1 729	485	1 290	2 149	1 625	1 663	489	466	1 212	1 241
1985	2 737	2 039	666	1 509	2 505	1 807	1 866	647	609	1 337	1 381
1986	2 979	2 178	763	1 619	2 642	1 853	1 932	727	677	1 377	1 436
1987	3 488	2 530	894	1 941	2 951	2 024	2 140	823	756	1 553	1 642
1988	4 301	3 063	1 135	2 370	3 331	2 199	2 372	972	879	1 702	1 836
1989	4 903	3 460	1 288	2 762	3 411	2 164	2 407	1 022	896	1 728	1 922
1990	5 093	3 569	1 323	2 962	3 514	2 171	2 463	1 055	913	1 802	2 044
1991	5 915	4 019	1 551	3 490	3 967	2 320	2 696	1 238	1 040	2 015	2 341
1992	7 447	4 844	2 010	4 839	4 854	2 637	3 157	1 598	1 310	2 634	3 154
1993	12 477	6 792	4 044	6 622	7 323	3 067	3 987	3 049	2 374	2 990	3 887
1994	14 281	7 372	4 352	8 017	7 241	3 075	3 738	2 740	2 207	3 344	4 065
Average annual growth (%)											
1980–8					9.51	7.22	8.08	16.42	15.43	10.17	10.37
1978–94					11.03	6.58	7.89	16.17	14.61	9.49	11.52

Sources: ZGJTN 1992, pp. 142–5; ZGJTN 1993, pp. 142–5; ZGJTZ 1949–84, p. 42; ZGJTZ 1987, p. 37; ZTN 1990, pp. 26, 414–15; ZTN 1994, p. 378; ZTN 1995, pp. 377, 388; Jefferson *et al.* (1992), p. 245.

Notes: The constant-price figures are calculated by using the gross-output deflators of Table 5.11.

Table 5.13 Labour Employment (Year-end Figures, 10 000 persons) at the Level of TAIAEs, 1978–94

	AEs	*SOEs*	*COEs*	*LMEs*
1978	4 529	3 041	1 488	1 725
1979	4 736	3 109	1 627	1 804
1980	5 028	3 248	1 749	1 903
1981	5 416	3 407	2 009	2 063
1982	5 563	3 503	2 060	2 119
1983	5 666	3 552	2 114	1 909
1984	6 157	3 708	2 401	2 139
1985	6 605 (6 425*)	3 858 (3 719*)	2 689 (2 653*)	2 204 (2 085*)
1986	7 040 (6 848*)	4 032 (3 886*)	2 939 (2 900*)	2 394 (2 265*)
1987	7 298	4 127	3 080	2 487
1988	7 518	4 257	3 144	2 629
1989	7 546	4 313	3 084	2 794
1990	7 663	4 390	3 092	2 936
1991	7 965	4 535	3 189	3 163
1992	8 008	4 522	3 167	3 433
1993	(8 300*)	(4 494*)	(3 231*)	(3 557*)
1994	(8 330*)	(4 261*)	(3 454*)	(3 373*)
Average annual growth (%)				
1980–8	5.16	3.44	7.61	4.12
1978–94	3.88	2.13	5.40	4.28

Sources: ZGJTZ 1949–84, pp. 71, 253; ZGJTZ 1987, p. 18; ZGJTN 1993, pp. 90–3; ZGJTN 1994, pp. 81, 84, 93, 120, 123; ZTN 1995, pp. 388, 401.

Notes: *Published year-average figures.

year-end employment figures of 1980 and 1984–92. The second is the 1978–94 figures (for AEs, SOEs and COEs, but not LMEs) of labour productivity, defined as GVIO at 1980 or 1990 constant prices divided by the year-average figures of employment. Because the constant-price GVIO data are available only for a limited number of years, we have to rely on the first series. Table 5.13 gives the employment data, while Table 5.14 gives the labour productivity data.

In Table 5.13, the 1978–9 and 1981–3 COEs figures are estimated from the ratio between numbers of workers in urban COEs alone and that in all COEs. The 1978–9 and 1981–3 LMEs figures are estimated by assuming the 1980 ratio between these enterprises and all enterprises remained the same. The 1994 AEs and SOEs figures are calculated by dividing value-added figures on labour productivity, both published data. That of COEs is estimated by multiplying the difference between AEs and SOEs by 0.8489 (which is the ratio between the true figure and the difference in 1993), and that of LMEs is assumed to be growing at the same rate as SOEs.

In Table 5.14, all figures for AEs and SOEs in 1978–94, and those for COEs in 1978–93, are published data. The 1994 COEs and LMEs figures are calculated by dividing their respective GVIO by the employment figures of Table 5.13. The 1980 and 1984–93 figures for LMEs are averages of large scale and medium scale enterprises weighted by their relative shares in the

Table 5.14 Labour Productivity (yuan per worker) of Enterprise Sectors at the Level of TAIAEs, 1978–94

	AEs	*SOEs*	*COEs*	*LMEs*
1978	8 458	11 131	5 733	10 603
1979	8 706	11 838	5 868	11 203
1980	8 952	12 081	6 549	14 441
1981	8 946	11 863	6 697	10 814
1982	9 364	12 133	6 969	11 704
1983	10 151	13 049	7 611	14 542
1984	11 190	14 070	9 227	16 613
1985	12 372	15 080	8 206	18 230
1986	12 609	15 451	8 600	18 684
1987	13 961	16 671	9 979	20 361
1988	15 835	18 056	12 195	22 214
1989	16 568	18 320	13 170	22 847
1990	17 408	18 639	14 258	23 411
1991	19 037	19 524	16 214	24 474
1992	22 773	21 803	21 189	27 039
1993	27 207	23 000	28 153	30 227 (29 977*)
1994	32 688	24 853	33 313	36 881
Average annual growth (%)				
1980–88	7.39	5.15	8.08	5.53
1978–94	8.82	5.15	11.63	8.10

Sources: ZGJTN 1993, pp. 144–5, 157–8; ZGJTN 1994, pp. 83, 86, 95, 120–3; ZTN 1993, p. 431; ZTN 1995, pp. 378, 380, 388, 401

Note: Labour productivity = GVIO at 1980 constant prices ÷ year average employment. *Published figure.

combined current-price GVIO, while the 1978–9 and 1981–3 figures are calculated by dividing the constant-price GVIO data in Table 5.10 by the employment data in Table 5.13. All 1991–4 figures are calculated from 1990 constant-price data, the conversion factor between 1990 and 1980 constant-price data being 1.508 for AEs, 1.655 for SOEs and 1.274 for COEs. The 1991–4 figures for LMEs are converted to 1980 constant prices by using the same conversion factor as SOEs.

Capital

Table 5.15 gives the original and deflated data of the value of fixed assets net of depreciation for the various enterprise sectors. All the 1994 original data are estimated by assuming the same ratios between the year-end figures and the year-average figures as 1993. Original data for COEs in 1978–9 are assumed to be the differences between AEs and SOEs divided by 1.033 (the ratio between the true figure and the difference in 1980), and in 1981–4 the

Table 5.15 Value of Fixed Assets Net of Depreciation of Enterprise Sectors at the Level of TAIAE, 1978–94 (Year-end figures, 100m yuan)

	K (original data)				*Deflator, P*	*K'(deflated)*			
	AEs	*SOEs*	*COEs*	*LMEs*	*(1978 = 100)*	*AEs*	*SOEs*	*COEs*	*LMEs*
1978	2 424	2 226	192	1 659	100.00	2 424	2 226	192	1 659
1979	2 630	2 379	243	1 800	101.34	2 627	2 377	242	1 798
1980	2 843	2 567	268	1 946	100.83	2 838	2 563	267	1 943
1981	3 064	2 709	336	2 081	100.63	3 058	2 704	335	2 077
1982	3 322	2 914	386	2 256	101.09	3 313	2 907	384	2 250
1983	3 624	3 161	438	2 461	101.76	3 610	3 150	435	2 451
1984	3 936	3 396	510	2 673	103.25	3 912	3 378	505	2 656
1985	4 725	4 026	660	3 004	116.92	4 587	3 917	633	2 939
1986	5 417	4 544	823	3 445	125.29	5 139	4 330	763	3 291
1987	6 347	5 242	1 017	4 033	131.78	5 845	4 860	910	3 737
1988	7 420	6 040	1 241	4 736	148.17	6 569	5 399	1 061	4 211
1989	8 752	7 033	1 478	5 700	181.00	7 305	5 948	1 192	4 744
1990	10 139	8 088	1 674	6 731	183.75	8 060	6 522	1 299	5 305
1991	12 020	9 507	1 919	8 155	191.32	9 043	7 264	1 427	6 049
1992	14 118	10 983	2 236	9 968	207.39	10 055	7 976	1 580	6 923
1993	18 428	13 304	2 988	12 383	267.41	11 667	8 844	1 861	7 826
1994	23 462	15 311	3 854	16 020	290.78	13 398	9 534	2 159	9 077
Average annual growth (%)									
1980–8						11.06	9.76	18.82	10.15
1978–94						11.28	9.52	16.33	11.21

Sources: ZGJTN 1992, pp. 65–6; ZGJTN 1993, pp. 103–6; ZGJTN 1994, pp. 82, 85, 94, 121, 124; ZTN 1995, pp. 249, 390;

differences divided by 1.058 (the ratio between the true figure and the difference in 1985). Original data for LMEs in 1978–9 are estimated by assuming the 1980 ratio between these enterprises and all enterprises (0.684) remained the same, while the 1981–3 data are based on the 1984 ratio (0.679).

The index of investment goods deflator (IID) is constructed on the basis of the following equation IID = 0.6DM + 0.4DB, where DM and DB are price indices of machinery and building materials, respectively. The relative weights are based on some official surveys which indicate that newly-installed fixed-capital assets were composed of 60 per cent machinery and 40 per cent structures in value terms (Jefferson *et al.* 1992). The conversion of the capital stock into constant-price measures involves the following three steps: first, $\Delta K_t = K_t - K_{t-1}$, where the variables are original data; second, $\Delta K'_t = \Delta K_t/P_t$; and, third, $K'_t = K'_{t-1} + \Delta K'_t$, where the variables are deflated data.

The Machinery Sector and Consumption Demand

For the purpose of testing the thesis of structural change as engine of growth, we need the output data of the 'new' industries, together with those of consumption demand. As explained, we use the machinery sector as the proxy for the 'new' industries. There are two series of output data of this sector, both at 1980 constant prices and at the level of township-and-above enterprises. The first is published by the state statistical authorities and covers all

Table 5.16 GVIO of the Machinery Sector and Value of Social Retail Sales, 1978–93 (100m yuan and percentages)

	C_1 *Amt*	*Amt* C_2	*(%)*	*Social retail sales* *Amt*	*(%)*
1978	1 018	996	(11.26)	1 559	(8.02)
1979	1 092	1 073	(7.75)	1 800	(13.19)
1980	1 122	1 062	(−1.10)	2 140	(12.15)
1981	1 080	997	(−6.08)	2 350	(7.23)
1982	1 225	1 108	(11.06)	2 570	(7.32)
1983	1 441	1 286	(16.12)	2 849	(9.21)
1984	1 757	1 523	(18.44)	3 376	(15.27)
1985	2 235	1 937	(27.16)	4 305	(17.20)
1986	2 372	2 062	(6.46)	4 950	(8.47)
1987	2 887	2 439	(18.29)	5 820	(9.57)
1988	3 609	2 986	(22.41)	7 440	(7.87)
1989		3 194	(6.97)	8 101	(−7.56)
1990		3 247	(1.65)	8 300	(0.35)
1991		3 870	(19.19)	9 416	(10.24)
1992		5 192	(34.17)	10 994	(10.77)
1993		7 014	(35.10)	13 593	(9.22)
Average annual growth (%)					
1978–93			13.90		9.10

Sources: ZGJTN 1989, p. 58; ZTN 1993, pp. 237, 611; ZTN 1994, pp. 231, 496; ZJGN 1994, p. VI–2.

Note: Figures in parentheses are real growth rates. The real growth rate of social retail sales is deflated by the retail price index. C_1 covers all township-and-above machinery enterprises while C_2 covers township-and-above enterprises affiliated to the Ministry of Machinery Industry, both at 1980 constant prices.

machinery enterprises at this level. The authorities, however, have ceased to publish the data after 1989. The second series, meanwhile, is published by the Ministry of Machinery Industry, covering enterprises under its affiliation and extending to 1993. Table 5.16 gives the two data series, together with data of the values and real growth rates of social retail sales.

Part III
Sector Studies

6 The Electronics Industry: State Industrial Policy and Development

In this and the next chapter, by means of two sector studies, I turn to examine more closely major characteristics of China's industrialization pattern and reforming economic institutions. The selection of the two industries to be studied, electronics and automobiles, is based on the observation that these are representative of the engine of growth in the 1980s and the 1990s, respectively. In addition, the development of the electronics industry has been especially revealing of the nature of market and institutional regulation in the industrialization process, while the organizational restructuring in the automobile industry has exhibited significant features of institutional reforms at the enterprise level. Thus, on the whole, the sector studies are likely to generate insights in to China's experience of economic development and reform, which are less discernible in the general analyses of the previous chapters.

THE ENGINE OF GROWTH OF THE 1980s

The Chinese electronics industry is representative of the group of 'new' (consumer durables) industries which formed the major impetus behind the spectacular growth of the economy over the past 16 years. Between 1980 and 1994, the industry registered an average growth rate of 23 per cent per annum. In the meantime, at the level of township-and-above independently accounting industrial enterprises, its share in the output of all industries increased from 1.6 per cent to 3.9 per cent while the ratio of its labour productivity (per worker gross output value) to that of all industries increased from 0.8 to 2.6 (Figure 6.1 and Table 6.1).

The rapid growth of the industry has been made possible by both technology imports and the expansion of domestic demand. This, however, has imposed on it, first severe foreign exchange constraints and later demand constraints. The crux of breaking the constraints rests on

Table 6.1 Output and Labour Productivity of the Electronics Industry (TAIAEs), 1980–94

	GVIO (100m yuan)			*Labour productivity (yuan per worker)*		
	(a)	*(b)*	*(a)/(b) (%)*	*(a)*	*(b)*	*(a)/(b)*
1980	76	4 703	1.62	8 106	9 658	0.84
1984	169	6 818	2.48	15 765	11 208	1.41
1985	244	8 435	2.89	20 931	12 389	1.69
1986	242	9 436	2.56	20 418	12 609	1.62
1987	339	11 382	2.90	28 605	13 961	2.05
1988	597	14 586	4.10	38 235	15 835	2.41
1989	551	17 474	3.15	38 193	16 568	2.31
1990	584	18 689	3.13	41 132	17 408	2.36
1991	765	22 089	3.46	50 970	19 037	2.67
1992	929	27 724	3.35	63 715	22 773	2.80
1993	1 299	39 693	3.27	82 065	27 207	3.02
1994	2 000	51 353	3.89	84 024	32 688	2.57

Sources: ZGJTN 1992, pp. 142, 154–5, 167; ZTN 1993, pp. 417–18, 432; ZGJTN 1994, pp. 81, 228; ZTN 1995, pp. 388, 401.

Notes: (a) = electronics and communication equipment industry; (b) = all industries; GVIO = gross value of industrial output at current prices; Labour productivity = GVIO at 1980 constant prices ÷ total employment. The conversion factor between 1990 and 1980 constant-prices output for the electronics industry is 1.03776 (ZJDGN-D 1991, p. II–15), and that for all industries is 1.50781 (ZTN 1993, p. 431).

improving its export competitiveness which, in turn, hinges upon the development of indigenous technological capabilities. In this regard, there has been important achievements, in terms of indigenizing imported technology and expanding exports. However, in view of the changing Chinese industrialization pattern in the 1990s, which involves even larger scales of technology imports (see Chapter 3), it is not certain that the achievements so far have placed the industry well on the way of rapid and sustained growth in the future. Everything depends on the mediation of the relevant institutions.

The achievements have been an outcome of a complex process of market and institutional regulation. Succinctly, due to the 'high-tech' nature of the industry and its peculiar configuration at the world level (acute oligopolistic competition and rapid technical change), the regulation of the market tends to induce Chinese enterprises and local authorities to focus on short-term profits rather than long-term development.

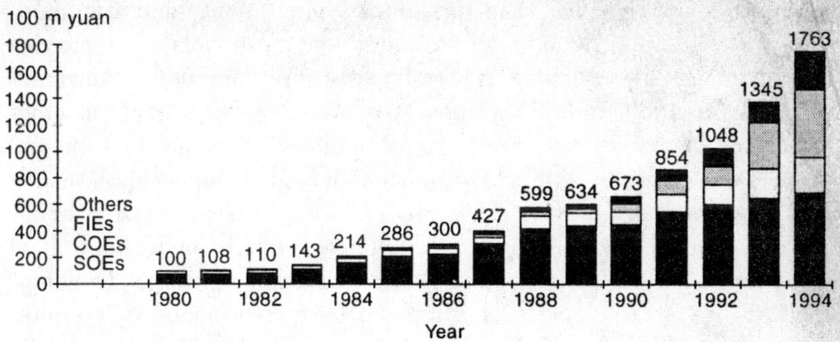

Figure 6.1 GVIO of Major Enterprise Sectors of the Electronics Industry (100m yuan, at 1980 constant prices), 1980–94

Sources: ZDGN 1986, p. III-4; ZDGN 1994, pp. II-2, II-10, II-26; ZJDGN-D 1990, p. II-13; ZJDGN-D 1991, p. II-15; ZJDGN-D 1992, p. II-21; ZDB, 27 January 1995, p. 4.

Notes: Figures cover enterprises under the Ministry of Electronics Industry. If electronics enterprises under other ministries are included, the 1993 figure would be 1686 million yuan, ie 25% greater than that shown in the chart. FIEs = foreign invested enterprises.

In this connection the intervention of the State, mainly through its industrial policy, has been indispensable. But the achievement of export competitiveness depends on not only technological development but also company-level efficiency. The improvement in efficiency has been to some extent ascribable to the increase in market competition. The wave of mergers and agglomerations among enterprises during 1989–92, largely initiated by the concerned local authorities for achieving economies of scale and building technological capabilities, has also been significant.

This chapter investigates the development of the Chinese electronics industry, and the actual forms and effects of the regulatory mechanisms thereof. Before we move on, it is helpful to look at the main technical and economic characteristics of the industry on a broader scale, that is the state of its development in the world setting. The following depiction draws on CASS-IJS (1988), Dicken (1992), Ernst and O'Connor (1992), Evans (1986, 1992), Fransman (1990), Henderson (1989), Hobday (1991, 1995), Mody (1990), Morgan and Sayer (1988), Schmitz and Cassiolato eds. (1992), Wade (1990) and Watanabe ed. (1993).

Technically, the electronics industry is divided into two main categories:

components and systems. The former can be split into active components, of which semiconductors are dominant products, and passive components; the latter category can be split into computers, consumer electronics and telecommunications. Among the systems, the consumer electronics sector is representative of modern mass production and consumption industries, while the computer and telecommunication sectors have pervasive effects on the technical change of a wide range of industries. It is perhaps the active components which, in technological terms, represent the core of the electronics industry at large. Developments in this sector have revolutionized the performance of computers, televisions and virtually all other electronics goods, and have radically reduced the costs of these downstream products. These effects are especially evident in the 'ASICs (application specific integrated circuits) revolution' since the mid-1980s. This 'revolution' represents a radical shift from commodity chips to design-intensive chips, and, in conjunction with the technology of electronic design automation, has lowered the technological and financial barriers to entry. Meanwhile, economically, the development of the electronics industry in general and the semiconductor sector in particular has been dominated by a phenomenal trend of competition-induced rapid *cum* abrupt technical change. This is largely due to the interaction of a number of peculiar features of the industry: high technology, heavy sunk investment and oligopolistic market structure in the world setting.

From the standpoint of late-comer electronics industries, therefore, the imperative for long-term visions and commitment, and appropriate targeting, in the face of abrupt changes, brings about demanding tasks to be accomplished by both the immediate manufacturers and the broader institutions. On the part of firms, to be able to participate in the competition of the world market and to eventually catch up with world advanced level, the prominent task is to shorten their lags from the ever-developing best practices (in economic terms) technology. This can involve a strategy of quick adaptation to new components or systems in the market. The precondition for quick adaptation, however, is that the firms must be extremely flexible. The applicability of the strategy is also likely to be limited to downstream assemblers where relatively little fixed investment and R&D contents are involved. Because adapting to the technical change of the world industry involves a process of learning, a further condition that is needed is the co-operation of component producers and users (systems producers) which facilitates knowledge sharing. In other words, there can be synergic gains from co-operation, though not necessarily through vertical integration. The same applies to divisions within the firm, particularly concerning the links between R&D institutions and the production units. The organization of firms in diversified business groups can also spread the risks and costs of developing a new and 'high-tech' industry like electronics.

Turning to the broader institutions, the need for long-term commitment rests not only on the immediate producers but also the externally-financing institutions. The firm needs to be well supported for coping with the enormous risks and violent cyclical fluctuations that are characteristic of the development of the industry. A further requirement on the part of the broader institutions is the co-ordination of joint R&D activities among firms, again because of the heavy costs involved in keeping up with the pace of technical change in the world market. Finally, in the context of late-comer electronics industry where firms are underdeveloped in terms of the capability to stand the world market competition, the State has an indispensable role to play – especially in areas such as protecting the infant industry, initiating the entry into specific technology and products, and promoting the industry to become competitive. The underpinning of this role, as is highlighted by Fransman (1990) in his study of the Japanese computers industry, is that, compared with firms, the State tends to have greater capacity to hold long-term visions and to undertake long-term commitments which are indispensable for the development of the industry.

To summarize, the economic importance of the electronics industry lies mainly in its pervasiveness in generating technical change, and its vast market demand which generates economies of scale and learning effects. In the context of late industrialization, however, the development of the industry often confronts a number of difficulties including the heavy sunk investment involved, the control of transnational corporations over technology, the problem of compatibility between domestic demand structure and the industry, and the risks caused by rapid technical change and acute competition in the world market. All these point to the need for building up indigenous technological capabilities and achieving competitiveness in the world market. There follows the need for the institutional preconditions delineated above.

THE DEVELOPMENT PATH

Between 1980–94, the Chinese electronics industry registered an average annual growth rate of 23 per cent, far faster than the rate of 13 per cent of all industries. This rate is comparable to those of the

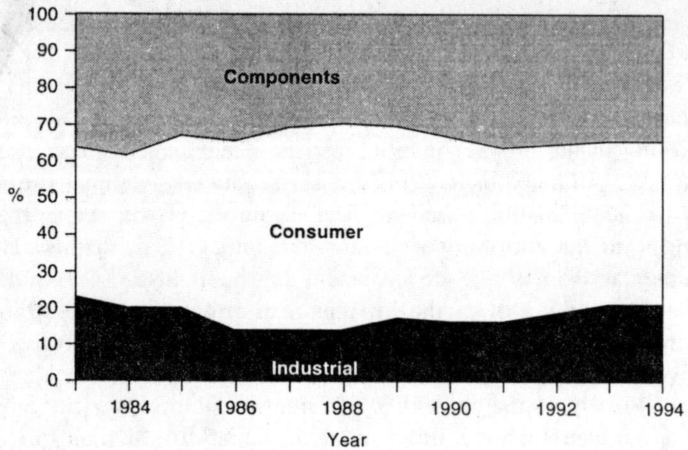

Figure 6.2 Output Composition of China's Electronics Industry, 1983–94 (sectoral shares at 1980 constant-price GVIO)

Sources: ZJDGN-D 1990, p. II-1; ZJDGN-D 1991, p. II-1; ZJDGN-D 1992, p. II-1; ZDGN 1994, p. II-1; ZDB, 31 January 1995, p. 5; ZJN, various years.

electronics industries of Japan, South Korea and Taiwan in their respective take-off periods. It thus seems that the Chinese electronics industry is on the way to catching up with the world advanced level. However, a closer comparison between the industry and its foreign counterparts reveals some shortcomings which are likely to hinder its future development.

One major shortcoming of the industry, as can be seen from Figure 6.2, is that it skews to the predominance of consumer electronics. Indeed, starting from almost nowhere in 1978, China became the world's largest TV receivers manufacturer by the mid-1980s, accounting for 23 per cent of world total output volume in 1988. In 1991, the sectoral composition of the industry among investment goods, consumer goods and components was at the ratio of 15.0:49.4:35.6. In contrast, the ratio of the electronics industry of the United States in the same year was 70.0:4.2:25.8, while that of Western Europe 73.7:8.8:17.5, that of Japan 46.0:18.9:35.1, and that of all newly industrialized countries combined 41.6:20.7:37.7 (*Financial Times*, 12 August 1992, p.16). The implication of this structure is that it threatens the secure supply of high performance machinery and components that are necessary for the international competitiveness of China's electronics industry as a whole.

A second shortcoming is fragmentation of the industrial structure and miniaturization of the firm scales. In 1991, the concentration ratio (by sales revenue) of the top five enterprises in the industry was merely 12 per cent. In the consumer electronics sector where scale economies are significant, the sum total of sales revenues of the top five enterprises in 1989 amounted to US$1.1b. This is much less than the USA's US$2.3b, South Korea's US$2.8b and Japan's US$22.3b (Wu 1992). Also, unlike the Japanese and South Korean diversified business groups, most Chinese enterprises concentrate heavily in a single sector. Of the top 20 electronics enterprises listed in Table 6.2, in 1989, only two – with their names ending with the term 'machinery' which indicates their previous status as military-related plants – diversified into more than one sector. Of these 20 enterprises, 16 concentrated in consumer electronics, especially TV receivers production. This makes the development of high capital intensity and high risk upstream sectors (eg in semiconductors) unable to count on the financial support of booming consumer electronics producers. It also hinders the sharing of information and knowledge between components producers and users.

The two features depicted above reflect the main character of the development of the industry in the 1980s: namely, short-termism. This refers to the focus on short-term profits instead of the cost-performance competitiveness of the industry in the world market. One typical case was the upsurge of colour television production during 1984–8.

Within a few years around 110 production lines were imported and installed in almost the same number of enterprises. The result was that none of them reached the minimum efficient scales by world standard. A World Bank survey in 1988 reveals that the average costs of production of the biggest Chinese colour TV producers were, in general, 70 per cent to 80 per cent higher than their foreign counterparts (DGFZY 1991). With most of the production lines imported in the form of turnkey plants and of virtually all the established brand names of the industrialized world, the industry became heavily dependent on imported components. The incompatibility among the brands also made it difficult for the development of upstream sectors. This led to unfavourable feedback effects on television production. The underdevelopment of integrated circuits (ICs), for instance, made TV manufacturers unable to design independently medium- to high-grade products. By 1988, while the industry was capable of producing 300-plus varieties and specifications of TV sets, these were only one-third of those turned out by Matsushita

Table 6.2 Top 20 Electronics Enterprises (Ranked by Sales Revenue), 1989–94 (100 m yuan)

1989 Rank	Enterprises	Sales	1994 Rank	Enterprises	Sales
1	Shanghai No. 1 TV	864	1	Shanghai Broadcasting Electr. Group	5347
2	Nanjing Radio	852	2	Shanghai Bell Tel. Equipment Ltd.	5119
3	Changhong Machinery	841	3	Changhong Electrical Ltd. (Holding)	5089
4	Wuxi TV	826	4	Beijing Legend Computers Group	4760
5	Shanghai No. 18 Radio	805	5	Panda Electronics Group	4221
6	Shanghai No. 4 Radio	727	6	Caihong Electronics Group	3563
7	Suzhou TV	691	7	Shenzhen Huaqiang Electronics Ltd.	3350
8	Tianjin Comm. & Broad. Equip.	657	8	Shenzhen Kangjia Electronics Group	2932
9	Changcheng Computers Group	621	9	Beijing Matsushita Colour Picture Tubes	2329
10	Beijing TV	578	10	Shenzhen SEG Electronics Ltd.	2271
11	Huanghe Machinery	569	11	TCL Group Corp.	1948
12	Shanghai Electr. Vacuum Tubes	552	12	Changcheng Computers Group	1785
13	Xiamen Huaqiao Electr. Ltd.	496	13	Beida Fangzheng Computers Group	1600
14	Hangzhou TV	479	14	Beijing Int'l Telephone Switching Ltd.	1573
15	Shanghai Broad. Equipment	467	15	Fujian Hitachi TV Ltd.	1552
16	Shaanxi TV Picture Tubes	462	16	Hangzhou Communication Equipment	1341
17	Fujian-Hitachi TV Ltd.	440	17	Tianjin Comm.&Broad. Equipment	1531
18	Dalian TV	402	18	Shanghai Yongxin Colour Picture Tubes	1470
19	Qingdao TV	367	19	Zhenghua Electronics Group	1356
20	Tianjin TV	339	20	Xihu Electronics Group	1341

Sources: ZJDGN-D (1990), p. II-33; JJRB, 28 March 1995, p. 12.

Notes: A number of the enterprises, particularly those which transformed themselves into joint stock companies or (through mergers and takeovers) business groups, changed their names during 1989–94. The following cases of correspondence can be identified. Rank 1st in 1994 = Rank 1st + 5th + 6th + 15th in 1989. Rank 3rd in 1994 = Rank 3rd in 1989. Rank 5th in 1994 = Rank 2nd + 26th in 1989. Rank 6th in 1994 = Rank 16th in 1989. Rank 20th in 1994 = Rank 14th in 1989.

of Japan alone. The underdevelopment of microelectronics-based machinery has hindered the automation of TV production: for each changeover of product specifications on the production lines, one day of time is needed, compared with Japanese producers' taking less than 15 minutes.

To trace the sources of short-termism amounts to delineating the essential features of the State development strategy and the reforming institutions in the 1980s. A precondition for the rapid expansion of the industry was the persistence of consumption booms. These booms, in turn, were a result of the State strategy which encouraged consumption rather than saving, and the expansion of consumer industries relative to capital goods sectors. On the supply side, the expansion was made possible by the institutional reform. The decentralization of economic power, together with trade liberalization, enabled local authorities and enterprises to build up the industry in a short period. Moreover, because the objectives of these economic agents were invariably short-term profits, the process was thus basically based on massive imports of downstream assembly lines.

This said, however, it needs to be balanced in assessing the development in the 1980s – it needs to be compared with the pre-reform experience. The pre-reform development strategy was basically one of 'technological dualism'. It was characterized by central planning and geared to military-related sectors. Alongside the centrally-managed sector there were also locally-managed enterprises which produced for the market. The development under this strategy had become increasingly unsatisfactory. It did not result in the formation of an economically beneficial electronics industry. On the one had, it led to heavy financial burdens on the State. On the other hand, the locally-managed sector remained technologically backward because of a lack of investment. In terms of technological progress, despite the fact that China had been able to generate major innovations in short intervals after the industrialized world (for example the first IC and the first semiconductor-based computer in 1965, both were introduced six years later than in the USA and one year later than Japan), the application was basically confined to small-batch rather than commercialized production.

By the 1980s, the limitations for pursuing a technologically-dualistic strategy became even more apparent. The market-oriented reform has largely reduced the ability of the State to allocate resources to specific industries. Also, following the reform, most medium-to-large scale enterprises which traditionally formed the backbone of the centrally-managed sector, have evolved towards the institutionalization of their own interests and the marketization of their operations. The regulatory mechanism, in short, has evolved into a planning-market 'economic dualism'. Thus, starting from the mid-1980s, there has been a reshaping of the character of State intervention in the electronics industry.

Central to the new forms of State intervention has been the implementation of an electronics industrial policy. This covers three broad areas. The first concerns rationalization. It has been particularly applied to consumer electronics, where the fragmentation of the industry and miniaturization of the scale of firms has been serious. The measures include promoting agglomeration and restricting new entrants. The second area is on assimilating and improving upon imported technology. One prominent measure is the State-enforced unified negotiation with transnational corporations (TNCs) for technology transfer. Both of these two areas of intervention are related to the emphasis on promoting the export competitiveness of the industry. The third area of intervention, which has been applied to the computer and semiconductor sectors, concerns targeting. This involves State-initiated developments of particular projects and technologies. The development lead of ASICs in the semiconductor sector, and micro-computers in the computers sector, are examples of this kind.

In response to the State policy, and the situation that the domestic consumption boom is cooling down and competition is tending to become acute, local authorities and enterprises have exhibited motivations for technical upgrading and exports. The reform of company organization and the broader institutional framework has also proved to be helpful in this respect. By the early 1990s, there have been a number of positive developments of which exports expansion is the most significant.

In 1990, China exported US$3.8b of electronics goods, a 15-times increase over the value of US$0.2b in 1985. This led to a reduction of trade deficit of electronics goods from US$3.3b just two years ago to US$1.4b in 1990. The exports and imports were finally balanced by 1994, with the deficits being only US$11m. Meanwhile, there is the exports expansion of a number of technologically sophisticated products, which indicates the standard the domestic production capability has attained. Whereas before 1987 China's colour TV exports had never exceeded the value of US$100m, in 1990, it exported 2.6m sets which were valued at US$405m. The good performance following the 1991 foreign trade regime reform, with the export value of colour TV being US$415m (2.6m sets in volume) and computer products US$460m in that year (Table 6.3), reflects the culminated result. By 1993, the exports of colour TV sets reached US$478m in value terms and 3.7m sets in volume term.

Table 6.3 Exports and Imports of Electronics Products, 1987–94 (US$100m)

	1987	*1988*	*1989*	*1990*	*1991*	*1992*	*1993*	*1994*
Electronics exports	7.45	19.95	27.57	37.87	49.00	68.72	81.10	123.60
Computer products	0.45	1.20	1.70	2.91	4.60	10.67	15.60	28.00
Electronics imports	. . .	52.79	51.74	51.46	60.13	80.30	106.00	134.80
Computer products	4.16	6.90	6.08	6.56	7.74	10.99	14.77	19.80

Sources: ZJDGN-D, various years; ZJN, various years; ZDB, 3 February 1992, p. 1; XXSB, 5 May 1994, p. 3; CD, 2 March 1994, p. 2; CD, 8 March 1995, p. 5; CD-BW, 19–25 March 1995, p. 8.

Along with the symptoms of achievement, of course, symptoms of failure still abound. The development lag of the semiconductor and computer sectors, both in terms of technological standard and price-performance competitiveness *vis-à-vis* the world advanced level, is especially serious in hindering the future development of the electronics industry as a whole. Even the relatively successful sector of consumer electronics has to confront the threat of slowdown in domestic demand expansion, and acceleration of technical change on the world scale (notably the development of high-definition TV), in the 1990s. All these imply the imperative for improving the regulatory mechanism of the Chinese electronics industry.

THE SUCCESS OF THE CONSUMER ELECTRONICS SECTOR

In 1993, China exported 9.4m television sets of which 3.7m were colour. These represent 31 per cent and 26 per cent, respectively, of domestic output volumes in that year. Amid the foreign trade reform of 1991, the ability and willingness to maintain exports reflect the interaction of at least three factors: (a) the intensification of competition in the domestic market; (b) the technological capability the industry has built up; and (c) the competitiveness of enterprises.

Of immediate effect, the expansion of Chinese TV exports has been propelled by a stagnant domestic market since the retrenchment period of 1989–91. The emergence of a sales slump was both abrupt and violent. It started in 1989: in that year, the volume of TV sets sold was 22m, down 18 per cent from the 1988 figure of 27m sets. The 1988 figure, in contrast, is 15 per cent over 1987; and the average annual growth rate over the eight-year period of 1980–8 is 28 per cent. The situation worsened in 1990 when total sales registered a decrease by

Table 6.4 Concentration Ratios (by Sales Revenue) of China's Electronics Industry, 1986–94 (bn yuan)

	1986	*1987*	*1988*	*1989*	*1990*	*1991*	*1992*	*1993*	*1994*	*1994/1986*
(a)	2.24	2.66	4.07	4.19	5.14	7.54	10.30	15.23	24.54	10.96
(b)	24.10	34.83	52.03	49.18	54.17	62.85	77.50	119.31	138.27	5.74
(a)/(b) (%)	9.3	7.6	7.8	8.5	9.5	12.0	13.3	12.8	17.7	
(c)	2.24	2.66	4.07	4.07	5.02	6.86	9.86	13.39	20.94	9.35
(d)	5.83	6.75	12.57	11.53	13.38	17.76	19.83	27.14	35.54	6.10
(c)/(d) (%)	38.4	39.4	32.4	35.3	37.5	38.6	49.7	49.3	58.9	

Sources: DZSC, 11 May 1987, p. 1; GLSJ, 1989 no. 1, p. 135; GLSJ, 1989 no. 6, p. 119; ZDGN 1994, p. II-32; ZJDGN-D 1990, pp. II-33–34; ZJDGN-D 1991, pp. II 38–40; ZJDGN-D 1992, p. II-46; JDRB, 25 February 1993, p. 2; JJRB, 28 March 1995, p. 12.

Notes: (a) = sales revenue of top 5 electronics enterprises; (b) = sales revenue of the electronics industry; (c) = sales revenue of top 5 TV manufacturers; (d) = sales revenue of top 25 TV manufacturers.

12 per cent. The modest rebound in 1991, up 5 per cent, despite the massive growth of the economy as a whole, did not lift sales back to their 1988 peak.

The major cause behind this dismal picture is the short-termist development pattern of the industry in the 1980s. Specifically, three features of the pattern are discerned. The first is the organizational inefficiency, and lack of economies of scale, on the part of enterprises. They were thus unable to drastically reduce production costs and product prices. The second feature is the weak R&D capability of enterprises, resulting in their inability to develop new and higher performance products and to diversify into other sectors, in order to offset the sales slump. Both of the two features are structural in nature. It is noted that, while the majority of the TV manufacturers were plunged into a predicament, there were some especially hard-hit and some others doing well. The increase in concentration ratios during 1989–92 (as opposed to those in 1986–9 which actually decreased) shown in Table 6.4 indicates the unevenness among enterprises under recession. The increase in concentration also indicates that a process of selection through market competition has taken place.

The third feature of the development pattern is generic: the serious over-capacity of the industry. In 1991, while the production capacity of colour TV reached 21m sets, the actual output was 12m. After a decade of persistent booms, the market is tending to be saturated. By year-end 1992, the volume of TV sets owned by the population was 228m, of which around 70 m were colour. This means 60 per cent of the households had TV sets, of which 20 per cent had colour

TV. The respective rates were even higher in the urban population: virtually all households had TV sets, and 75 per cent had colour TV. As the income of the average rural household is much lower, their demands have concentrated on black and white TV sets. The stagnation trend is likely to be long-lasting. This has been evident in the situation following the termination of the retrenchment period. In contrast to the rapid expansion of the economy, the growth of TV output has been sluggish. In 1991–4, while the industrial sector as a whole grew by 106 per cent, the output volume of colour TV sets grew by 40 per cent. Overall, the expansion of Chinese TV exports is to a considerable extent attributable to the deteriorating domestic sales that gave enterprises the incentive to export.

Incentive alone, however, is unlikely to have been the main impetus behind the exports expansion. For a technically-sophisticated product such as the colour TV set, which is also a product of acute competition in the world market, the expansion is more ascribable to the economic and technological strength of the Chinese industry. In this connection, the vast size of the domestic market, and its tremendous expansion in the 1980s, have proved to be advantageous. They have provided the industry with a major source of capital accumulation and hence the financing for technical renovation. They have also enabled the growth of some enterprises eventually up to internationally competitive scales (Table 6.5).

For a mature product like a TV receiver, the sustainability of exports competitiveness ultimately rests on the technological capability. This stems from the fact that the competition in the world market has taken place largely among a small number of TNCs, often in the form of rapid product and process innovations. In this regard, the experience of the Chinese TV industry can be judged as a basic success. By late 1990, when the industrial authorities held the 'fifth national working convention on the indigenization of colour TV technology', the industry had been transformed from an assembler of imported SKD/CKD (semi- or completely-knocked down) kits just a few years ago to one capable of using CAD/CAM (computer-aided design and manufacturing) technology in product and process development and of turning out products with more than 95 per cent local contents. The transition has involved the development of a range of support industries, particularly ICs and automation technology, and the production of high-tech components like picture tubes (kinescopes). It is on this basis that China intends to join the international race for the development of high definition television (HDTV) in the 1990s, which it is believed will bring about

Table 6.5 Output Volumes of Television Receivers and Picture Tubes, 1975–94 (thousands)

	TV receivers		*Picture tubes*	
	total	*colour*	*total*	*colour*
1975	178	3	149	. . .
1980	2 492	32	670	. . .
1981	5 394	152	1 310	. . .
1982	5 920	288	2 510	136
1983	6 840	531	4 150	580
1984	10 038	1 340	5 820	974
1985	16 677	4 353	8 230	1 060
1986	14 594	4 146	9 780	1 121
1987	19 344	6 727	11 150	1 211
1988	25 051	10 377	13 950	1 448
1989	27 665	9 400	17 440	1 718
1990	26 847	10 330	20 780	3 535
1991	26 914	12 051	21 030	7 507
1992	28 678	13 331	24 160	8 769
1993	30 330	14 358	23 650	9 267
1994	32 833	16 892	29 900	12 910
Average annual growth (%)				
1982–88	27.2	81.7	33.1	48.3
1988–94	4.6	8.5	13.5	44.0

Sources: ZDB, 27 January 1995, p. 4; ZDGN 1986, p. III-15; ZDGN 1994, p. III-68; ZJDGN-D 1990, p. II-18; ZJDGN-D 1992, p. II-30; ZGJTN 1994, pp. 52–3; ZTN 1995, p. 417.

Notes: Colour picture tubes figures cover enterprises under the Ministry of Electronics Industry.

revolutionizing technical change for a wide range of industries.

Of the thousands of TV parts and components, the most technically sophisticated is the picture tube. In view of the underdevelopment of electronics technology in China, it was thus natural that in the booming years of the 1980s the regulation of the market tended to skew to imports rather than domestic production. In the face of the foreign exchange constraint, and hence domestic production of picture tubes becoming not just necessary but rather profitable, the regulation of the market also tended to focus on importing turnkey plants instead of indigenizing technology. Both of these were rejected by the state. By the mid-1980s, the then Ministry of Electronics Industry (MEI) formulated a 'three unified' policy for building up an indigenous picture tube industry. This encompassed three measures:

(a) unified planning, in order to avoid duplication of projects
(b) unified negotiation with TNCs, in order to strive for favourable terms in technology transfer
(c) unified setting of technical standards, in order to bring about competition among TNCs and to avoid fragmentation of the industry.

In addition, there was the intention to form a specialized team in the construction process that would be capable of mastering not only picture tubes production but also the technology of equipment manufacturing, design and R&D for product and process innovations. The concrete target was to have the local contents of the producing equipment reaching 40 per cent or above.

The implementation of the 'three unified' policy took the form of three rounds of negotiation with TNCs in the second half of 1986. Consequently, of the eight TNCs joining the competition, Toshiba of Japan won the contracts of constructing the three projects in Xianyang (near Xian), Nanjing and Shanghai with Matsushita winning the contract of the fourth project in Beijing. Because of the unified negotiations, the costs were reduced – from the amount of US$800m originally quoted by the TNCs to a half of that – and the technical standards were unified. For technology transfer, the focus was on the Xianyang plant (ranked 16th in 1989 and sixth in 1994 among electronics enterprises, see Table 6.2). Unlike the other three which were Sino-foreign joint ventures, this plant was solely owned by China and was set with the highest target of local contents: 76 per cent in physical terms, and 49 per cent in value terms. The MEI recruited 18 machinery enterprises to participate in the project. Toshiba also sent out 120 experts to give technical advice. By 1990, when the Japanese firm gave its approvals, the plant had built up not only the capacity of producing colour picture tubes but also the capability of keeping up with technical changes in the world market. The target of technology indigenization was thus basically achieved.[1]

Meanwhile, the enthusiasm of local authorities to introduce turnkey plant persisted. This was induced by the sales booms in the domestic market. In 1988 alone, China spent US$1.1bn of foreign exchange to import 9m colour picture tubes; and in that year, the price of each tube in domestic sales was 2.9 time the import price at official exchange rate. For profit-seeking local authorities, this inducement was strong enough to lead them to build up production capability. Thus, despite repeated state stipulations to prohibit new projects, by 1990, there were in total, 18 projects under construction. This means that upon completion, by the mid-1990s, the combined capacity would reach 21m which, as in the case of colour TV, would far exceed domestic demand (the actual output volume of colour TV sets was 17m in 1994, and colour picture tubes 13m, see Table 6.5). Not only were most of the projects imported turnkey plans, but also they all had an individual capacity ranging between one million and two million tubes per annum. This was well below the minimum efficient scale by world standards, believed to be around three million tubes per annum. Clearly, what the local authorities targeted at was solely short-term profits, at the expense of long-term development.

In this connection, the construction of colour TV picture tube production capability in Guangdong province is especially a case illustrative of the short-termism. Under the original planning of the central government, none of the four designated plants would be situated in the province, because of the consideration for acquiring technology – Guangdong is not a base of linked capital goods industries. However, by 1990, the province had already set up four plants which were promoted by provincial and lower level authorities. At one point, the MEI and three other ministries jointly dispatched a document and sent a task force to Guangdong to stop the construction, but were rejected by the provincial authorities. Just like other non-designated projects, all the Guangdong plants were imported in turnkey forms and were with individual capacity ranging from 1.2m to 1.6m tubes. The fact that two of the four projects were imported from Hitachi of Japan, which had failed to win the contracts in the unified negotiation, casts doubt on their cost-benefits from the point of view of the country as a whole.

From the above description, it is possible to assess the respective roles of the State and the market in the indigenization of picture tubes and other kinds of colour TV production technology. To the extent that the profit-seeking behaviour of local authorities (and TNCs) is regarded as an essential element of the market, the regulation of the market can be judged as a failure.[2] Of course, it might be argued that this is not really the market, as local authorities and even enterprises in China are not purely economic agents. Thus it is necessary to add a qualification – the market is conceptualized in such a way that it refers to the regulatory mechanism which would have emerged if the state gave up its intervention. This was the profit-seeking behaviour of enterprises and local authorities, plus the constraints from the world market (consumption demonstration effects and the controls of a small number of TNCs over technology), which failed in fostering the development.

The formation of technological capability, though, is a necessary but not sufficient condition for the development of the electronics industry. To be an economically beneficial sector, the industry needs eventually to become competitive in the world market. In addition to technology, the economic strength of the industry and efficiency of enterprises are also essential. In this regard, the relative success of China's consumer electronics industry must be attributed not only to the promotion of the State but also the favourable structural conditions (the sales booms) and the competitiveness of at least quite a number of enterprises. The wave of mergers and agglomerations in 1989–92, which was mainly aimed at enhancing enterprise competitiveness, thus can be regarded as entrepreneurial. By 1994, there were five Chinese colour TV manufacturers with individual output volume exceeding one million sets per annum, of which the biggest (Changhong Machinery) produced almost two million. In view of the rigidity of the Chinese industrial system in general, and the serious fragmentation of the colour TV industry just a few years ago in particular, this is no small achievement.[3]

That the mergers and agglomerations took place almost exclusively among enterprises of the same regions reflects the crucial role of local authorities. Indeed, since the retrenchment period of 1989–91, there have been signs of some local authorities striving to emphasize long-term development instead of short-term profits. In the electronics industry, there were cases of local authorities initiating joint R&D activity among manufacturers to enhance the capacity for product and process innovations. The indigenization of colour TV technology in Shanghai, initiated by the municipal government, is a case in point. The joint R&D activity has involved the development of customized ICs and the employment of CAD technology. By 1990, the city was capable of exporting not only TV sets but also SKD/CKD kits and production lines.

Thus the regulatory mechanism of the Chinese economy has become more complex than that before 1989. Evidently, the economic agents learn. Many local authorities which were seriously prone to short-termism in the 1980s have in recent years exhibited changes (SCESR 1992). Insofar as they exhibit both profit-seeking behaviour and developmental concerns, their economic role appears to be close to the concept of 'institution'. In other words, they are capable of undertaking activity from a long-term development perspective, and are willing to do so under certain circumstances. This is akin to the character of Japanese and South Korean business groups, and thus might be explained by the theory of internalization: where the market fails, institutions replace it by internalizing the transactions.

There remains the need to consider the conditions under which local authorities would behave in an entrepreneurial way, rather than being overwhelmed by the profit-seeking, short-termist objective. In the case of the Chinese TV industry, it is believable that the entrepreneurial activities of the early 1990s were undertaken against the background of increasingly acute market competition. But whether they validate the notion (of transaction cost theory) of the market as the creator of efficient institutions, or the Schumpeterian notion that entrepreneurship is peculiar to certain institutions and is not reducible to the market, remains unclear.[4]

THE FAILURE OF THE SEMICONDUCTOR SECTOR

In contrast to the relative success of television production, the development of the Chinese semiconductor industry over the past decade can be judged a failure. One indicator is that, in 1991, China produced 170m ICs, which was far less than the target of around 400m once laid down in the Seventh Five-Year-Plan (1986–1990) of the MEI.

Concerning technological development, amid the completed transition among world semiconductor manufacturers to the mass production of large and very large-scale integrated circuits (LSI and VLSI), in 1991, China did not produce in batch VLSI, while LSI accounted for merely 11 per cent of its total output volume. Also, while the processing technology of most world-class manufacturers had reached a standard of as large as 6 inches or above wafer size and as small as 1 micron or below linewidth, the dominant Chinese products were 3 inches wafer size and 3–5 microns linewidth. Compared with South Korea and Taiwan, both of which had leap-frogged from a low technological level into VLSI production within just a few years, the development of the Chinese semiconductor industry has been very sluggish.

It is true that the sluggish development has been largely ascribable to constraints from the demand side. Above all, in view of the fierce competition in the world market, it is impossible for China to follow the Japanese and South Korean models – mass-production of standardized chips, exporting at aggressively low prices. Moreover, unlike the case of TV sets, there has not existed a vast and rapidly expanding domestic market for semiconductors. But, the reality is more complex. In 1991, domestic sales of ICs did exceed 600m units. The Chinese enterprises, while facing serious under-utilization of capacity, supplied just 20 per cent of domestic sales. This indicates some deeper problems with the industry.

Table 6.6 Semiconductors Output Volume: Discretes and Integrated Circuits, 1975–93(m)

	National total			*Enterprises under MEI*				
	(a) discretes	*(b) ICs*	*(b)/(a) %*	*(a) discretes*	*(b) ICs*	*(c) ASICs*	*(b)/(a) %*	*(c)/(b) %*
1975	315	6	1.8	292	6	...	2.0	...
1980	696	17	2.4	677	17	...	0.2	...
1981	996	13	1.3	928	13	2.6	1.4	20.3
1982	675	14	2.0	634	14	2.5	2.1	18.5
1983	822	26	3.2	734	24	7.5	3.2	31.8
1984	1176	42	3.5	1054	39	18.1	3.7	46.1
1985	1479	64	4.3	1304	53	30.2	4.1	56.9
1986	1099	57	5.2	990	46	33.0	4.6	72.2
1987	1514	95	6.3	1379	77	56.7	5.6	73.9
1988	1977	132	6.7	1876	93	71.9	4.9	77.7
1989	2480	132	5.3	2395	96	78.6	4.0	81.5
1990	3338	108	3.2	3111	97	80.7	3.1	83.6
1991	5469	170	3.1	5058	118	100.0	2.3	84.5
1992	6719	161	2.4	5647	143	...	2.5	...
1993	9506	201	2.1	6906	178	...	2.6	...

Sources: ZDGN 1986, p. IV-164; ZDGN 1994, p. III-59; ZGJTN 1994, pp. 52–3; ZJDGN-D 1990, p. II-18; ZJDGN-D 1992, p. II-30; ZJN, various issues.

One problem is the mis-match between the output of the industry and the demand structure. Chinese industry normally needs 20 000 specifications of ICs, of which domestic producers supply only 3 000. This stems from the development pattern of short-termism of the electronics industry. The imports of assembly lines from a wide range of foreign brands in downstream sectors, notably TV sets, have fragmented the market for semiconductors. The rapid changeovers of downstream products, induced by consumption demonstration effects, tend to threaten established ICs production capabilities with becoming obsolete.[5] Because the demands for individual specification of ICs are far too small to support economies of scale, domestic production becomes unviable. Meanwhile, there are some deficiencies which can be regarded as mainly supply-side problems. In particular, most of the imported products which fill the supply-demand gap are LSI and VLSI. Both of these are related to the technological backwardness and lack of economies of scale of the industry.

To analyze the institutional framework that has governed the development depicted above, I start with the State. The two 'national conventions on ICs development strategy', held in 1986 and 1989, respectively, have resulted in an industrial policy encompassing four measures:

(a) to build up several big ICs production bases, which would enhance scale economies
(b) to prioritize the development of ASICs
(c) to concentrate resources on several key R&D projects
(d) to promote the acquaintance of 1 microns technology in top research institutes, 3 microns among flagship enterprises, and 5 microns among the rest in 1986–90.

In addition, starting from 1987, there has been a broader industrial policy for the electronics industry at large. This focuses on targeting: to accelerate the development of the four sectors of ICs, computers, computer software and programme-controlled telephone switching. The measures adopted include sales tax exemption, income tax reduction, R&D subsidies, and tariff exemption for imports of equipment and instruments.[6]

The outcome of the industrial policy has been mixed, but unsatisfactory on the whole. The development of ASICs production, which increased its share in the total from 20 per cent in 1981 to 85 per cent in 1991, is in line with state promotion. Correspondingly, there has been a remarkable development of design activity, especially CAD technology. Both of these signify the search for a development strategy that takes into account the structural constraints of limited size (and fragmented demands) of the domestic market and fierce competition in the world market of standardized chips. The concentration of resources on key R&D projects has also yielded remarkable results. Of particular note is the success in turning out a large-scale ICCAD three-tier system (integrated circuits computer-aided design, combined with testing and manufacturing functions, that is ICCAT and ICCAM) and breakthroughs in VLSI technology – the 1.5 microns processing technique and 1M read-only memory chips, all in 1991. The significance of the breakthroughs is that, in line with traditional practice, they help to ease Western restrictions on transfer of technology of advanced levels below what China has attained.

With regard to commercialized production, the outcome has been disappointing, The State industrial policy has not been effective in pulling the industry out of the vicious circle of financial predicament *cum* sluggish technological progress. Thus, apart from the sluggish development mentioned above, another overall indicator is the dismal financial performance of the industry: in 1991, its (pre-tax) profit-to-sales ratio registered a depressing –2.1 per cent, compared with that of 8.1 per cent for the electronics industry as a whole.

A number of factors can be identified as accounting for the dismal outcome, one of which being thc continuous fragmentation of the industry. By 1991, there were in total 23 ICs manufacturers which, despite being less than the figure of 42 in 1985, are far too many in comparison with other countries. Most of them did not reach the minimum efficient scale. An official survey reveals that, in 1989, only three had individual capacity exceeding 20m ICs, one exceeding 10m and a further six reaching 5m. Moreover, the capacity was seriously underutilized: of these ten, only five had actual output exceeding 5m. The State industrial policy has not been effective in rationalizing the industrial structure. Another crucial factor is that the plan of constructing several flagship production bases during the Seventh Five-Year-Plan period did not materialize. One indication is that the output concentration ratio of the top enterprises did not increase substantially. For the three localities where the new production bases are designated to be situated in – Jiangsu, Shanghai and Beijing – the share in China's total ICs output volume was 46 per cent, 15 per cent and 9 per cent, respectively, in 1987. By 1991, the respective share declined to 33 per cent, 13 per cent and 6 per cent (and further to 30 per cent, 11 per cent and 5 per cent, respectively, in 1993). Amid the expansion of the total, this trend of decreasing concentration indicates an increase in the utilization of production lines previously left idle. But it also indicates slow progress in the expansion of capacity of the designated production bases.

Especially worth noting is the case of Huajing Microelectronics Group, the country's largest ICs producer. In late 1990, in addition to its original capacity of 26.5m ICs, another 23.5m was installed. This project was in fact a major constituent of the Seventh Five-Year-Plan for the semiconductors industry. In the meantime, however, the enterprise has seen its output share in the national total shrinking. In 1988, it produced 35m ICs which represents 38 per cent of the national total. By 1991, the volume decreased to 33m and the share was reduced to 28 per cent. The same situation persisted: the volume increased to 46.5m in 1993, but the share decreased to 26 per cent. Of the various factors accounting for the decreases, a major one was lack of investment which resulted in capacity constraint and weak capability in product innovation. By 1994 when Huajing finally completed its Seventh Five-Year-Plan project, which involved one billion yuan of investment and added to it the capacity of another 50m 2–3 microns VLSI chips a year, eleven years had already passed – the completion date was, in fact, initially planned to be in 1990. Yet Huajing is already an exceptional case in the sense that the State has channelled the bulk of its investment in the semiconductor industry to this project.

From the above depiction, it is possible to make some assessments on the role of the State. On the whole, the failed development of the semiconductor industry must imply the failure of the State. This is so despite the achievements in basic research, the development lead of ASICs, and the assimilation and diffusion of imported technology among enterprises. After all, it is the economic performance of the industry that counts.[7] Unlike the experiences of Japan, South Korea and Taiwan, where state financing has catalyzed the inflows of private resources, in the case of China's semiconductor industry, the State policy has not led to the same response from enterprises and local authorities. The State has been unable to govern a market whose regulation tends to discourage semiconductor production in China, due to the huge investment and high risk involved. Yet in view of the transitional nature of China's economic system, where Schumpeterian entrepreneurship is underdeveloped – or, where the market is imperfect for coping with high risk and huge investment – the State is supposedly the sole agent capable of remedying the market failure. The failure of State intervention was largely due to insufficient financing. The policy of prioritizing ICs production was not put into effect, as the major portion of State investment in the electronics industry in 1986–90 was channelled to the TV component sector, which was added to top priorities of the electronics industry Seventh Five-Year-Plan in 1987, in addition to or indeed replacing for the original targets on ICs, computers, software and telephone switching.[8]

In 1992, the State authorities announced the launch of a VLSI project. Targets include the industrial production capacity of megabit-or-above access memories, 32-digits mini-computer CPU, and ICs for digital TV and HDTV, with processing technology of 0.3–1 microns. Significantly, as a constituent of the economy's overall Eighth Five-Year-Plan (1991–5), the project would involve State investment of more than 2bn yuan, which almost doubles the fixed-asset value of the ICs industry. This reflects a recognition of the need for increasing State investment. But, again, the reality is complex. Amid the latest round of rapid economic growth during 1992–94, which exerts heavy pressure on State finance (this is peculiar to Chinese industrialization where the burden of curing the bottlenecks arising from unbalanced growth often falls on the State, see Chapter 3), the project has been effectively shelved. By the summer of 1993 when a half of the Eighth Five-Year-Plan period had already passed, there was still no sign of State investment forthcoming.[9] Evidently, just like its encouragement of consumption at the expense of accumulation (and squeezing the technologically advanced sector) in the 1980s, the State is also prone to short-termism – at times.

A related assessment can be made concerning the role of local authorities, using the development of semiconductor production in Shanghai as an illustration. For two decades it was China's ICs manufacturing centre, but by the early 1980s, the city's output volume accounted for half the national total and its product specifications accounted for 70 per cent. The position deteriorated sharply from the mid-1980s, mainly due to insufficient investment and competition of imported products. The annual output volume has stayed at 10–15m ICs, resulting in the reduction of its share in the national total to 11 per cent in 1993. Also, the Shanghai semiconductor industry, which encompassed four specialized enterprises – No. 5, No. 7, No. 14 and No. 15 Radio Works – and another 17 smaller factories and research institutes, has continuously suffered from financial losses. In the face of this dismal situation, a conspicuous move of the municipal authorities is to set up two Sino-foreign joint ventures. These have involved Philips of Holland and ITT of Belgium, with the former incorporating No. 5 and No. 7 Radio Works and the latter incorporating No. 14 Radio Works. Based on this, the authorities hope to pull the industry out of the predicament of technological backwardness *cum* financial losses.

Viewed closely, however, this move of establishing joint ventures to substitute for the existing enterprises carries a strong implication of market-oriented import substitution. For the two European TNCs have their own logic of operations. As the Shanghai authorities are well aware, the technology which the TNCs transferred to the joint ventures is by no means advanced by world standard. And the products turned out by the joint ventures would be mainly supplied for the domestic market, not for exports. Clearly, the target of the authorities is to reap the profits from the foreseeable booms in domestic sales, or at least to get rid of the financial burden of keeping the industry alive, not the developmental concern of catching up. Given the fact that the semiconductor industry has extremely high capital-intensity, and hence the developmental concern is indeed very demanding (far more demanding than the indigenization of TV technology), it is natural that the Shanghai authorities choose the easy way of market-oriented import substitution. Yet it is precisely at this point that the limitation of the economic functioning of local authorities, as entrepreneurial institutions, is exposed.

By 1994, the completion of the Huajing project and the formation of another four flagship manufacturers – Shaoxing Huayue, Shanghai Beiling (ITT), Shanghai Philips and Shougang-NEC, the latter three being Sino-foreign joint ventures – largely transformed the Chinese ICs industry. The dominant technology now reached 2–3 microns in mass production and 0.8–1.2 microns in research institutes. Based on the capability, the MEI authorities set the targets of helping the manufacturers to apply 0.8–1.2 microns technology in mass production within the Eighth Five-Year-Plan period (1991–95) and 0.5 microns technology by the end of the century. The output volume is also planned to reach 1bn ICs by the year 2000. However, in view of the continued lack of State investment, and, more important, the fact that the flagship firms are now dominated by TNCs, the future prospects for the development of the industry are very uncertain.

CONCLUDING REMARKS

If, just like the depiction in Chapter 3, the future prospects for Chinese industrialization rest on either a drive of secondary import substitution or another consumption revolution, some important lessons can be derived from our analysis of the experience of the electronics industry. In the first place, because of the need to import foreign technology on a scale far greater than that of the 1980s, the development pattern of short-termism is unlikely to be feasible anymore. The fragmentation of the industry and miniaturization of firm scales, and, more generally, the development along the line of market-oriented import substitution (and hence the focus on import-dependent, downstream manufacturing activities), are likely to result in the industry becoming a drag on the economy, rather than assuming the role of a dynamic industry.

In this regard, it is arguable that a developmental State is indispensable. This is especially true for the development of the high capital-intensity and high risk semiconductor industry, and perhaps that of HDTV as well, which goes well beyond the visions or planning horizons of purely profit-seeking economic agents. But precisely because the industrialization in the 1990s is characterized by capital deepening, the task of promoting dynamic industries to become internationally competitive is likely to be so demanding as to outstrip the capacity of the State as well (in the same way as the failure of State intervention in the development of semiconductors in the 1980s). Unlike the 1980s when State intervention barely managed to correct the economy from exhausting the impetus of growth, in the 1990s, the development of Schumpeterian entrepreneurship must come to the play. In other words, the future prospects rest on the reform of the institutional framework, particularly the reform of large scale, mostly State-owned enterprises.

7 The Motor Industry: Institutional Reform and Development

THE ENGINE OF GROWTH OF THE 1990s

The massive expansion of the Chinese automobile industry in the first half of the 1990s is both spectacular in its own right and symbolic of the change in the country's industrialization pattern. Put in a nutshell, this change involves two prominent features. The first is the exhaustion of dynamism of the engine of growth of the 1980s: the so-called 'new' (consumer durables) industries which, having expanded enormously for a decade, face a significant slowdown in growth. The second is the rise of a range of technically sophisticated industries, which either serve investment demands or produce consumer durables of even higher grades (for an analysis of China's changing industrialization pattern in the 1990s, see Chapter 3; see also SCESR 1992).

At a glance, the contrast between the 'new' and the 'old' has already been evident. In 1994, China produced 1.4m motor vehicles, 2.8 times the output volume of 1990. If we combine both domestic outputs and the volume of net imports, which indicates the size of domestic demands, the ratio is around three (Table 7.1). In contrast, for the three items representative of the 'new consumer durables' of the 1980s – colour TV receivers, household refrigerators and washing machines – the output volume in 1994 is 1.6, 1.7 and 1.7 times, respectively, of that of 1990. Put another way, against the background that the average annual growth rate of the country's gross industrial output during this period registers 24 per cent, that of the output volume of motor vehicles registers 29 per cent and the three consumer durables 12–14 per cent. Taken together, these exhibit a trend that is quite different from the 1980s when the output volumes of the 'new consumer durables' grew far faster than both that of motor vehicles and overall industrial output.

Put in a broader context, as is analyzed in detail in Chapter 3, one can speculate that the prospects for Chinese industrial development in

Table 7.1 China's Motor Vehicles Output Volume, 1978–94 (thousands)

	(a) Output volume		*(b) Net imports*		*(a) + (b)*	
	All vehicles	*Cars*	*All vehicles*	*Cars*	*All vehicles*	*Cars*
1978	149.1	2.6	24.4	0	173.5	2.6
1979	185.7	4.2	32.1	0.7	217.8	4.9
1980	222.3	5.4	51.0	19.6	273.3	25.0
1981	175.6	3.4	40.8	1.4	216.4	4.8
1982	196.3	4.0	15.8	1.1	212.1	5.1
1983	239.9	6.0	23.3	5.8	263.2	11.8
1984	316.4	6.0	85.8	21.7	402.2	27.7
1985	443.4	5.2	352.3	105.8	795.7	111.0
1986	372.8	12.3	145.9	48.3	518.7	60.6
1987	472.5	20.9	61.1	30.5	533.6	51.4
1988	647.0	36.8	90.1	57.4	737.1	94.2
1989	586.9	28.8	76.3	45.0	663.2	73.8
1990	509.2	42.4	56.6	34.1	565.8	76.5
1991	708.8	81.1	28.9	54.4	737.7	135.5
1992	1 061.7	162.7	203.6	1 47.6	1 265.3	310.3
1993	1 296.8	229.7	300.5	1 82.2*	1 597.3	411.9*
1994	1 353.4	350.0	272.9	1 70.2	1 626.3	520.2
Average annual growth (%)						
1979–90	9.6	23.4	5.3	42.4	9.1	28.4
1990–4	27.7	69.5	48.2	49.5	30.2	61.5

Sources: ZQGN 1991, pp. 124, 536–7; ZQGN 1995, pp. 87, 89; RMRB, 31 May 1993, p. 1, and 8 February 1994, p. 2; CD-BW, 20–26 February 1994, p. 8; CLES, various issues; CTR, various issues; ZQB, 22 February 1995, p. 1; CD, 30 March 1995, p. 5; JJRB, 1 March 1995, p. 2.

Notes: Output figures are from the auto industry authorities and are slightly smaller than figures from the State Statistical Bureau, the latter being 714.2, 1082.2, 1310.1 and 1402.0, respectively, for the years 1991–4. Output figures include CKD production, which accounted for 6.7% of total output in 1986, 7.7% in 1990 and 13.5% in 1994. Net imports figures also include CKD kits, and thus there is some degree of double counting. The 1978–90 net imports figures are slightly understated, because whilst the imports figures are customs statistics those of exports are compiled by the the foreign trade authorities which include motor vehicles sold in the domestic market but in foreign currencies. *According to ZQB, 21 February 1994, p. 2, taking into account smuggling, China in fact imported 405 000 cars in 1993.

the 1990s rest on either a newer round of 'consumption revolution' (just like the 1980s) or a drive of 'secondary import substitution' (development of investment goods industries). This speculation can be gauged by looking at the trends of consumption, investment and outputs at the aggregate level. The severe slump of market sales during 1989–91 exposes the problem of weak consumption demand. Subsequent rapid industrial growth since the second half of 1991 has also been clearly investment-led. It can thus be further hypothesized that the prospects for Chinese economic growth rest on dramatic improvement of the international competitiveness (in terms of productivity) of its industry, which is crucial for sustaining the massive imports of high value-added machinery and industrial inputs. The fact that the economy is increasingly liberalized, and with it the increase in the competitive pressure from foreign firms even in the domestic market, further necessitates the improvement of competitiveness. This is especially the case for technically sophisticated, high value-added industries in which China does not have the international comparative advantage and hence must rely on institutional mediation to narrow down the competitive gap from the world advanced level.

With the recognition of the strategic position of China's automobile industry, this chapter aims to analyze the specific forms and effects of market and institutional regulation thereof. The focus is on the interplay between the State, local authorities, enterprises and transnational corporations in shaping the development of the industry and the reform of its institutions. We begin with a brief review of the state of development of the industry in the world context, drawing possible lessons from the experiences of other latecomer auto industries. The depiction below draws on Altshuler *et al.* (1984), Bloomfield (1991), Cusumano (1985), Dankbaar (1990), Dicken (1992), Gwynne (1991), Hill (1989), Jenkins (1985), Jones (1988), Schmitz and Carvalho (1989), Watanabe (1987) and Womack *et al.* (1990).

The automobile industry is perhaps the best known classic case of modern mass production. With the potential of mass consumption which fosters the generation of learning effects in the production process, as well as strong linkages with a wide range of industries, the industry acquires a strategic position in the economy. However, the fact that it often involves huge fixed investment poses the question as to whether late-industrializing countries should participate in its development. A number of considerations have been raised in the relevant literature for answering this question.

Regarding the world context, the motor industry is one of the most internationalized. Since the 1970s, there has been a trend of industrial relocation by TNCs to the developing world, especially in search for market outlets. As a consequence, the distribution of the industry in the developing world has been very uneven: it concentrates in regions that have, or are close to, large markets. Thus, the development of late-comer auto industries has taken place mainly in the context of import substitution. The industries are largely characterized by fragmentation and miniaturization, because the target of TNCs is the protected local markets, not the competitive world market. At another level, this pattern of international distribution reflects some peculiarities of the world auto industry. These include the oligopolistic market structure and the persistence of excess capacity which result in extremely acute market competition, with the competitiveness tending to hinge upon continuous technological and organizational innovation. Overall, it is extremely difficult for latecomer auto industries to enter the world market, and, as is particularly evident in Latin America and Eastern Europe (before 1989), there has been the danger of the established production capability becoming technologically obsolete.

It is in East Asia that the development of late-comer automobile industries has been successful. The experiences of Japan and South Korea suggest a model of development that is essentially a combination of import substitution (ISI) and export-oriented industrialization (EOI). For ISI, it is often pointed out that when the two countries started developing their industries the capital intensity involved was well beyond their international comparative advantage, and deliberate promotions by the State had to come into play. In the case of South Korea, which started much later, the State ruthlessly restricted the number of automobile firms in the pursuit of economies of scale. This alleviated the problem of fragmentation and miniaturization that is characteristic of late-comer motor industries. As for EOI, the Japanese and South Korean model is known for 'pre-mature' exports. From the beginning the capacity, and actual output volumes, of the industries have far exceeded domestic sales. This has exposed the automobile producers to world market competition, thus pressing them for efficient performance and technological progress.

The fact that the Japanese and South Korean automobile industries have become cost and quality competitive *vis-à-vis* traditional US and European firms within a fairly short period of time indicates some further features of the model which go beyond the combination of ISI and EOI. The most prominent is the innovation capacity of the production system. A study in the early 1980s indicates that, of the cost advantage of Japanese car-makers *vis-à-vis* the American, technological lead played an insignificant role and wage differentials accounted for only 25 per cent of the total, whilst 'management systems and techniques' accounted for 63 per cent. This organization efficiency arose from renowned operational practices like quality circles and just-in-time (*kanban*) supply lines.

At a deeper level, however, it has been revealed that the Japanese and South Korean operational practices in fact involve a whole set of preconditions in the institutional respect: collective work organization, long-term employment relationship, subcontracting relations, bank-dominated financial system, and so on. It is in this connection that there has emerged a vast literature on the contrast between 'Toyotism' (after Toyota) and 'Fordism' (after Ford), a contrast that signifies the transition of the world techno-economic paradigm from mass (rigid) production to flexible production. This contrast is summarized by the term 'lean production', which proposes that, whereas Fordism assumes that there is only one best way of doing things, Toyotism emphasizes multiple ways and that there is always a better way of doing things. The essence of the Japanese system is thus considered to be continuous innovation based on collective learning.

From the above depiction, it appears that the automobile industry especially embodies the essence of late industrialization. This is associated with the economic dynamism it exhibits, the patterns of international division of labour it has undergone, the various development paths that have been witnessed, and the changing production organization that has attracted extensive studies. All these lie at the heart of the late industrialization literature.

THE DEVELOPMENT PATH

In the seminal MIT study on the world motor industry, Womack *et al.* (1990, p. 268) state: 'for the moment the Chinese industry is still focused inward, pursuing a combination of extremely rigid mass production in its two volume-production complexes in Changchun (No. 1 Auto Works) and Hubei (No. 2 Auto Works) and inefficient low-quality craft production in about a hundred additional vehicle-manufacturing facilities spread throughout China.' At a glance, this statement seems true enough. By 1990, the Chinese automobile industry was composed of around 2 600 manufacturers, including 117 assembly plants, of which only two (the No. 1 and No. 2, or First and Second) had annual output volume exceeding 100 000 vehicles and another four (Beijing Jeeps, Beijing Light Commercials, Nanjing Auto and Shanghai Volkswagen) exceeding 10 000. In view of the sharp contrast with its Japanese counterpart, whose per worker output volume of vehicles were almost 70 times greater, the industry stood at almost nowhere in the world scene.

The reality is more complex. The situation depicted above, while indicating the technological backwardness of China's motor industry, cannot be fully relied upon in gauging its development potential. The potential appears to be more favourable, if we see it in historical perspective. It is noted that, by 1992, the fixed assets of the entire industry were valued at 36bn yuan, which is equivalent to just one-twelfth of that of General Motors of the USA, one-eighth of Japan's Toyota or one-quarter of Germany's Volkswagen (FZRB, 10 January 1993, p. 1).[1] This is a major source of the productivity gap. With the industry being placed at a strategic position, and hence earmarked or actually allocated massive investment, the situation is certain to change in the 1990s.

Likewise, it is noted that, at least up to 1990, the country's developmental condition had not been especially supportive of the industry. Even in the booming years of 1978–90, its pace of growth was not much faster than the industrial sector at large – on average 15 per cent and 12 per cent per annum, respectively (Table 7.2). In view of the experience of China's electronics industry, which – starting from almost nowhere – has taken a big step to international competitiveness after a decade of rapid growth (see Chapter 6), it seems appropriate to say that the motor industry is also likely to greatly change its technological backwardness should the development conditions turn to its favour. The conditions have indeed changed enormously since 1990. In value terms, the industry grew at an average annual rate of 39 per cent in the subsequent four years to 1994. It is reasonable to believe that this trend is to persist throughout the 1990s.

Thus, what remains of paramount importance concerning the development prospects for the Chinese automobile industry is the institutional aspect. According to the studies of the world motor industry which we have reviewed above, in the context of acute competition and rapid technical change, the institutional dimension is indeed crucial in promoting the development of the industry. In particular, for late-comer motor industries, the ability of rapidly improving organizational and technical efficiency (especially in the form of assimilating and improving upon imported technology) is the primary factor which they can rely upon for catching up with the world advanced level. As

Table 7.2 GVIO of All Industries, the Auto Industry and Auto LMEs, 1978–94 (100m yuan)

	(a)	*(b)* x	*(c)*	*(b)/(a)* %	*(c)/(b)* %
1978	4 237	64		1.5	
1979	4 681	74		1.6	
1980	5 154	86		1.7	
1981	5 400	71		1.3	
1982	5 811	82		1.4	
1983	6 460	118		1.8	
1984	7 617	168		2.2	
1985	9 716	274		2.8	
1986	11 194	213	111	1.9	52.4
1987	13 813	273	156	2.0	57.2
1988	18 225	407	247	2.2	60.1
1989	22 017	481	298	2.2	62.0
1990	23 924	493	319	2.1	64.8
1991	28 248	...	...	...	...
1992	37 066	...	...	...	...
1993	52 692	1 792	1 511	3.4	84.3
1994	76 909	2 183	1 973	2.8	90.4
Average annual growth (%)					
1978–90	12.0	15.0	—		
1990–4	24.0	38.6	49.6		

Sources: Table 5.9; ZQGN 1983, p. 146; ZQGN 1988, pp. 109–11, 123; ZQGN 1991, p. 118; ZQGN 1994, p. 53; ZQGN 1995, p. 61.

Notes: Value figures at current prices; growth rates calculated at 1980 constant prices. (a) = all industries, including village-and-below enterprises; (b) = auto industry; (c) = LMEs of auto industry.

for China, a further requirement on the institutional framework is to cure the problems of fragmentation of the industry and miniaturization of plant scales.[2]

In this connection, it is helpful, briefly, to trace the sources of the fragmentation and miniaturization of the industry back to the pre-reform era. In a nutshell, two terms can be highlighted: technological and economic dualism. The former refers to the co-existence of firms with vast variation in technological sophistication, financial performance and, above all, production scale. This stems from the peculiarity of China being an underdeveloped Soviet-type economy. In the face of severe resource constraints, yet constantly under the political-economic pressure of the world market, the State has had to concentrate resources on building up strategic industries and projects. The result is a situation where some relatively advanced enterprises exist side-by-side with a vast number of backward plants.

The technological dualism has been transformed into a planning-market economic dualism under reform. The development of the Chinese motor industry in the reform era has been especially shaped by local authorities and enterprises. The complementary relationship between the centrally-managed sector and the locally-managed sector has changed to one of competition. By gaining autonomy and with the marketization of operations, most large- and medium-scale enterprises, which traditionally formed the backbone of the centrally-managed sector, have also gradually consolidated their own interests. In this context, these economic agents have both the power and incentive to expand high- and quick-returns industries. The persistence of 'auto boom' in the domestic market and the availability of Western technology have further fuelled the expansion. Thus, there have been several nationwide drives to import technology from Western TNCs. At one point in the mid-1980s, there were 17 Chinese parties simultaneously negotiating with Honda of Japan and 22 others with Ford of the USA to seek for the supply of technology for producing sedan cars. In a total, around 200 sets of technology were imported in the 1980s, of which most were assembling projects. Table 7.3 gives the major projects of auto technology imported in the 1980–90s.

The focus of the newly-empowered economic agents has been on short-term profits. Hence, in the second half of the 1980s, the situation of fragmentation and miniaturization did not improve. It was rather exacerbated because of the availability of imported technology. One indication is that the concentration ratio of the top five motor manufacturing enterprises actually declined from the very low level of 26 per cent in 1987 to 25 per cent in 1990, the period when the 'auto boom' of the 1980s reached its peak (Table 7.4).

Conspicuously, however, the abrupt jump of the concentration ratio to reach 50 per cent in 1992 indicates that a massive scale of structural adjustment has taken place in the recession period of 1989–91. Given that the situation of fragmentation and miniaturization has been seriously hampering the productivity of the industry, this is no small achievement. A question thus arises: what has accounted for the structural adjustment? Specifically, given our depiction of the detrimental effects of the institutional framework, we need to ask what changes have taken place in this respect that result in the observed twist. In the meantime, as will be depicted below, along with the tendency towards rationalization,

Table 7.3 Imports of Foreign Auto Technology in the 1980s–90s: Major Projects

	Project imported	*Foreign supplier*	*Nature of business*	*Contract signing year*
Beijing Jeep Corp.	Cherokee jeeps	AMC/Chrysler, USA	joint venture	1984
Jiangxi Auto Works	Isuzu light vehicles	Isuzu, Japan	licensing	1984
Shanghai VW Ltd.	Santana cars	VW, Germany	joint venture	1985
Guangzhou Peugeot Ltd.	cars & trucks	Peugeot, France	joint venture	1985
Nanjing Auto Works	Iveco S-series light trucks	FIAT, Italy	licensing	1985
Qingling Motor Co.	Pickup trucks	Isuzu, Japan	licensing	1985
Tianjin Minibus Works	Charade cars	Daihatsu, Japan	licensing	1986
Inner Mongolian Second Auto Works	33-07 series heavy trucks	TEREX, UK	licensing	1987
Jinbei Auto Ltd.	Hiace light vehicles	Toyota, Japan	licensing	1987
	S10 light vehicles	GM, US	joint venture	1991
Heavy Vehicle Corp.	Steyr heavy-duty vehicles	Steyr-Daimler-Puch, Austria	licensing	1988
Beijing No. 2 Auto Works	130-series light vehicles	Isuzu, Japan	licensing	1988
FAW	Audi & Jetta cars	VW, Germany	licensing	1988
	Golf cars	joint venture		1990
Southwest Isuzu Auto Co.	Isuzu light vehicles	Isuzu, Japan	licensing	1989
SAW	Citroën ZX cars	Peugeot, France	joint venture	1990
Zhengzhou Nissan Co.	Pick-up trucks	Nissan, Japan	joint venture	1993
Hainan Mazda Co.	Pick-up trucks	Mazda, Japan	joint venture	1993
Guizhou Auto Works	Subaru cars	Fuji Heavy Ind., Japan	licensing	1993
Liuzhou Minibus Works	Alto cars	Suzuki, Japan	licensing	. . .
Jiangnan-Hunan Auto Co.	Alto cars	Suzuki, Japan	licensing	1993
Chang'an Machinery Works	Alto cars	Suzuki, Japan	joint venture	1993
Sanjiang-Renault Auto Co.	Trafic minibuses	Renault, France	joint venture	1994
Nanfang Auto Co.	Multi-purpose vans	Mercedes-Benz, Germany	joint venture	1995
Jiangxi-Isuzu Auto Co.	Vans and cars	Ford, US	joint venture	1995

Sources: press reports and official releases.

Table 7.4 Concentration Ratio (by Sales Revenue) of China's Auto Industry, 1987–94 (m yuan)

	1987	*1988*	*1989*	*1990*	*1991*	*1992*	*1993*	*1994*	*1994/1987 (inc.)*
(1) Industry	27 409	41 300	43 364	44 192	64 674	95 000	183 430	185 348	6.76
(2) Top 5 firms	7 215	10 465	10 894	11 056	20 353	47 727	86 584	88 580	12.28
(2)/(1) (%)	26.3	25.3	25.1	25.0	31.5	50.2	47.2	47.8	

Sources: GLSJ, 1989, no. 1, p. 133; 1989, no. 5, p. 103; 1990, no. 5, p. 69; 1991, no. 5, p. 78; 1992, no. 4, p. 98; 1994, no. 5, p. 106; CTR, October 1993, p. 14; JJCK, 28 January 1993, p. 2; ZQGN 1991, p. 154; ZQGN 1994, p. 97; ZQGN 1995, pp. 41–50, 61, 120; ZQB 4 November 1994, p. 1; ZGN 1992, p. 264.

the production system of China's motor industry has also exhibited significant improvement in flexibility (that is the ability of quick response to the demand for improving product quality and upgrading output-mix). This is especially true for volume motor manufacturers.

The observed trends towards rationalization and flexibility put the statement made by Womack *et al.* (1990), which is a widely-held and reasonable view, to the test in the context of the 1990s.[3] These underscore the need for unravelling the specific forms and effects of the changes in the institutional respect. The following sections aim to undertake this task by analyzing the respective roles of the state, local authorities, enterprises and TNCs.

STATE INDUSTRIAL POLICY AND SECTORAL MANAGEMENT

The motor industry is the first among China's industries to have a formal State industrial policy, first formulated in 1987 and later largely revised in 1994. The evolution from the first version of the policy to the second reflects the authorities' changing thinking about the prospects for the development of the industry, as well as the requirements on the part of State intervention. More important, however, the 1994 version was a result of the contradictions and problems that have emerged after the implementation of the 1987 policy.

The 1987 automobile industrial policy emphasizes three points:

(a) to shift the product-mix of the industry from commercial vehicles to passenger cars
(b) to boost economies of scale by restructuring the industry from the situation of fragmentation and miniaturization towards concentration
(c) to seek for technology transfer by inviting the participation of TNCs.

A major measure that follows these emphases is the stipulation to restrict the number of auto firms. Especially for cars, the number of manufacturers is restricted to six – the 'big three plus small three', the former referring to the three Sino-foreign joint ventures of Shanghai Volkswagen, First Auto Works Volkswagen (FAW-VW) and Second Auto Works Citroën (SAW-Citroën), while the latter being the two joint ventures of Beijing Jeep (which involves Chrysler) and Guangzhou Peugeot plus Tianjin Minibus which produces Daihatsu-designed cars under license. Together with Heavy Vehicles Corp. and four designated production bases of light commercials, these enterprises would form the backbone of the industry and were expected to carry forward the line of development as laid down in the policy.

It turns out that the implementation of the 1987 motor industrial policy has not resulted in marked achievements. The performance of the industry was especially bad in the recession period of 1989–91. This indicates that the demand-side condition in the domestic market is yet to be sufficiently supportive for the industry to become an engine of growth. Technical progress has also remained sluggish. Despite the auto booms in 1986–8 and 1992–4, enterprises have tended to invest in capacity expansion – for reaping short-term profits from the buoyant sales – instead of technological upgrading. The foreign investors that have a stake in the 'big three plus small three' Chinese motor enterprises, mostly European TNCs, have exhibited the same inclination, and have been reluctant to transfer new technology.

The latest round of rapid growth in 1992–4 has again given rise to the proliferation of small scale projects, mostly assembly plants which rely heavily on foreign supply of parts and components. For car production, the number of producers has increased to, at least, ten. In addition to the designated six, there have emerged another four – Chang'an, Guizhou, Hunan-Jiangnan and Liuzhou, all sourcing technology from Japan – which established themselves first and pressed the State leadership to grant approvals. A number of non-approved entries have also been reported. In the case of light commercials, despite the stipulation to focus on the four production bases of FAW, Beijing, Nanjing and Southwest, by 1992, the number actually increased to around 50.

A major reason for the ineffectiveness of the 1987 automobile industrial policy is the lack of State investment. In fact, despite its being placed at a strategic position, the industry received only 1.5 per cent of total State investment in Chinese industry available during 1986–90, compared with that of 2.8 per cent in the previous five years. In the two years of 1991–2, State investment in the industry was valued at 6bn yuan, which is equivalent to a mere 12 per cent of the planned total for the Eighth Five-Year-Plan period of 1991–5 (JJRB, 14 January 1993, p. 1). The lack of State investment has led to long periods of congestion of the construction of the designated production bases, which in turn resulted in the vast demand-supply gap when the new round of 'auto boom' in the domestic market erupted in 1992–4. It is also because of this that the State leadership has not had the economic means to direct the massive investment by local authorities along the line of rationalization.

The institutional framework has also proved to be ineffective in enforcing the policy. In 1987, in line with the market-oriented reform, the state-enterprise intermediary China National Automotive Industry Corporation (CNAIC) was rescinded. This entity, which has undergone several times of rescission and reinstatement since its creation first in the 1960s, is a central managing agent characteristic of the Soviet-type industrial system. Its rescission once again in 1987, together with the transfer of 39 flagship motor plants previously affiliated to it to local authorities, reflects the belief that simply by means of the market mechanism the development of the industry would be directed along the prescribed line. But this has proved to be overly optimistic.

The 1994 auto industrial policy was adopted to reverse the unfavourable trends. It involves two salient features: to rationalize the production system and, less definitive but still of paramount importance, to promote domestic demand. It indicates that the situation of the buyers of cars being mainly Government bodies and State-owned enterprises is insufficient for sustaining the expansion of the industry, and that the prospects rest on private consumption. It thus clearly stipulates that local and ministerial authorities should not continue to hinder the private purchase of cars. Nevertheless, the policy also exhibits some caution, and does not set out any concrete measures. It just indicates that measures would be formulated in the future, in accordance with changes in the market and development of the industry. An important step that has already been taken, however, is permission to develop a 'family car'. In a joint study presented to world-class auto TNCs in late 1994, the State Planning Commission and CNAIC (which was reinstated in 1990) predict that by the year 2010 China would produce 3.5m cars and the total stock of cars in the country would reach 22m, of which around two-thirds would be privately owned. This study has aroused considerable debate in China, but what is especially important is that it has resulted in the state's giving the 'go-ahead' for the development of a family car. There follows the scramble among Chinese car-makers and the concerned TNCs, which have formed or have sought to form strategic alliances with the former, for constructing projects for family car production.

As far as rationalization of the production system is concerned, four problems are identified as main obstacles. These are:

(a) the proliferation of plants and the fragmentation of investment
(b) the chaotic situation of local and ministerial authorities' approval of projects
(c) the duplicated imports of technologically backward projects
(d) the sluggish development of backbone enterprises and the slow progress in the local contents of foreign-designed vehicles which these enterprises produce.

Accordingly, the 1994 industrial policy stipulates that the central Government is to support the development of a few 'national champions'. For enterprises that turned out 300 000-plus vehicles in 1995, and allocated no less than 3 per cent of sales revenue for R&D, the State supports their expansion to a scale of more than 600 000 by the end of the century. For enterprises turning out 150 000-plus vehicles in 1995, and having 2.5 per cent revenue for R&D, the target is to expand to a scale of 300 000. In this way, it is hoped that, by the year 2000, there would be 2 to 3 enterprises of the first category and 6 to 7 of the second. The combined sales of the biggest three manufacturers of passenger cars, commercial vehicles and motorcycles will each account for 70 per cent of the sector total. The State would also promote agglomeration among the enterprises, so that by the year 2010 there would be 3 to 4 automobile industrial concerns that are internationally competitive.

A range of measures would be adopted to achieve the targets. Starting from 1996, enterprises belonging to the two categories would enjoy the following preferential treatments:

(a) exemption of adjustment taxes in fixed-asset investment
(b) priority arrangements in shares issuing and listing in stock markets
(c) priority access to bank credits
(d) priority arrangements in utilizing foreign investment
(e) upon approval, the financial companies of the enterprises can expand the scope of business.

Besides, enterprises producing economy cars or key parts can have access to policy loans. The state would also subsidize joint R&D activities by enterprises in vital projects. In conjunction with the rationalization measures, the State seeks to direct the construction of new projects. The policy stipulates that the vehicles produced by new joint ventures or licensing plants must be of world advanced technological standard. These enterprises must set up in-house R&D centres that are capable of developing new models, must treat equally foreign and locally-produced parts and components, and must balance their foreign exchange requirement by exporting their products. For joint ventures that manufacture vehicle bodies or engines, the stake of foreign investors must not exceed a half.

To prevent the possible anti-competition behaviour of established auto firms that might result from the protective measures, the new policy stipulates that the ban on new joint ventures and new cars and light commercials projects would come to an end by 1996. This represents a shift away from the 1987 policy which emphasizes protection. The emphasis is now on constructing a market structure that is characterized by 'effective competition', that is competition among a small number of big firms.

Turning to the institutional dimension, it seems clear from the experience of 1987–93 that the enforcement of an industrial policy aimed at concentration and selectivity requires substantial direct State involvement. Once again, CNAIC was reinstated in 1990. But unlike previous zigzags between decentralization and recentralization, whereby the economic power shifted, basically, between the central and local authorities, the emphasis was now on State management over the sector instead of enterprises. To achieve the target model of 'state regulating the market, the market coordinating enterprises', there is the emphasis of forming industrial concerns, which has in fact been experimented with since the mid-1980s and is considered to be in line with the Japanese and South Korean model of development.[4]

By the early 1990s there were, in total, eight industrial concerns of this kind, of which the most important were the three assigned the privileged status of 'separate planning': the Jiefang Group based on FAW, the Dongfeng Group based on SAW, and Heavy Vehicle Corp. (HVC) based on three heavy-duty trucks manufacturing plants in Shandong, Sichuan and Shaanxi. By 'separate planning' it refers to a package of preferential treatments granted by the central authorities, which cover the allocation of bank credits, raw materials and fuels, the prioritized access to foreign technology, and more operational autonomy. This has in some ways proved to be effective in fostering the rationalization of the production system.

A case in point is the development of HVC. Dating back to the early 1980s, the State decided to develop heavy-duty vehicles production by setting up a conglomerate, which was to be based on three existing manufacturers and to carry out technical renovation through the introduction of the Steyr-series technology from Austria. The formation of HVC resulted in a new firm structure: the imported Steyr technology was dissociated into 14 sub-projects and was distributed to 12 enterprises situated in five provinces, and the group was composed of 15 closely-linked enterprises and another 22 collaborating enterprises. This posed a difficult task for management. In this regard, the 'separate planning' status of HVC played a crucial role. Because of its prioritized access to resources, especially the imported Steyr technology, in the course of the assimilation of the technology, the group was basically able to articulate with its members in the development along the line of specialized division of labour.

But access to imported technology alone was insufficient to consolidate HVC. As the group in fact accounted for almost 60 per cent of heavy vehicles production in China, individual members had strong incentives to build up self-sufficient production systems. Meanwhile, the 'separate planning' arrangement was also intended to be transitional in nature. It was adopted as a means to promote the gradual evolution of enterprises from the traditional status of administratively-managed units to pure economic entities. The privileged position granted to enterprises was expected to wither over time.

Thus in the course of assimilating imported technology, HVC was encouraged by the state to experiment with various measures of organizational restructuring. These included the building up of centralized institutions like financial company, trading company and R&D centres, all aimed at maintaining the structure of a conglomerate. By 1990 when the group completed the assimilation of the Steyr technology and started batch production (the local content of products being 67 per cent that year), it was capable of centralizing the management of its core members (for profile of HVC, see Table 7.5). The foundation of the achievements, however, has been fragile. While the production system of Steyr vehicles has developed along the line of specialized division of labour among member enterprises, those of the old products are still self-contained within individual members. This reflects a problem at the deeper level of property rights: that the substitution of the Steyr system for the old systems has been resisted by the members because it involves a redistribution of interests among them and between the HVC centre and individual members.

Table 7.5 Profile of Heavy-duty Vehicles Corporation (HVC), 1982, 1987, 1990, 1993

	1982	*1987*	*1990*	*1993*
(a) Number of member enterprises	13	15	17	16
% of national total	0.53	0.64	0.65	0.65
(b) Output of completed vehicles (000s)	6.5	7.9	10.9	18.2
% of national total	3.32	1.66	2.14	1.41
(c) GVIO at current prices (bn yuan)	0.44	0.89	1.81	5.94
% of national total	5.40	3.27	3.67	3.32
(d) GVIO at 1980 constant prices (bn yuan)	0.45	0.75	1.52	4.07
% of national total	5.19	3.21	4.44	3.94
(e) Employment (year-end, 100 persons)	469	576	644	719
% of national total	4.98	4.27	4.11	3.72
(f) Net fixed-asset value (year-end, m yuan)	457	628	927	1 425
% of national total	7.93	5.50	5.15	4.02
(g) Registered working capital (year-average, m yuan)	270	686	788	3290*
% of national total	6.57	6.25	3.76	3.58
(h) Total realized profit + tax (m yuan)	—	55	94	416
% of national total	—	1.37	2.19	2.33
(i) Profit rate = (h)/[(f)+(g)] (%)	—	4.21	5.45	8.83
Proportion to national total	—	0.23	0.50	0.63
(j) Output volume per worker = (b)/(e) (unit)	0.14	0.14	0.17	0.25
Proportion to national total	0.67	0.39	0.52	0.38
(k) Output value per worker = (d)/(e) (100 yuan)	96	130	236	567
Proportion to national total	1.04	0.75	1.08	1.06

Sources: ZQGN 1983, pp. 133–7, 145, 154, 219–21; ZQGN 1988, pp. 111–12, 127, 155–8; ZQGN 1991, pp. 95, 124, 160–3; ZQGN 1994, pp. 50, 73, 107–8.

Note: Figures cover the layer of 'closely cooperating' member enterprises of the corporation. 'National total' refers to the auto industry as a whole. *Year-end figure.

By late 1993, in line with the new drive of enterprise reform whereby eight Chinese industrial concerns were restructured to become truly internally integrated entities, the HVC centre was designated by the State to take full control over member enterprises, that is to become the representative of the State-owner, in order to be able to complete the rationalization. This unexpectedly threw the group into crisis. One of its core members, Jinan Auto Works, announced its withdrawal from the group. What made the issue even more complex is that this move was backed by the local authorities concerned. This gave rise to the controversy on the ownership relations between the central Government and local authorities over State-owned enterprises. The development of HVC was thus at a crossroads between disintegration, and with it the breakdown of the system of specialized division of labour, and further integration. This, symbolically, puts the entire Chinese enterprise reform to the test.

From the depiction above, it is evident that the 1987 State industrial policy has failed to achieve its target of rationalizing the production system. The failure is associated with the short-sightness of the State – it has not invested sufficiently to induce the development of the industry along the prescribed lines. The resurgence of investment fervour of local authorities (which worsens the fragmentation) and the tremendous expansion of vehicles imports under the 1992–4 'auto boom', therefore, represent the price paid for this short-sightedness. In the institutional respect, the practice of sectoral management based on the formation of industrial concerns has seemed to be more successful. This is evident in the case of HVC, whereby State intervention has played an indispensable role. To appreciate the point more fully, we need to conceive what would have happened in the absence of State intervention. This leads us to examine the role of local authorities, the agents which have been particularly influential in shaping the development of the industry.

LOCAL AUTHORITIES, TNCs AND TECHNOLOGICAL DEVELOPMENT

The trend towards fragmentation and miniaturization is a consequence of short-termism – the focus on short-term profits instead of, and often at the expense of, long-term development. The several nationwide drives to import foreign technology suggest that the behaviour of local authorities, which have become profit-oriented under reform, is strongly prone to short-termism. Nevertheless, it is observed that there have been cases where local authorities also exhibit the capability and willingness to pursue long-term development. This is particularly evident in the assimilation of imported technology.

Technological development stands as a major emphasis in both the

1987 and 1994 versions of the automobile industrial policy. This has led to the policy of differentiated tariff rates on imported vehicles and CKD/SKD kits, the rationale being to encourage increasing local contents of vehicles assembled by domestic manufacturers. In the case of cars, by 1992, the tariff on whole vehicles imports was 180–220 per cent, while that on CKD/SKD varied according to the local contents of the vehicles: 50 per cent tariff on vehicles with 40 per cent local contents, 48 per cent on those with 60 per cent local contents, and 32 per cent on those with 80 per cent local contents (SJXB, 24 November 1992, p. 2. As part of China's drive to re-enter the GATT/WTO, the tariff rate on imports of whole vehicles was reduced to 110–150 per cent in 1994; see RMRB, 27 February 1994, p. 2). The 1994 policy further revised the differentiated tariff rates for different levels of local content: three levels for passenger cars (40 per cent, 60 per cent and 80 per cent), commercials and motorcycles (30 per cent, 70 per cent and 90 per cent), and major auto parts (50 per cent, 70 per cent and 90 per cent). Thus, for instance, in the case of Shanghai VW's Santana cars, whose local contents exceeded 80 per cent by 1993, imported parts and components have enjoyed tariff exemption since that year. For other cars whose local contents fall in the range of 60–80 per cent, the tariff rate on imported parts is 32 per cent; and for local contents of 40–60 per cent and below 40 per cent, the tariff is 48 per cent and 50 per cent, respectively. The policy also sets the minimum scales for new projects: 150 000 for passenger cars of engine capacity below 1600 cc, 100 000 for light trucks, 50 000 for vans, 10 000 for heavy-duty trucks, and 200 000 for motorcycles of engine capacity below 150 cc.

A second aspect of the emphasis on technological development concerns selecting TNCs for co-operation. The main criterion is the willingness of technology transfer. It is noted that, over the 1980s, those selected were mainly European firms. In contrast, before 1990, the Chinese authorities had at least twice turned down the proposals from Japanese car-makers for setting up joint ventures. This contrast indicates some difference in investment strategies. Unlike the Japanese and the Americans, the production networks of European car-makers are far less globalized and as a result their shares in major world automobile markets are far smaller. In the face of the competitive pressure from their rivals, European car-makers are thus eager to extend their reach. This accounts for their higher willingness of technology transfer. In the case of Volkswagen's investment in Shanghai, for instance, the German car-maker went so far as to announce that the plant is not just to target at the Chinese market but rather to be a bastion for the company to compete against Japanese and South Korean auto firms in the whole East Asian market.

This announcement can be deceptive. The Santana B-series technology that the Shanghai plant receives is, after all, simply not internationally competitive; the German firm itself has rather abandoned the model since the mid-1980s. In mid-1991, VW announced to set up a joint venture in Taiwan, a move which contradicts its previous investment strategy in China in two ways. First, as VW made it clear, with the establishment of the joint venture in Taiwan, the plants in mainland China (Shanghai VW and FAW-VW) were no longer to be its sole producers for the East Asian market – they were rather assigned to produce mainly for the Chinese domestic market. Yet previously VW had claimed to give all future orders obtained from the whole Asian market to the two plants. Second, the joint venture in Taiwan was planned to be an assembler. Yet in 1990 VW had invited a Taiwanese motor group to set up parts-producing plants in the mainland for boosting the export competitiveness of the two mainland plants. Now that VW plans to establish an assembly plant in Taiwan, the target appears to be shifting towards the promotion of competition, not co-operation, between the two sides of the Taiwan strait. This case thus indicates that technology transfer from TNCs is not automatic. It rather involves continuous, tough bargaining.

Given the specific environment of the Chinese State leadership's attempt to promote technological development on the one hand, and the ambivalence of TNCs on the other hand, the mediation of local authorities becomes crucial. In this regard, the performance has been disappointing. The persistence of the drive to import turnkey plants and to construct new ventures indicates it. Because most of the plants are small in scale and turning out products with little local content, the cost of production has remained high. In the case of Shanghai VW, the production cost in 1993 was around 85 000 yuan per car (and domestic sales prices around 200 000 yuan), which at official exchange rate almost doubled the sales prices of the same car in the world market. Yet Shanghai VW is already the country's biggest car-maker, with output volume exceeding 100 000 cars and local contents reaching 80 per cent in 1993 (XFSB, 12 May 1993, p. 1). As for the newly-approved car-maker, Chang'an, which turned out around 10 000 cars with 20 per cent local contents, the domestic sales price was almost four times higher than that in the world market (ZQB, 2 July 1993, p. 1; ZJMB, 13 July 1993, p. 3). It is reported that, in 1992, Shanghai VW confronted heavy pressure from other car-makers when it tried to

Table 7.6 Local Contents of Foreign-designed Cars and Jeeps, 1987–94 (percentages)

		1987	*1988*	*1989*	*1990*	*1991*	*1992*	*1993*	*1994*
Shanghai VW	Santana cars	12.6	12.8	31.0	60.1	70.4 (68.0)	75.3	80.5	85.8
FAW	Audi-100 cars	—	—	6.7	13.7	21.9 (24.2)	30.7	42.6	62.5
	Jetta cars	—	—	—	—	3.0	. . .	7.0	40.5
SAW/DAC	ZX cars	—	—	—	—	—	—	4.0	15.2
Beijing Jeep	Cherokee jeeps	18.7	30.0	35.5	43.5	44.8 (55.6)	57.3	60.5	80.2
Guangzhou Peugeot	PU-505 cars	6.3	11.8	12.8	27.6	29.8 (39.6)	51.5	61.7	62.1
Tianjin Minibus	Charade cars	9.7	11.2	40.7	40.7	45.7 (50.5)	47.4	61.8	83.8

Sources: ZJGN 1994, p. I-13; ZQGN 1991, pp. 495, 510; ZQGN 1995, p. 59; press reports.

Note: Figures in parentheses are official planned targets.

reduce its delivery price by 20 per cent: because of the high cost of production, the others simply could not afford to reduce prices by such a margin. This move was finally prohibited by the motor industrial authorities (ZGSB, 30 June 1993, p. 1).

Table 7.6 shows the local contents of major models of cars produced or assembled in China. The figures indicate the progress in assimilating imported technology. In general, with the exception of Shanghai VW, the progress is unsatisfactory: it took five years for the local contents to reach 50 per cent, while in the world market the product life cycle of a model is normally around 3–4 years. It is, therefore, no wonder that most of the China-produced cars are of outdated models.

The Shanghai cars, for instance, are of the second-generation Santana-series, while in its German mother company the production of the fourth-generation was already underway by the early 1990s. For Chang'an, the cars which it has been assembling since 1991 are of the first-generation Alto model, whilst the technology-supplier, Suzuki of Japan, has been turning out third-generation products. Perhaps most conspicuously, in 1991, Guangzhou Peugeot bought from its French investor the entire production line of Peugeot-505 cars, the model being what had just been abandoned by the latter.

The assimilation of imported technology is no easy job. The quality standard of parts and components is much higher than domestically-designed vehicles. The supply of parts and components is also not normally economical for lacking economies of scales. To accomplish the job successfully it is necessary to transcend the consideration of short-term profitability. It is precisely in this respect that the different orientations of enterprises and the concerned local authorities are evident. A case in point is the comparison between Shanghai VW and Guangzhou Peugeot, which both started producing cars in the same year. It is clear from Table 7.6 that, regarding the achievement in local contents, the Shanghai plant has far outperformed its Guangzhou counterpart. By 1991, the local contents of Shanghai cars reached 70 per cent, while the Guangzhou cars remained at 30 per cent which was well below the planned target. This indicates the different orientations of not only the enterprises but also the local authorities, because of the fact that the progress requires the co-operation of large number of parts-producers normally situated in the same localities. For Shanghai VW, in 1990, of its 60 per cent local contents, 18 per cent were parts from in-house production while the remaining 42 per cent from outsourcing. Likewise, for Guangzhou Peugeot, in 1989, of the 13 per cent local contents 10 per cent were contributed by parts from outsourcing. The achievement in local contents thus requires the assistance of the concerned local authorities.

Achievement in local contents, or mastering the production techniques, is perhaps just the first step in the indigenization of imported technology. In view of the experiences of successful latecomer automobile industries, especially Japan and South Korea, what seems more crucial is the formation of the capability to independently develop new technology. In this regard, the Chinese industry is even more backward. Despite the imports of around 200 sets of technology over the 1980s, by 1992, the industry was still incapable of developing new models of vehicles to a reasonably high standard. It was also unable to develop key parts like the gear box, engine and vehicle body. Amid the increased competition in the domestic market, the enterprises and local authorities have also exhibited different orientations in this respect. While most of them tend to rely on further imports, there are phenomenal attempts to develop new models based on the indigenized technological capability, Shanghai VW's collaboration with VW's Brazilian subsidiary (Autolatina) to modify and improve the Santana model being a case in point. This project has been supported by the Shanghai government which, in the face of the German car-maker's unwillingness to further transfer technology, has invited (and encouraged by providing cheap credits) several TNCs to participate in the technological upgrading of 23 main parts-producers (SGJB, 11 June 1993, p. 1; ZQB 16 June 1993, p. 1).

To summarize, regarding technological development, which is crucial for late-comer auto industries to catch up with the world competitive level, it seems that China's institutional framework is inadequate. The short-termism of enterprises and local authorities is incapable of accomplishing the task. Indeed, precisely because of the sacrifice of short-term profits, as well as heavy investment and enormous risk, the task is likely to outstrip the atomistic firm in general. The regulation of the market would fail to achieve it, and hence State intervention is indispensable if the industry is to become an economically beneficial sector. But Chinese local authorities are far more complex than the notional atomistic firm. The fact that some of them have shifted to emphasize long-term development, instead of short-term profits, indicates that they are changeable. Likewise, the wave of mergers and agglomerations in 1989–92, which was largely initiated by local authorities and have largely increased market concentration, indicates the entrepreneurial facet of their orientation. Finally, due to their strong links with enterprises, local authorities in general have long-term commitment to their development. This, as will be discussed in more detail below, can be conducive for the organizational flexibility of enterprises.

FIRM ORGANIZATION: RATIONALIZATION AND FLEXIBILITY

The restructuring of the internal organization of the firm is a neglected issue in the literature of studies on Chinese economic reform. Economists tend to conceptualize firm-level reforms in a simplistic framework of enterprise autonomy versus bureaucratic intervention. However, in the literature of studies on the world market, the organization of the production system has been placed at the centre of competitiveness. This is especially the case for the motor industry, where flexibility on top of cost-price competitiveness is most crucial. In this connection, it is worth noting the statement in the MIT study (Womack *et al.* 1990) that China's two volume-production auto firms, FAW and SAW, are engaged in 'extremely rigid mass production'. The question arises as to whether this is a valid characterization of the reality, and to what extent the situation has changed under reform.

This section attempts to unravel the implications of the organizational restructuring in terms of rationalization and flexibility. This will be done by paying a close look at SAW and the industrial concern Dongfeng Auto Corp. (DAC) of which SAW is the core member. The restructuring has been carried out mainly at three levels. First, at the shopfloor level, the organization of work has evolved around the principle of fostering a continuous flow of work-in-progress. This has culminated in the application of the *yigeliu* (continuous flow) practice, a modified version of the Japanese *kanban* (just-in-time) system, at 50-plus production lines. The practice sequences the production process in a way aiming at continuous flow of semi-finished products, synchronization of speed among different processes of the same sequence, and zero buffer stocks.

Second, regarding the restructuring of SAW's intra-firm divisions and workshops, the evolution has eventually converged to the M-form (multi-divisional) model. This is a three-tier structure comprising the headquarters responsible for strategic decision-making, product- or geographically-differentiated divisions as profit centres, and workshops as cost centres. The rationale is not just to strike a balance between the pre-reform system of centralized management and the decentralized system which SAW adopted in the early reform period of 1979–86 – the latter was felt unsatisfactory because the divisions and workshops, as profit centres and with autonomy of investment and trading with entities outside SAW, tended to focus on their own profitability while disregarding the proper operation of SAW as a whole. The M-form structure is aimed rather at fostering both competition (for investment funds and the promotion of divisional staff) among divisions and co-operation among workshops of the same production chain.

Third, at the inter-firm level, the formation of DAC is aimed at expanding SAW's production capacity, and promoting specialized division of labour for the group as a whole. The group is composed of three layers. The first, the closely-co-operating layer, comprises several core members that are under centralized management over allocation of investment, output sales and production planning. The second, with 30-plus enterprises, is linked together by means of cross-shareholding or joint venture. The third layer is composed of more than 200 members which join together mainly through subcontracted parts-production. In the early years of its formation, and in line with the status of 'separate planning', the conglomerate was encouraged by the State authorities to set up internal financial companies, unified trading companies and R&D centres. By 1993, in line with the general policy of enterprise reform, SAW was empowered to be the representative of the State-owner, that is being responsible for the management of the assets of core members. The first layer has become a fully-integrated entity, and SAW was formally renamed DAC.

The effect of the various measures of organizational restructuring depicted above can be gauged with reference to the observed performance of SAW and DAC (Table 7.7 gives some basic indicators). At one level, we can focus on the immediate effect of the application of individual measures. It is reported that the application of the *yigeliu* practice on universal-joints production, for instance, has led to a remarkable improvement in productivity: increasing output volume by 29.8 per cent, reducing the number of workers by 28 per cent, reducing product stocks by 79.9 per cent, reducing the ratio of sub-quality products by 68 per cent, and reducing machine stoppage hours by 84 per cent.[5] It is also reported that the formation of DAC has resulted in SAW's ratio of outsourcing of parts increasing from 25 per cent in 1981 to more than 50 per cent by 1990.

At a more comprehensive level, the flexibility which DAC (that is, the transformed SAW) exhibited in 1993 in response to severe market fluctuations is especially revealing. In the second quarter of that year, the company found that the demand for five-ton trucks to which it planned to devote the bulk of its production capacity rapidly diminished, whereas that for six-ton and eight-ton engineering vehicles suddenly surged. The company decided to switch the output-mix, which took it some two weeks to accomplish. The output volume of six-ton and eight-ton vehicles in the first half of the year registered 28 600 units, as opposed to the original planning of 10 000 units for 1993 as a whole. This switching brought DAC a net increase in sales revenue of 2bn yuan. Then, entering the third quarter, there came a new state austerity drive which instantly led to the fall in demand for all kinds of ordinary vehicles. In response, DAC scaled down the production of ordinary vehicles from the traditional level of 80–90 per cent of its total outputs to a low level of just 27 per cent. It turned to the production of special-purpose vehicles. By October, 75 different varieties of special-purpose vehicles were being produced in the company. Amid the abrupt shrinkage of market demand for motor vehicles, in 1993, DAC's total sales revenue reached 12bn yuan (up 22 per cent) and output volume 178 000 units (up 16 per cent) (RMRB, 4 January 1994, p. 2). The simultaneous achievement of output expansion and changes in output-mix thus indicates the organizational flexibility which the company has built up.

The fact that SAW has exhibited considerable flexibility along with the realization of economies of scale is significant not only for its competitiveness but also for revealing the effects of the institutional reforms with which it has experimented. It is clear that flexibility-

Table 7.7 Profile of the Second Auto Works and Dongfeng Auto Corporation, 1982, 1987, 1990, 1993

	1982		*1987*		*1990*		*1993*
	DAC	*SAW*	*DAC*	*SAW*	*DAC*	*SAW*	*DAC*
(a) No. of member enterprises	9	—	7	—	5	—	11
% of national total	0.37	—	0.30	—	0.19	—	0.44
(b) Output of completed vehicles (000s)	53	51	124	100	121	105	231
% of national total	27.0	26.1	26.3	21.1	23.8	20.5	17.8
(c) GVIO at current prices (bn yuan)	1.23	1.11	3.72	3.20	5.11	4.51	19.6
% of national total	14.9	13.5	13.6	11.8	10.4	9.2	11.0
(d) GVIO at 1980 constant prices (bn yuan)	1.50	1.36	3.37	2.88	3.77	3.31	8.33
% of national total	17.3	15.6	14.4	12.3	11.0	9.7	8.06
(e) Employment (year-end, 100 persons)	705	531	849	708	924	791	1252
% of national total	7.48	5.63	6.30	5.25	5.90	5.05	6.48
(f) Net fixed-asset value (year-end, m yuan)	1475	1380	1844	1700	2129	1903	3241
% of national total	25.6	23.9	16.2	14.6	11.8	10.6	9.1
(g) Registered working capital (m yuan)	365	261	786	584	2173	1416	8225
% of national total	8.89	6.34	7.20	5.32	10.4	6.8	9.0
(h) Total realized profit + tax (m yuan)	—	—	932	—	645	—	2446
% of national total	—	—	23.1	—	15.1	—	13.7
(i) Profit rate = (h)/[(f)+(g)]	—	—	35.4	—	15.0	—	21.3
Proportion to national total	—	—	1.97	—	1.37	—	1.52
(j) Output per worker = (b)/(e) (unit)	0.75	0.96	1.47	1.41	1.31	1.32	1.85
Proportion to national total	3.61	4.63	4.20	4.01	4.03	4.06	2.75
(k) GVIO per worker = (d)/(e) (100 yuan)	213	256	397	406	409	418	665
Proportion to national total	2.31	2.77	2.29	2.35	1.87	1.91	1.24

Sources: Same as Table 7.5; ZQGN 1983, pp. 534–5; ZQGN 1988, pp. 692–3; ZQGN 1991, pp. 658–9.

Note: 'National total' refers to the auto industry as a whole. DAC figures cover the layer of 'closely cooperating' member enterprises of the corporation.

orientated practices like *yigeliu*, which by lifting buffer stocks implies rigorous demand for on-site quality control and problem-solving, cannot be successfully instituted without the active participation of major agents of the production system, particularly the workers. SAW's policy of promoting quality circles and encouraging workers to raise management suggestions also seems to have been helpful. The formation of the DAC union, the first enterprise-union permitted in China, is likely to have been conducive for promoting a co-operative atmosphere and hence for motivating workers. Yet what seems the most fundamental is the long-term commitment of workers. In this regard, the rigidity of the employment relationship – a central feature of China's enterprise system even after reform – can be seen in a more favourable light. The soft financing of the bank and the protection of local authorities, another two central features, which, by cushioning enterprises from the threat of severe short-term fluctuations in the market environment, can also be helpful.

Meanwhile, however, the adoption of the M-form model of firm structure and the formation of conglomerates in the pursuit of rationalization cannot have taken place without the mobility of productive inputs. This needs to overcome the fragmentation of the industrial system associated with the domination of local authorities. In this regard, the contractual management system which has been applied to Chinese enterprises since 1987 seems to have been helpful. The system has helped to institutionalize the interests of enterprise on the one hand, and to define the Government–enterprise relationship in more formal, contractual terms on the other hand. The policy of adopting corporatization of State-owned enterprises as the main approach of reform during 1991–5 seems to further shape the Government–enterprise relationship along the same lines. The relatively successful organizational restructuring so far, in short, suggests that an appropriate balance (however fragile) between the two principles of flexibility and rationalization under reform has been reached.

CONCLUDING REMARKS

In this chapter, we have depicted the experience of the Chinese motor industry as a mix of achievements and shortcomings in a developmental sense, and an even more complicated mix of market and non-market features at the institutional level. Is there any way to thereby draw some lessons on market and institutional regulation? If we focus on the three issues of rationalization, flexibility, and technological development, it is arguable that a series of institutional features which can be considered as market imperfections have in fact been indispensable in bringing about the achievements.

Regarding State intervention, the argument is that the regulatory mechanism which would have emerged if the State gave up its intervention has indeed proved to be incapable of accomplishing the three tasks. Nevertheless, the achievement of rationalization through the wave of mergers and agglomerations in 1989–92 is largely attributable to the efforts of local authorities. The achievement of flexibility also appears to be largely a consequence of intra-firm organizational restructuring. These achievements have been underpinned by institutional features such as the rigidity of the employment system, the strong link between local authorities and enterprises, and the soft-financing of the bank – all being at odds with the principle of the 'pure' market.

Nevertheless, the series of institutional features also have their detrimental facets. Indeed, as is discussed in detail in this chapter, the serious shortcomings widely evident in the Chinese automobile industry have been endemic to the same institutional framework. All the three economic agents, the State, local authorities and enterprises, have been in one way or another prone to short-termism. The most important lesson which can be drawn from the experience of the industry, therefore, is that future economic reform needs to strike an appropriate balance between the achievements and the shortcomings. People who uphold the notion of the 'pure' market are likely to deny such a possibility. But the achievements so far, in terms of rationalization, flexibility and technological development, indicate that there is no *a priori* reason to believe that this is impossible in the first place.

8 Conclusions

The process of Chinese industrialization under reform is a complex one. It is not collapsible to any all-embracing concepts, such as the market. What we have witnessed is the interaction of various forces which have shaped the past outcomes and will continue to shape the future prospects. Specifically, our analysis points out that the growth pattern over the past 16 years was based on structural changes where the rise of the 'new' consumer durables industries and the massive imports of Western technology played a central role. This pattern has produced contradictions, being favourable to growth on the one hand while giving rise to structural problems on the other hand. The problems have not only undermined the sustainability of the growth but also tended to produce unfavourable effects on long-term development, especially in terms of the international specialization of the economy.

In this connection, the mediation of State strategy and institutions has been crucial in determining the final outcomes. The 1988–9 cyclical crisis and the subsequent predicament during the retrenchment period reflect the failed side of the mediation. The sustained growth and increasing competitiveness of the economy for the 1978–94 period as a whole, despite the serious shortcomings, reflect the successful side. The combination of the two sides means vast uncertainty for the future prospects which will face far more severe challenges under the new pattern of industrialization. On the whole, by explicitly taking a development criterion to analyse the growth experience, our study should be more appropriate than the mainstream approaches which start from, and basically stop at, the abstract conception of the 'pure' market: that is attributing everything good to the market and everything bad to the observed 'imperfections', thus placing the market in a reified position of non-falsifiability.

Turning to the dimension of systemic reform, the reified nature of the market-centred approaches is as apparent. Commenting on the finding of substantial productivity growth of a sample of SOEs under survey, Gordon and Li (1991, p. 204), for instance, assert: 'thus, decentralized decision making, even with badly distorted incentives, raised productivity in the state sector.' Likewise, Fang (1993) complains that many TVEs in industrialized coastal provinces are mimicking the institution and behaviour of SOEs. The implication of this mode of thinking is two-fold: first, the actual economic outcome would have been better if the imperfections were cleared away, and, second, future reforms should follow more closely the principles of the 'pure' market. But, even if this approach is accepted, it is likely to be felt simplistic by people who want to make sense of the complexity of the experience. For one thing, how can we account for the fact that SOEs have outperformed non-SOEs in a number of respects in booming times, but have been outperformed under recession? And what about the extremely uneven development within State industry? Any exposition which does not explain these phenomena is unlikely to provide convincing inference for the two central issues arising from the Chinese experience: (a) the impetus behind past growth and the prospects for future growth; and (b) the role of market and institutional regulation during this process of economic development.

In contrast, in the preceding chapters, we have attempted to explicitly integrate the analysis of enterprise reform with that of the pattern of growth. Our emphasis is on technical change, through collective learning. This involves the premise that organizational rigidity, albeit in some ways being detrimental to allocative efficiency, can have the virtue of facilitating productivity growth and flexibility in the product market. The crux is to strike an appropriate balance, and to institute an appropriate form of rigidity. It is from this perspective that the series of institutional reforms and organizational restructuring in LMEs are seen to be significant. But the actual significance (the net effects of the rigidity) depends on the growth pattern. Specifically, the realization of the merits of organizational rigidity is dependent on the expansion of market demand, the continuous upgrading of product-mix and the possibility for 'borrowing' (technology). Thus, for LMEs, the productivity growth associated with their organizational rigidity has been basically able to compensate for their higher operation cost. This is less true in the recession period when the contraction of market demand, and hence production scale, reduces the benefits of learning and raises costs. It is also not true for small scale SOEs which, while having similar institutions as LMEs, benefit far less from collective learning because of lacking economies of scale. This explains the observed contrast of performance between SOEs and the organizationally more flexible non-SOEs, and between LMEs and small scale SOEs.

From the above depiction, we can then turn to assess China's economic reform, its achievements and problems. To the extent that the reformed enterprise system has exhibited the flexibility to accommodate the series of organizational restructuring and entrepreneurial behaviour which we have analyzed, the achievements cannot be overlooked. It should be noted that, in the debate over the transformation of the Soviet-type economic system, even dissident writers (the self-proclaimed evolutionary economists) consider the system as not reformable – because of its systemic feature of public ownership, it cannot accommodate organizational innovations like the adoption of the M-form model and just-in-time practice which are regarded as the key to the success of economic development of the advanced capitalist countries. The Chinese experience, however, indicates that this view is premature. In the meantime, the experience refutes such ill-founded assertions as 'China's reform has been least successful in the urban state sector, especially in large and medium-sized enterprises despite their importance' (Lee 1993, p. 179; see also Fischer 1993).

This said, however, we must add that the achievements so far have been fragile and the reformed Chinese enterprise system is far from being capable of guaranteeing future success in productivity growth and market competition. Indeed, the fragility has been clearly exposed by the dismal performance of SOEs since the recession period of 1989–91. This performance, in turn, has been caused by deficiencies of the enterprise system. Specifically, the three central issues which I have analyzed – soft-budgeted behaviour, Government intervention, and labour immobility – are far from reaching appropriate settlements. The re-emergence and intensification of *ad hoc* bargaining in the conclusion of the second round of the contractual management system indicates the problems. As is revealed by a number of studies (for example Du 1992; Du and Guo 1993), enterprises are in general weak in coping with severe market fluctuations and as a result they have exhibited the tendency of returning to seek for Government protection in times of adversity. This implies serious obstacles for the development of Schumpeterian entrepreneurship, whereby firms are capable of overcoming the regulation of the market in the pursuit of long-term development.

The foremost difficulty for future reform is that it is inextricably interwoven with the condition of economic strength of the enterprise. Indeed, one precondition for the emergence of Schumpeterian entrepreneurship is that firms are strong enough to shape the market. Note that the dismal performance of SOEs under recession also has its roots in the unfavourable policy regime which they face – the State's squeeze of their capital accumulation and hence the vast insufficiency of investment in technical renovation, which has seriously weakened their capability to withstand market fluctuations. Thus there is no easy way for the reform, and the price must be paid for the development of entrepreneurship. Future reform of the enterprise system inevitably involves the broader context of restructuring the financing regime, the State taxation system and the social security system.

To summarize the propositions and findings of this study, the following points can be noted:

(a) that China's rapid economic growth over the past 16 years has been based on a structural change associated with the explosive expansion of the 'new' consumer durables industries, a growth pattern that is akin to market-oriented import substitution
(b) because of the foreign exchange 'gap' and demand constraint, the growth pattern has tended to undermine its own sustainability, and it is especially in this connection that institutional regulation has played an indispensable role
(c) based on the afore-mentioned growth pattern, Chinese industrial enterprises of all ownership sectors have markedly improved their measured input-output efficiency
(d) in particular, large-and-medium scale enterprises which represent the core of Chinese industry as well as China's Soviet-type economy have contributed no less than market-orientated township-and-village enterprises to overall economic growth
(e) the good performance of large-and-medium enterprises has been based on a series of institutional reforms which combine both market and non-market features, thus forming a reform model that is far different from (indeed contradictory to) what has been prescribed by orthodox economists for the transformation of the Soviet-type economic system.

These propositions, to be sure, are preliminary, and more empirical evidence – on top of what is compiled in the previous chapters – is needed to substantiate them. In particular, the efficiency performance of Chinese enterprises is an issue of continuous debate, and I claim no superiority for my findings over those of others, including the 'big bang' group. But, what I have focused upon is the performance of State-owned enterprises, especially large-and-medium enterprises *relative to* the rest of Chinese industry, particularly township-and-village enterprises. Part 2 of the book shows that the performance of LMEs has been comparable to, if not superior than, TVEs. To dismiss the performance of State-owned enterprises thus necessarily implies dismissing that of the rest of the economy as well. Of course, by using certain notional constructs (for example the measurement of total factor productivity by some economists before 1988, a tradition that has been revived by 'big bang' writers like Woo *et al.* 1994), it might be possible to argue that Chinese industry as a whole has performed badly. But this is unlikely to be a credible argument. After all, China's economic development under reform, despite all its shortcomings, is outstanding in international comparison, especially when compared with countries of the former Soviet bloc which have adopted the 'right' reform strategy.

This said, however, I do not mean that there has been no significant failure in the Chinese experience. Nor does the study say that the Chinese economic system has reached a point where future success is guaranteed. On the contrary, the preceding chapters reveal many failures over the past 16 years, and that the foundation of the achievement so far has been fragile – particularly in terms of the development of entrepreneurship in enterprises, which is central in determining the future prospects for Chinese industrialization. The task which this book undertakes, therefore, is rather to clarify the specific forms and effects of market and institutional regulation in the past experience, and to thereby point out some directions for future economic development and reform (note that in prescribing policy for the future most economists including the evolutionary writers tend to move back to the notional 'pure' market, urging China to complete its transition to the market, to establish the 'full market system', and so on).

Given our undertaking, this study must be viewed as the first step of a fully-fledged research programme. A number of issues which are significant for substantiating our conclusions have not been analyzed in-depth, or have been ignored. These include, above all, rigorous analysis of the determination of various aspects of intra-enterprise organization and their effects on efficiency performance. This is the weakest link in the study, where the reasoning is basically composed of propositions and hypotheses articulated with stylized facts. Other prominent issues are the modelling and investigation of technical change in China's dynamic industries, the spatial dimension of Chinese industrialization (especially the disparity of performance of different local authorities), the role of foreign capital (especially TNCs) in the past growth and in the future. Some of these issues are technical in nature, requiring refinement of analytical tools. Some others are related to China's specific political economy during the reform era, which is clearly of central importance and which requires insights into the Chinese reality.

Nevertheless, based on what has been done so far, this study still claims some merits in clarifying the Chinese experience of economic development and the actual forms and effects of market and institutional regulation thereof. At least, it warns against the prevailing practice of simply applying the notional 'pure' market on the interpretation of the experience and based on which prescribing policy that affects the livelihood of a significant proportion of humankind, that is people in China and countries of the former Soviet bloc.

Notes

1 OVERVIEW

1. These include McMillan and Naughton (1992) and Wang (1993) on the reform-growth dynamics, Byrd (1991) on the allocative function of the market-planning dual track system, Singh (1992) on State industrial policy, a series of joint studies by the Chinese Academy of Social Sciences, University of California at San Diego and University of Oxford on the reforms of State-owned enterprises, Weitzman and Xu (1994) on the property rights of rural enterprises, and Qian and Xu (1993) on the effect of the fragmented administrative framework on reform. The syntheses of these earlier studies by Naughton (1995) and Jefferson and Rawski (1994, 1995), among others, are likely to gain the position of a paradigm at least for some years.
2. Part two criticizes the TFP approach on both theoretical and empirical grounds. I argue that, for the purpose of comparing SOEs and TVEs, the approach is flawed because it cannot take into full account the varied vintages of technology/capital (and skill/labour), in the context of structural change. At another level, measured TFP cannot be regarded as determined by enterprise efficiency alone; it is also affected by the macroeconomic and developmental settings, which in the Chinese case have involved a complex mix of market and institutional regulation. Finally, in a context of underemployment of productive inputs, it is not clear that the importance of TFP growth must supersede the growth of output *per se*. Even if it is true that Chinese SOEs have experienced slow TFP growth and, further, that this really reflects inefficiency, it is still not clear that the massive output decline of SOEs in countries of the former Soviet bloc represents a model that is superior to the substantial output growth of Chinese SOEs.
3. In this connection, it is worthwhile to say a few words on the recent policy debate over the issue of competitiveness of national economies. Krugman's (1994a, 1994b) critique of the arguments for (and implied policy prescriptions from) focusing on competitiveness, while not without merits, does not convince me that the concept must be discarded altogether. In particular, he simply ignores (or at some points dismisses in a casual way) the central proposition put forth by the writers whom he criticizes: that the productivity growth of the economy as a whole is affected by the economic structure – that is, by the development of high growth-potential industries, which are normally involved in acute competition in the world market (see, eg Tyson 1993).

2 TOWARDS AN ALTERNATIVE PERSPECTIVE ON SYSTEMIC TRANSFORMATION

1. It should be noted that the emphasis on (world) market determination of specialization is unambiguously central to the orthodox writings. The

catchphrase 'getting the relative prices right' further specifies comparative advantage – at a point in time and changes over time – as being 'given' by the relative scarcity of factors inputs. Beyond this, there is the division over what exactly the 'factor inputs' refer to. Little (1982), following the Heckscher-Ohlin-Samuelson theory, regards comparative advantage as being determined by a nation's endowment of 'capital' and 'labour'. Balassa (1977, 1981), in contrast, broadens the coverage to include labour, skill, physical capital and technology.

2. Romer (1990) attempts to model increasing returns at the firm level. But the conclusion which he arrives at is rather ambiguous with respect to whether perfect competition still can be preserved. On the whole, he tends to conclude that it cannot. Romer (1994, p. 19) finally proclaims that perfect competition should be abandoned by growth theorists: 'we have gone through a progression that starts with models based on perfect competition, moves to price-taking with external increasing returns, and finishes with explicit models of imperfect competition'. In this connection, it is noted that while Romer considers the construction of 'an alternative to perfect competition and Pareto optimality' as the primary achievement of new growth theory, Solow (1994) claims that perfect competition is not essential to neoclassical growth theory. This gives rise to the vexed question as to what actually constitutes the core of neoclassical economics. Fortunately, we need not dwell on this question, because in the industrialization debate the orthodox position is clear enough: let the market reign.
3. The causation between the trajectory of innovations and the organization form, as Piore (1992) notes, rests on the fact that the division of labour involves not only specialization but also re-integration. For mass production, with detailed division of labour: 'the conceptual categories in terms of which the elements of production were performed were distinct from the categories of the final product. This created a problem of re-integration, which led in turn to a hierarchical organizational form' (p. 169). For flexible specialization, re-integration is achieved through network organization. Here, the degree of horizontal interaction across specialties is too intense to permit a market, ie purely arm's-length exchanges (see also Best 1990).
4. Amsden (1990, p. 10) criticizes: 'we know in retrospect from the failure of dependency theory that the dynamics of growth in the Third World cannot be analyzed satisfactorily in terms of the categories of "centre" and "periphery". To the extent that Lipietz employs these categories, he is a dependency theorist, and no more successful than they in explaining Third World industrialization.' Whether a theory is 'successful' or "failed" depends on the purpose which one expects it to serve. With its focus being placed at the global level, the regulationist approach is unlikely to be able to account for the diverse industrialization experiences of individual developing nations – nor is it intended to serve this aim (Lipietz 1987, p. 4). But what about treating it as a theory of global trends, non-deterministic?
5. In general equilibrium analysis the protection of one sector necessarily discriminates against another, so any imports protection amounts to a trade

regime with 'anti-export bias'. It is often asserted that the protection of upstream industries, eg machinery, would preclude downstream industries from getting imported inputs that they need to become export competitive. More generally, Balassa (1981, p. 5) puts it, 'the higher the rate of protection, the lower will be the exchange rate necessary to ensure equilibrium in the balance of payments, and the lower the amount of domestic currency exporters receive per unit of foreign exchanged earned'. Thus, in empirical research, trade regime neutrality is often defined as the ratio between the effective exchange rate for exports and that for imports being close to one, ie $EER_e/EER_m \approx 1$.

6. Rodrik (1992, p. 310), an occasionally non-orthodox writer, dismisses the Prebisch-Singer thesis and claims: 'a deterioration in primary commodity prices will naturally reorient an economy's resources toward industry (and services). Industrialization will be the automatic consequence of the shift in relative prices'. This ignores not just the arguments of forced specialization and path-dependency in radical political economy, but indeed all market-failure arguments over the regulation of the world market. In his understanding, 'market failures' (which he refers to as 'market distortions' like minimum wage law) rarely occur in trade and trade protection is hardly an appropriate corrective policy.
7. The position of information-economic theorists is less definitive regarding the nature of innovation and the efficacy of market regulation. Dasgupta and Stiglitz (1988) develop another game-theoretical model which departs more radically from neoclassical theory: if the nature of innovation is not transmissible knowledge but rather some kind of firm-specific learning, there would be cost advantage to incumbent firms which, in conjunction with positive entry/exit cost, would lead to monopoly. Market failure would be inevitable. They then ask: what accounts for the capability of the incumbent firms of being 'far-sighted' enough to accept initial loses in anticipation of eventual gains? They do not attempt an answer to the question. It is precisely at this point, ie the relationship between firm organization and innovation capacity, that the exploration of the late industrialization literature starts (see Thomson ed. 1993).
8. The argument concerning the conflicts between productive and allocative efficiency can be carried forward to the 'political structure' of the firm, ie the pattern of accountability of the managerial leadership. The 'managerial analogue of the classical capitalist firm model', a term coined by Putterman (1984) referring to the work of Jensen and Meckling, says that, to be able to obtain external financing, the firm must be organized in a hierarchical manner. Otherwise, if the firm follows the principles of labour management or co-determination, the risk of using the financial resources is diluted and the lenders would be unwilling to lend. Hansmann (1990) calls this the 'cost of the internal politics of the firm'. In contrast, in the spirit of economics of information, Gintis (1990) argues that the capital market, even if perfectly competitive, has the bias of favouring externally accountable firms, a bias that has no efficiency basis. At this point, one can push further to argue that, by discriminating against the active participation of workers, the capital market runs counter to the logic of the learning firm.

9. The term 'evolutionary' is subject to different interpretations. I retain the usage here just for convenience – it is highlighted by the self-styled evolutionary writers in the transformation debate. It is noted that traditionally there are evolutionary writers, notably those of the European neo-Schumpeterian school, who hold a historical perspective and emphasize the centrality of institutions (including the state) in economic development.
10. Boycko (1991) provides a purely political explanation to the existence of shortages. He claims that shortages are generated by prices being deliberately set below equilibrium level. This arises from the totalitarian nature of the State and the self-interests of bureaucrats: shortages play the role of rewarding privileges to those subordinate and loyal, and of maximizing bribes to bureaucrats. It follows that price decontrol would not cause any real economic effect. This explanation of shortages is unusual in the literature. One explanation, made famous by Kornai (1980), is that shortages stem from the soft budget constraint of enterprises, which, in turn, is underpinned by the domination of workers. Another explanation holds that the fundamental cause is the State's obligation, in implicit contracts, to subsidize virtually the entire urban population. A third explanation, especially for the severe shortages since the late 1970s, is under-development and external shocks, just like those debt-burdened developing nations. For a comprehensive collection of the literature, see Davis and Charemza eds. (1989).
11. This economic message, as Lazonick notes, goes with the neo-liberal political message of 'free to choose'. Since control over the allocation of resources is widely dispersed among households (assumed synonymous with individuals) in a free market economy, individuals are free from inherent personal commitment and dependence on the will of others. The exercise of social power, therefore, is considered to be playing no role in the operation of the capitalist economy. An elaboration, held by many East European intellectuals and in line with the property rights theory, is that private ownership is a 'basic human right' (see Kornai 1990; and the contrasting view in Bowles and Gintins 1993).
12. This argument is derived from neo-liberal political economy: the state is no more than a collection of self-interested bureaucrats. Its ignores the aspects of legitimation and ideology in shaping the character of the state (Toye 1987).
13. Kornai (1990, pp. 70–3) dismisses any form of 'property reforms' in the context of the Soviet-type economic system, ie public ownership and centralized redistribution. He criticizes proponents of the reforms of not accepting the truth that any reforms not following the principle of natural-personal ownership are doomed hopeless. This, as we have argued, is not convincing both theoretically and empirically.

3 CHINESE INDUSTRIALIZATION IN STRUCTURALIST PERSPECTIVE

1. The description here runs counter to Chen *et al.* (1992, p. 221) who state: 'administrative interference, price manipulation and corruption, as well as

attempts to monopolize production and trade at the local level, underscore the need for checks and balances in an effective market economy'. In so asserting, they perceive the 'distortions' or 'imperfections' as purely politically induced (as the headline 'The Importance of Checks and Balances and the Difficulty of Achieving These under a Communist Regime' further indicates). This is a thesis of neo-liberal political economy, based on the notion of the 'pure' market as being incompatible with all those 'authoritarian' features (see Chapter 2).

2. Regarding the mechanisms that enabled the investment expansion, a major one was the expansion of bank credits (on average around 20 per cent growth per annum), especially fixed-asset loans (30 per cent per annum). In principle, the central authorities had the power to control credits. In practice, however, local authorities also could influence the growth, especially because local banks were soft-budgeted and were economically dependent on the former. The central authorities have imposed restrictions on extra-budgetary investment, such as the need for approval for projects exceeding a certain amount or in particular industries. But this has been ineffective. One conspicuous result has been the expansion of extra-budgetary fixed-asset investment in excess of the planned target. During 1986–90, the actual investment was 1975bn yuan, 27 per cent in excess of the planned volume, of which extra-budgetary investment in capital construction exceeding the planned target by 117 per cent (SSB 1991). For elaborated accounts, see Tsang (1990) and Yenal (1990).
3. The product range of 'new' consumer goods is too wide to list. Suffice it to say that, for electrical and electronic equipment and appliances alone, there emerged from almost non-existence in the pre-reform period such products as tape recorders (25m sets annual output by 1988), electric fans (45m), electric irons (22m), electric cookers (9m), microwave ovens (2m), electric water heaters (2m), space heaters, vacuum cleaners, electronic pianos, electronic games, etc.
4. On the whole, and especially in the period prior to the 1989–91 austerity and readjustment, the lack of economies of scale, low technical efficiency and lack of R&D capability of the plants, accounted for the huge gap between their performance and the world competitive level. The case of microwave ovens production was a conspicuous example in the peak years of the 'new' industries-led boom. In 1987–8 the newly established production capacity jumped to 2m sets per annum. This capacity was distributed among 20 plants, all assembling plants as most of the key components are in fact 'high-tech' products. And while the output volume accounted for only 1 per cent of the world total, the number of plants was equivalent to two-thirds of Japan, South Korea, the US and Western Europe combined (YGXB, 11 March 1991, p. 1).
5. The local authorities-promoted upsurges in downstream processing industries also, in many cases, hindered specialized division of labour. In a sense, the expansion was akin to the 'Great Leap Forward' campaign of the late 1950s. In the case of the textile industry, China's production capacity of cotton yarn jumped from 18m spindles in 1984 to 36m in 1988, despite the decrease in the output volume of cotton from 626m tons to 415m in the meantime. This forced one-third of the spinning machines to lie idle;

and the most hard-hit were technologically advanced SOEs, as raw cotton was taken away by TVEs under local authorities protection. But TVEs employed mainly unskilled labour and backward production equipment (a major proportion being those scrapped by SOEs). The result was a steady deterioration of the overall efficiency of materials utilization and product quality. (For reports on the proliferation of TVEs and its unfavourable impact on the textile industry as a whole, see JJXB, 6 September 1990; JJRB, 18 August 1990; ZJXW, 13 June 1990; and JJCK, 25 March 1991).

6. It appears to be no coincidence that China's outstanding foreign debts by 1988 amounted to US$40bn, or 10.6 per cent of GNP (the liability ratio) and 84.4 per cent of foreign exchange earnings (the foreign debts ratio) that year, which equalled exactly the trade deficits that had accumulated during 1984–8. Nevertheless, because of the rapid growth of exports in the subsequent years, the foreign indebtedness has been within manageable limits: by 1994, outstanding foreign debts amounted to US$93bn, with the liability and foreign debts ratios being 17.6 per cent and 77.8 per cent, respectively. The ratio of payments of interest plus amortization to exports of goods and services, or the debt service ratio, has meanwhile increased from 6.3 per cent in 1988 to 9.1 per cent in 1994 (ZTN 1995, p. 225).
7. See JXDT, April 1992, pp. 15–16, and June 1992, pp. 3–4; ZGJW, April 1992, pp. 61–2. True that the sales slump of 'new' consumer durables was initially caused by the State austerity drive, especially the rise in interest rates for saving and the imposition of sales taxes. But the subsequent relaxation and abandonment of the measures did not result in the improvement of sales. In contrast to the massive economic rebound since the second half of 1991, the sales and production of the 'new' consumer durables have been lagging far behind.
8. The Guangdong ten-year development plan was issued by the provincial government in April 1991 and can be found in *Nanfang Ribao* [Southern Daily], 22 April 1991. For an analysis of the plan, see *Economic Research Report on Guangdong – A Review of the 1980s and the Prospects for the 1990s* (Hongkong: CERD Ltd, 1991). For the model of 'secondary import substitution', and the application to South Korea and Taiwan, see Schive (1990).
9. It must be noted that the State–market relationship in China during the 1980s was far more complex, and the argument here is not meant to be a comprehensive assessment. Only in the sense that the development of the linked upstream industries, and the indigenization of imported technology, could not have taken place under the unfettered regulation of the market, can the State strategy be regarded as a success. But the success was achieved at considerable cost: in the sample case, the successful development of picture tube production was largely responsible for the lack of funding, thus failed development, of other electronics sectors (especially semiconductors) that are arguably more important for the economy as a whole. This is not entirely a success from a structuralist point of view (see Chapter 6). From the neoclassical standpoint, it is an indication of bad policies and practices that 'mitigate against the development of labor-intensive sectors that accord with China's international comparative advantage'. (Chen *et al.* 1992, p. 219) Meanwhile, back to our context, the concept of the

'market' here refers to the specific situation of China in the 1980s: ie the regulation mechanism which would have emerged if the state gave up its intervention. Conceivably, in a different institutional and structural framework – eg the existence of big business groups in the styles of Japan and South Korea – it might still be possible that market regulation could enable the successful development of high-tech industries that are not in line with the given comparative advantage (Mody 1990).

4 (RE)INTERPRETING CHINESE ENTERPRISE REFORM

1. Most new entrants of LMEs are joint ventures between foreign investors and SOEs and, especially after 1992, corporatized former SOEs. Taking this into account, the output share of SOEs in LMEs is likely to have remained at the 90 per cent-plus level.
2. It thus can be misplaced to criticize the approach adopted here on the ground that we are 'comparing orange with apple'. In any event, the fact that Chinese LMEs have done well over most of the 1980s and that the vast majority of which have been SOEs says it all. Shock therapy advocates would certainly not be happy with privatizing small SOEs only, while leaving large enterprises in the state sector.
3. We express the output of LMEs as a share of township-and-above enterprises, rather than the national total. The reason is that village-and-below enterprises, whose output accounted for 3.5 per cent of the national total in 1980, 10 per cent in 1985 and 21 per cent in 1992, concentrate mainly in industries which are different from those where the state sector operates (there are no LMEs at this level). They are not the competitors of LMEs. If this category is taken into account, the share of LMEs in the national total increased from 41.7 per cent in 1980 to 42.3 per cent in 1985 and further to 43.0 per cent in 1992.
4. Nevertheless, it is probably this dismal performance that has prompted the State to rethink the industrialization strategy of the 1980s which was characterized by expanding the technologically backward sector at the expense of the advanced sector. There follows the series of measures adopted or announced since 1991 which are aimed at revitalizing LMEs. Especially important are the reduction of income tax rate from 55 per cent to 33 per cent, the exemption of contribution to the 'two funds', the application of the 1 per cent ratio of sales revenues for R&D expenditure, the replenishment of enterprise working capitals, and the increase in depreciation rates. All these have been put into effect step-by-step within three years from 1991.
5. More precisely, interest payment is a burden on SOEs because it is not treated as part of the cost of production by the state – the owner of the enterprises. Meanwhile, it might be argued that bank borrowing cannot be harmful to SOEs because they always have the option of not to borrow (while COEs might not have the option to borrow in the first place). This counter-intuitive argument, however, might not be valid because it fails to take into account the difference between the (long-term) interests of the enterprise and the (short-term) interests of its inside members. There are

many reports by Chinese press of managers who complain that to borrow would lead to unbearable financial burdens for the enterprises in the long term, but not to borrow would result in enterprises stopping operation immediately. Finally, precisely because of recognizing the long-term danger of this 'double squeeze' on SOEs, in early 1995, the State authorities announced a package of measures to transform SOEs debts into State-owned equity. This covers the borrowing by all SOEs during 1984–8 (amounting to 66bn yuan) and the borrowing by selected SOEs, mainly those designated for experimenting further reforms in the second half of the 1990s, in subsequent years (see JRSB, 7 October 1995, p. 1).

6. This caveat is necessary because the analytics used here are not the received wisdom. Put plainly, while it is safe enough to claim without support that soft budget constraint is bad, our claim that it can also be good must draw on some well-developed (albeit non-orthodox) theories. More generally, while mainstream writings can treat marketization and private ownership as by assumption good for economic development (examples abound, just take two: Chen *et al.* 1992, and even Naughton 1994), our contention about the possible detrimental effects must be argued. Of course, it is not my intention to jump to the other extreme of totally denying the conducive effects of market competition in the Chinese experience; I rather seek to provide an account that is more balanced than the single-minded emphasis on the market, and dismissal of non-market.
7. It goes without saying that the lending-for-appropriation reform is alone adequate in constraining soft-budgeted behaviour. Indeed, some Hungarian economists have pointed out that the experience in their country is different: enterprises continue to exhibit soft-budgeted behaviour after the substitution of bank lending for State appropriation as the main source of external financing. In the light of the discussion here, one possible explanation for this divergence of experience is that the financial reform in China has been carried out within a wider context of the formation of the nexus of control, whereas Hungarian enterprises are in the main still dealing with a single-state agency and hence can have the expectation of trying to capture the agency (this point comes out from a discussion with Hugo Radice, see also Lo and Radice 1995).
8. In accounting for input-output performance, neoclassical theory focuses on allocative efficiency. Recent writings on endogenous growth incorporate increasing returns into analysis, but still focus on market competition. In contrast, structuralist development economics emphasizes the effect of macro-conditions on micro-level efficiency (eg the effect of income distribution on firms' capacity utilization; see Taylor 1985), while the late industrialization literature extends its investigation to the organizational capability of the firm and the role of market-governing, Schumpeterian entrepreneurship (Lazonick 1991; Teece 1993). On the whole, all these different strands tend to accept that the assumption of global production functions is not tenable and that technological development deliberately promoted by economic agents explains much of the observed experiences of development and underdevelopment (for two schematic expositions which though of contrasting theoretical persuasions have arrived at this same point, see Romer 1994, and Piore 1992; see also Chapter 2 for a survey).

9. With the market condition and technological opportunities depicted above, the observed behaviour of LMEs to enhance their innovation capacity can be seen as entrepreneurial. One indication is their R&D activity. Between 1985 and 1993, the number of LMEs with in-house R&D centres increased from 1913 to 9503, or 29 per cent and 51 per cent respectively of the total. Of the total amount of investment funds for R&D activity, the proportion of funds raised by enterprises themselves increased from 31 per cent to 68 per cent. By 1993, the number of Government-contracted R&D projects accounted for 32 per cent of the total, with the remainder being initiated by enterprises in response to market demand (ZTN 1994, p. 602; Ma 1993). At another level, the increased innovation capacity of LMEs are also based on the widespread application of flexibility-orientated measures such as the Japanese just-in-time practice, in both intra-firm work organization and the co-ordination between assembling firms and parts producers. Again, this is possible because of the long-term commitment of the participants (see chapter seven).

5 TESTING ALTERNATIVE EXPLANATIONS OF GROWTH

1. The official price index for GVIO at the level of national total (which we use to deflate the current-price NVIO of township-and-above independently accounting enterprises in the text), and that for NVIO at the level of township-and-above enterprises, in the years of 1979–85 are given below (ZGJTZ 1949–1984, p. 41; ZGJTZ 1986, p. 136; Table 5.11):

	1979	*1980*	*1981*	*1982*	*1983*	*1984*	*1985*
GVIO deflator	101.54	102.31	102.77	102.58	102.56	103.99	109.27
NVIO deflator	101.38	98.81	100.14	99.81	99.92	102.67	105.40

It can be seen that the GVIO deflator persistently exceeds that of NVIO, implying that we have over-deflated the output figures in the text. Meanwhile, the official price index for fixed-asset investment in the years of 1991–4 is 109.5, 115.3, 126.6 and 110.4, respectively, while our constructed one is 104.1, 108.4, 128.9 and 108.7, respectively (ZTN 1993, p. 269; ZTN 1995, p. 250; Table 5.15). Again, the official deflator tends to exceed the constructed one, implying that we have under-deflated the figures of capital stock in the text.

2. Note that the problem of simultaneity bias can also be present in production function analysis. If productivity growth is at least partially demand-driven, ie if Verdoorn's law as interpreted by Kaldor is to some extent valid, then TFP growth would be both a cause and a consequence of output growth. Thus, TFP analysis and Verdoorn's law can be seen as two extreme cases, the former assuming purely supply-driven growth while the latter assuming purely demand-driven growth. Again, in both cases, simultaneity bias is just a potential problem and whether it is present or not is an empirical issue. Our estimation results of equations (3) and (5) suggest

that, in the case of Chinese industry, both of the two approaches have significant explanatory power and both might to some extent suffer from the problem of simultaneity bias.

6 THE ELECTRONICS INDUSTRY: STATE INDUSTRIAL POLICY AND DEVELOPMENT

1. Subsequent developments of the Xianyang plant (which adopts the name of Caihong Electronics Corp.) have been spectacular. By 1994, of the nine manufacturers of colour picture tubes in the country, eight were Sino-foreign joint ventures – the exception being Caihong. That year, Caihong turned out 4.4m tubes (of which 1.1m were exported), accounting for one-third of the national total. The local content of its products reached 90 per cent, that of producing equipment 82 per cent and main structure materials 60 per cent.

   More important is the technology capability which Caihong has built up. In 1992, it successfully developed the production technology of high definition picture tubes. It is only with this breakthrough that Japanese TNCs have become willing to transfer similar technology to China. In 1994, Caihong independently upgraded its two production lines to reach a capacity of 2.4m tubes a year each. The total cost actually incurred was 18.5m yuan, far less than Toshiba's quotation: 2bn yen! In 1995, Toshiba finally entered into an agreement with Caihong to jointly develop a range of international frontier products, which would use the brandnames of both of the two companies (RMRB, 7 November 1995, p. 1).
2. It can be generalized from our depiction of the indigenization of colour TV technology that, because of the huge investment and high risk involved, the achievement of the task can be well beyond the capacity of the short-term profit-seeking, atomistic firm of the Walrasian 'pure' market. This is indeed a conclusion drawn by Mody (1990) from the development experiences of the electronics industries of Taiwan and South Korea.
3. The conglomerate Shanghai Broadcasting Electronics Group, which emerged in 1992, was formed through a system of mutual share-holding among four TV manufacturers and three trading companies in the municipality: No.1 TV Works, No.18 Radio Works, No.4 Radio Works, and Shanghai Broadcasting Equipment Works, which by sales revenue ranked the 1st, 4th, 5th and 11th, respectively, in the country's TV industry in 1989. Nanjing Radio Works of Jiangsu province, which in 1989 ranked the 2nd took over Nanjing TV Works, ranked the 18th, to maintain its position as the 2nd in 1992. It was later renamed Panda Electronics Group. Beijing TV Works (ranked the 9th in 1989) merged with Beijing Dongfeng TV Works (17th) to become the Mudan TV Group, which ranked the 7th in 1992, and 21st in 1994.
4. The success of the consumer electronics sector was based on enormous costs, and, in terms of opportunity cost, it is unclear that its development is a desirable choice for the Chinese electronics industry (and indeed the economy) as a whole. Initial estimation of investment in the four designated picture tubes projects amounted to 2.38bn yuan. This increases to

4.14bn yuan if three of the four Guangdong projects are taken into account, and to around 10bn yuan for all the 18 projects. But picture tubes investment accounts for only part of the total investment in indigenizing colour TV technology. An official report puts the total investment in the Sixth and Seventh Five-Year-Plan periods (1981–90) at 11.4bn yuan, of which US$2.1bn was in foreign exchange. Even these conservative estimates account for a big proportion of the investment in the electronics industry as a whole during the same period: 18bn yuan, including US$3bn foreign exchange. This explains the lack of investment in the semiconductor and computer sectors. From the standpoint of prioritizing dynamic industries, where TV production is hardly qualified for such an overwhelming position, it also points to the limitation of market-oriented import substitution (see Chapter 3).

5. In an interview with officials of Shanghai electronics industrial authorities in August 1993 I was told that, because of the abrupt change of market demand towards very large screen TV sets, the technology indigenized through joint R&D activity was under the threat of becoming obsolete.
6. Within the three years 1987–9, there were 235 enterprises belonging to the four prioritized sub-sectors which enjoyed the preferential treatments of tax reduction and R&D subsidies, amounting to a total of 601m yuan. This funding has enabled the enterprises to invest in technical renovation, resulting in the increase of output value by 200 per cent, realized profits by 180 per cent and export earnings by 13 times. A related feature is the attempt of the State to put into effect the principle of reciprocity between itself and the subsidized enterprises. The latter has had to strive for good performance in technological and economic terms in order to obtain the preferential treatments of the former. Thus, in 1991, of the 223 subsidized enterprises, 131 were incumbents while another 92 were newly entitled, meaning that 104 incumbents had lost their favourable positions for not meeting the condition.
7. One indication is that by 1991 the actual output volume of ICs was far closer to the design capacity than that before the implementation of the State industrial policy – in 1987, of the 30-plus production lines imported in the first half of the 1980s, only three were running while the rest lay idle due to the inability of the enterprises to master the technology.
8. The Chinese computer industry, which was originally given top priority in the electronics industry Seventh Five-Year-Plan, also failed in achieving its targets. In 1990, China produced 78 000 micro-computers, 478 mainframe and mini computers and 320 000 peripherals, which represent 78 per cent, 60 per cent and 54 per cent, respectively, of the planned targets (ZJDGN-D, 1991, p. I-21). That the development lag of semiconductors and computers was largely due to insufficient investment, in contrast to the TV-and-related sector, is widely reported by Chinese press.
9. This was disclosed in an interview by industrial officials of Shanghai, which is supposed to be a participant of the VLSI project. Also, there was no sign that the state investment in the HDTV project was forthcoming by August 1993.

7 THE MOTOR INDUSTRY: INSTITUTIONAL REFORM AND DEVELOPMENT

1. This comparison is of course not precise, because it involves the question as to how accurate the official exchange rate is in the representation of the purchasing power of China's currency. The fixed-assets of the Chinese motor industry encompass both tradable goods like machinery and non-tradable goods like construction.
2. By miniaturization, we refer to two related phenomena. One is that the plant scales are well below the minimum efficient scales by world standards. Another is the formation of new plants which replicate existing plants (eg using the same machinery) but on a smaller scale.
3. The 1991–4 auto boom, together with the wave of mergers and takeovers prior to it, has significantly eased the problems of fragmentation of the industry and miniaturization of plant scales. By 1994, the output volume of the biggest four firms – DAC, FAW, Tianjin Auto and Shanghai Auto – reached 182 284, 178 299, 122 490 and 115 326 motor vehicles, respectively. In that year, there were another three firms whose output volume exceeded 50 000 motor vehicles (ZQGN 1995, p. 57)
4. In late 1993, CNAIC's power of sectoral management was transferred to the newly-established Auto Industrial Bureau under the Ministry of Machine-building Industry (MMI). In a sense, this can be seen as a move of further centralization, thus indicating further direct State involvement. Unlike CNAIC, whose power is limited within the jurisdiction of the MMI, the new bureau is empowered to manage the entire sector, ie including automobile enterprises affiliated to other ministries such as aerospace and defence industries (JDRB, 13 November 1993, p. 1).
5. The adoption of the just-in-time practice is not confined to SAW. In the case of FAW, it is reported that the application of the practice on gear box production has yielded the following results: per worker output value increasing from 99 000 yuan to 163 500 yuan, total output increasing from the designed capacity of 68 000 units to 120 000 units, sub-quality products reduced by 33.5 per cent, and the proportion of quality products lifted from 80 per cent to more than 95 per cent. FAW adopted the practice directly from Toyota of Japan (JJCK, 17 July 1993, p. 1).

Sources of Data

YEARBOOKS AND OTHER STATISTICAL PUBLICATIONS

Beijing Gongye Nianjian [Beijing Industry Yearbook] (BGN); *China's Latest Economic Statistics* (CLES); *Huadong Diqu Tongji Nianjian* [Statistical Yearbook of East China] (HDTN); *Shanghai Jingji Nianjian* [Shanghai Economic Yearbook] (SJN); *Zhongguo Caizheng Tongji* [China Finance Statistics] (ZCT); *Zhongguo Dianzi Gongye Nianjian* [China Electronics Industry Economy Yearbook] (ZDGN); *Zhongguo Gongye Jingji Tongji Nianjian* [Statistical Yearbook of China's Industry Economy] (ZGJTN); *Zhongguo Gongye Jingji Tongji Ziliao* [China Industrial Economics Statistical Information] (ZGJTZ); *Zhongguo Gongye Nianjian* [China Industrial Economy Yearbook] (ZGN); *Zhongguo Jingji Nianjian* [Almanac of China's Economy] (ZJN); *Zhongguo Jingji Tizhi Gaige Nianjian* [China Economic System Reform Yearbook] (ZJTGN); *Zhongguo Jixie Dianzi Gongye Nianjian: Dianzi Juan* [Yearbook of China's Machinery and Electronics Industry: Electronics Volume] (ZJDGN-D); *Zhongguo Jixie Dianzi Gongye Nianjian: Jixie Juan* [China Machinery and Electronics Industry Yearbook: Machinery Volume] (ZJDGN-J); *Zhongguo Qiche Gongye Nianjian* [China Automobile Industry Yearbook] (ZQGN); *Zhongguo Shangye Waijing Tongji Ziliao* [China's Commerce and Foreign Trade Statistical Information] (ZSWTZ); *Zhongguo Tongji Nianjian* [China Statistical Yearbook] (ZTN); *Zhongguo Tongji Zaiyao* [China statistical survey] (ZTZ).

NEWSPAPERS

China Daily (CD); *China Daily, Business Weekly* (CD-BW); *Dianzi Shichan* [Electronics Markets] (DZSC); *Fazhi Ribao* [Legal Daily] (FZRB); *Guoji Shanbao* [International Business News] (GJSB); *Jiefang Ribao* [Liberation Daily] (JFRB); *Jingji Cankao* [Economic Information] (JJCK), renamed *Jingji Cankao Bao* in 1992; *Jingji Daokan* [Economic Herald] (JJDK); *Jingji Gongzuozhi Tongsun* [Bulletin for Economists] (JGT); *Jingji Ribao* [Economic Daily] (JJRB); *Jingji Wanbao* [Economic Evening Post] (JJWB); *Jingji Xinxi Bao* [Economic Information News] (JJXB); *Jingrong Shibao* [Financial Times] (JRSB); *Nanfang Ribao* [Southern Daily] (NFRB); *Renmin Ribao* [People's Daily] (RMRB); *Shanghai Gongye Jingji Bao* [Shanghai Industrial Economic News] (SGJB); *Shoudu Jingji Xinxi Bao* [Capital Economic Information News] (SJXB); *Xinan Dianli Bao* [Southwest Electricity Bao] (XNDB); *Xiaofei Shibao* [Consumption Times] (XFSB); *Xinxi Shibao* [Information Times] (XXSB); *Xiaofei Shibao* [Consumption Times] (XFSB); *Yuegang Xinxi Bao* [Guangdong-Hongkong Information] (YGXB); *Yatai Jingji Shibao* [Asia-Pacific Economic Times] (YJSB); *Zhongguo Dianzi Bao* [China Electronics Industry News] (ZDZB); *Zhongguo Gongshang Bao* [China Industry and Commerce News] (ZGSB); *Zhongguo Jidian Bao* [China Machinery and Electronics Industry News] (ZJDB),

Zhongguo Jixie Bao before 1988 and renamed *Jidian Ribao* (JDRB) in 1993; *Zhongguo Jingji Xinwen* [China Economic News] (ZJXW); *Zhongguo Junzhuangmin Bao* [China Defence-turn-Civilian Industry News] (ZJMB); *Zhongguo Meitan Bao* [China Coal Mining Industry News] (ZMTB); *Zhongguo Qiche Bao* [China Automobile Industry News] (ZQB); *Zhongguo Tongji Xinxi Bao* [China Statistical Information News] (ZTXB); *Zhongguo Xiangzhen Qiye Bao* [China Township-Village Enterprises News] (ZXQB).

MAGAZINES

China Trade Report (CTR); *Guangli Shijie* [Management World] (GLSJ); *Jingji Guangli* [Economic Management] (JJGL), monthly; *Jingji Yanjiu* [Economic Research] (JJYJ), monthly; *Jingjixue Dongtai* [Developments in Economics] (JXDT), monthly; *Zhongguo Gongye Jingji Wenti* [Problems of China's Industrial Economy] (ZGJW), monthly; *Zhongguo Gongye Jingji Yanjiui* [Studies in China's Industrial Economy] (ZGJY), monthly.

Bibliography

1. IN ENGLISH

Alchian, A. and H. Demsetz (1972) 'Production, Information Costs, and Economic Organization', *American Economic Review*, 62 pp. 777–95.

Altshuler, A., M. Anderson, D. Jones, D. Ross and J. Womack (1984) *The Future of the Automobile: the Report of MIT's International Automobile Programme*, London: George Allen & Unwin.

Amsden, A. (1989) *Asia's Next Giant: South Korea and Late Industrialization*. New York: Oxford University Press.

—— (1990) 'Third World Industrialization: "Global Fordism" or a New Model?', *New Left Review*, no. 182, pp. 5–31.

Aoki, M. (1990) 'Toward an Economic Model of the Japanese Firm', *Journal of Economic Literature*, vol. 28, pp. 1–27.

Aoki, M., B. Gustafsson and O.E. Williamson (eds.) (1990) *The Firm as a Nexus of Treaties*. London: SAGE Publications.

Auerbach, P. (1988) *Competition: The Economics of Industrial Change*. Oxford: Basil Blackwell.

Balassa, B. (1977) 'A Stage Approach to Comparative Advantage', Staff Working Paper no. 256, World Bank. Reprinted in B. Balassa (1981) *The Newly Industrializing Countries in the World Economy*. New York: Pergamon Press.

—— (1981) 'The Process of Industrial Development and Alternative Development Strategies', in B. Balassa (1981) *The Newly Industrializing Countries in the World Economy*. New York: Pergamon Press.

—— (1986) 'China's Economic Reform in a Comparative Perspective', World Bank Development Research Department Discussion Paper, no. 177. Reprinted in Balassa (1989) *New Directions in the World Economy*. London: MacMillan.

Berglof, E. (1990) 'Capital Structure as a Mechanism of Control: a Comparison of Financial Systems', in Aoki *et al.* (eds.) (1990).

Best, M. (1990) *The New Competition: Institutions of Industrial Restructuring*. Cambridge: Polity Press.

Bina, C. and B. Yaghmaian (1990) 'Post-war Global Accumulation and the Transnationalization of Capital', *Review of Radical Political Economics*, vol. 22 (1), pp. 78–97.

Bliss, C. (1989) 'Trade and Development', in H.B. Chenery and T.N. Srinivasan eds. *Handbook of Development Economics*, vol. 2, Elsevier Science Publishers B.V.

Bloomfield, G. (1991) 'The World Automotive Industry in Transition', in Law ed. (1991).

Borensztein, E. and M. Kumar (1991) 'Proposals for Privatization in Eastern Europe', *IMF Staff Papers*, vol. 38, no. 2, pp. 300–26.

Bowles, P. and X. Dong (1994) 'Current Successes and Future Challenges in China's Economic Reforms', *New Left Review*, no. 208, p. 49–76.

Bowles, S. (1985) 'The Production Process in a Competitive Economy: Walrasian, Neo-Hobbesian, and Marxian Models', *American Economic Review*, 75, pp. 16–36.

Bowles, S. and H. Gintis (1993) 'The Revenge of Homo Economicus: Contested Exchange and the Revival of Political Economy', *Journal of Economic Perspectives*, vol. 7, no. 1, pp. 83–102.

Boycko, M. (1991) 'Price Decontrol: The Microeconomic Case for the "Big Bang" Approach', *Oxford Review of Economic Policy*, vol. 7, no. 4, pp. 35–45.

Boyer, R. (1988) 'Technical Change and the Theory of "*Regulation*"', in G. Dosi *et al.* (eds.) *Technical Change and Economic Theory*. London: Pinter Publishers.

Boyer, R. and P. Petit (1991) 'Kaldor's Growth Theories: Past, Present and Prospects for the Future', in E. Nell and W. Semmler (eds.) *Nicholas Kaldor and Mainstream Economics: Confrontation or Convergence?* London: Macmillan.

Byrd, W. (1991) *The Market Mechanism and Economic Reforms in China*. New York: M. E. Sharpe.

—— (1992a) 'Chinese Industrial Reform, 1978–89', in W. Byrd (ed.) *Chinese Industrial Firms under Reform*, Oxford: Oxford University Press.

—— (1992b) 'The Second Motor Vehicle Manufacturing Plant', in W. Byrd (ed.) *Chinese Industrial Firms under Reform*, Oxford: Oxford University Press.

Chen, K., G. Jefferson and I. Singh (1992) 'Lessons from China's Economic Reform', *Journal of Comparative Economics*, vol. 16, pp. 201–25.

Chen, K., H. Wang, Y. Zheng, G. Jefferson and T. Rawski (1988) 'Productivity Change in Chinese Industry: 1953–1985', *Journal of Comparative Economics*, vol. 12, pp. 570–91.

Chenery, H.B., S. Robinson and M. Syrquin (1986) *Industrialization and Growth: A Comparative Study*, New York: Oxford University Press.

Coombs, R., P. Saviotti and V. Walsh (1987) *Economics and Technological Change*. London: Macmillan.

Cusumano, M. (1992) *The Japanese Automobile Industry: Technology and Management at Nissan and Toyota*. Cambridge, Mass: Blackwell.

Dankbaar, B. (1990) 'International Competition and National Institutions: the Case of the Automobile Industry', in C. Freeman and L. Soete (eds.) *New Explorations in the Economics of Technical Change*. London: Pinter Publishers Ltd.

Dasgupta, P. (1988) 'Patents, Priority and Imitation or, the Economics of Races and Waiting Games', *The Economic Journal,* vol. 98.

Dasgupta, P. and J. Stiglitz (1988) 'Learning-by-Doing, Market Structure and Industrial and Trade Policies', *Oxford Economic Papers,* vol. 40, pp. 246–68.

Davis, C. and W. Charemza (eds.) (1989) *Models of Disequilibrium and Shortage in Centrally Planned Economies*. London: Chapman and Hall Ltd.

Demsetz, H. (1983) 'The Structure of Ownership and the Theory of the Firm', *Journal of Law and Economics*, 26, pp. 375–90. Reprinted (1988) in *Ownership, Control and the Firm*. Oxford: Basil Blackwell.

Dicken, P. (1992) *Global Shift: the Internationalization of Economic Activity*. Second edition, London: Paul Chapman Publishing Ltd.

Dosi, G. (1988a) 'Institutions and Markets in a Dynamic World', *The Manchester School*, vol. 56, no. 2.

—— (1988b) 'Sources, Procedures, and Microeconomic Effects of Innovation', *Journal of Economic Literature*, vol. 26.

Dosi, G., C. Freeman, R. Nelson, G. Silverberg and L. Soete (eds.) (1988) *Technical Change and Economic Theory*. London: Pinter Publishers.

Dutt, A.K. (1984) 'Stagnation, Income Distribution and Monopoly Power', *Cambridge Journal of Economics*, vol. 8, pp. 25–40.

Dutt, A.K. and K. Jameson (eds.) (1992) *New Directions in Development Economics*. Aldershot: Edward Elgar Publishing Ltd.

The Economist (1992) 'China: the Titan Stirs', 28 November 1992.

Ernst, D. and D. O'Connor (1992) *Competing in the Electronics Industry: The Experience of Newly Industrialising Economies*, Paris: OECD.

Evans, D. (1989) 'Alternative Perspectives on Trade and Development', in H.B. Chenery and T.N. Srinivasan ed. *Handbook of Development Economics*, vol. 2, Elsevier Science Publishers B.V.

Evans, D. and P. Alizadeh (1984) 'Trade, Industrialization, and the Visible Hand', *Journal of Development Studies*, vol. 21, no. 1, pp. 22–46.

Evans, P. (1986) 'State, Capital and the Transformation of Dependence: The Brazilian Computer Case', *World Development*, vol. 14, no. 7, pp. 791– 808.

—— (1992) 'Indian Informatics in the 1980s: The Changing Character of State Involvement', *World Development*, vol. 20, no. 1, pp. 1–18.

Fischer, S. (1993) 'Socialist Economy Reform: Lessons of the First Three Years', *American Economic Review*, vol. 83, no. 2, pp. 390–5.

Frank, A.G. (1981) *Crisis in the Third World*. London: Heinemann Educational Books.

Fransman, M. (1990) *The Market and Beyond: Co-operation and Competition in Information Technology Development in the Japanese System*. Cambridge: Cambridge University Press.

Freeman, C. and C. Perez (1988) 'Structural Crises of Adjustment, Business Cycles and Investment Behaviour', in G. Dosi *et al.* (eds.) (1988) *Technical Change and Economic Theory*. London: Pinter Publishers.

Fröbel, F., J. Heinrichs and O. Kreye (1980) *The New International Division of Labour: Structural Unemployment in Industrialized Countries and Industrialization in Developing Countries*. Cambridge: Cambridge University Press.

Gintis, H. (1990) 'The Principle of External Accountability in Competitive Markets', in M. Aoki *et al.* (eds.) (1990).

Gordon, D. (1988) 'The Global Economy: New Edifice or Crumbling Foundations', *New Left Review*, no. 168.

Gordon, R. and W. Li (1991) 'Chinese Enterprise Behavior under the Reforms', *American Economic Review*, vol. 18, no. 2, pp. 202–6.

Groves, T., Y. Hong, J. McMillan and B. Naughton (1994) 'Autonomy and Incentives in Chinese State Enterprises', *Quarterly Journal of Economics*, vol. 109, no. 1, pp. 183–209.

Gwynne, R. (1991) 'New Horizons? The Third World Motor Vehicle Industry in an International Framework', in Law ed. (1991).

Hansmann, H. (1990) 'The Viability of Worker Ownership: An Economic Perspective on the Political Structure of the Firm', in Aoki *et al.* (eds.) (1990).

Harvey, D. (1989) *The Condition of Postmodernity: An Enquiry into the Origins of Cultural Change*. Oxford: Basil Blackwell.

Hay, D., D. Morris, G. Liu and S. Yao (1994) *Economic Reform and State-Owned Enterprises in China, 1979–1987*. Oxford: Clarendon Press.

Henderson, J. (1989) *The Globalization of High Technology Production: Society, Space and Semiconductors in the Restructuring of the Modern World*. London: Routledge.

Hill, R. (1989) 'Divisions of Labor in Global Manufacturing: the Case of the Automobile Industry', in A. MacEwan and W. Tabb (eds.) *Instability and Change in the World Economy*. New York: Monthly Review Press.

Hobday, M. (1991) 'Semiconductor Technology and the Newly Industrializing Countries: The Diffusion of ASICs (Application Specific Integrated Circuits)', *World Development*, vol. 19, no. 4, pp. 375–97.

—— (1995) *Innovation in East Asia: The Challenge to Japan*, Aldershot: Edward Elgar.

Hymer, S. (1971) 'The Multinational Corporation and the Law of Uneven Development', in J. Bhagwati ed. *Economics and World Order* (New York, Macmillan), reprinted in R. Cohen, N. Felton, M. Nkosi and J. van Liere (eds.) (1979) *The Multinational Corporation: a Radical Approach*, Cambridge: Cambridge University Press.

Jefferson, G. (1988) 'The Aggregate Production Function and Productivity Growth: Verdoorn's Law Revisited', *Oxford Economic Papers*, vol. 40, pp. 671–91.

Jefferson, G., T. Rawski and Y. Zheng (1992) 'Growth, Efficiency, and Convergence in China's State and Collective Industry', *Economic Development and Cultural Change*, vol. 40, no. 2, pp. 239–66.

Jefferson, G. and T. Rawski (1994) 'Enterprise Reform in Chinese Industry', *Journal of Economic Perspectives*, vol. 8, no. 2, pp. 47–70.

—— (1995) 'How Industrial Reform Worked in China: The Role of Innovation, Competition, and Property Rights', *Proceedings of the World Bank Annual Conference on Development Economics 1994*, pp. 129–56.

Jefferson, G. and W. Xu (1991) 'The Impact of Reform on Socialist Enterprises in Transition: Structure, Conduct, and Performance in Chinese Industry', *Journal of Comparative Economics*, vol. 15, pp. 45–64.

—— (1994) 'Assessing Gains in Efficient Production among China's Industrial Enterprises', *Economic Development and Cultural Change*, vol. 42, no. 3, pp. 597–615.

Jenkins, R. (1984) 'Divisions over the International Division of Labour', *Capital and Class*, no. 22, pp. 28–57.

—— (1985) 'Internationalization of Capital and the Semi-industrialized Countries: the Case of the Motor Industry', *Review of Radical Political Economics*, vol. 17 (1/2), pp. 59–81.

—— (1987) *Transnational Corporations and Uneven Development: Internationalization of Capital and the Third World*. London: Methuen.

—— (1991) 'The Political Economy of Industrialization: a Comparison of Latin American and East Asian Newly Industrializing Countries', *Development and Change*, vol. 22, no. 2, pp. 197–231.

Jones, D. (1988) 'Structural Adjustment in the Automobile Industry', OECD *STI Review*, no. 3, pp. 7–64.

Kaldor, N. (1966) 'Causes of the Slow Rate of Economic Growth in the United Kingdom', originally published by Cambridge University Press, reprinted in Kaldor (1978) *Further Essays on Economic Theory*, London: Duckworth.

Kaplinsky, R. (1985) 'Electronics-based Automation Technologies and the Onset of Systemofacture: Implications for Third World Industrialization', *World Development*, vol. 13, no. 3.

Kay, C. (1989) *Latin American Theories of Development and Underdevelopment*. London: Routledge.

Kay, N. (1988) 'The R and D function: Corporate Strategy and Structure', in Dosi *et al.* (eds.) (1988).

Kornai, J. (1980) *Economics of Shortage*. Amsterdam: North Holland.

—— (1990) *The Road to a Free Economy. Shifting from a Socialist System: the Example of Hungary*. New York: W.W. Norton and Company.

Kornai, J. and Z. Daniel (1990) 'The Chinese Economic Reform – as Seen by Hungarian Economists', in Kornai (1990) *Vision and Reality, Market and State: Contradictions and Dilemmas Revisited*. Hemel Hempstead: Harvester Wheatsheaf.

Krueger, A.O. (1984) 'Trade Policies in Developing Countries', in R. Jones and P. Kenen (eds.) *Handbook of International Economics*, Elsevier Science Publishers, B.V.

—— (1985) 'The Experience and Lessons of Asia's Super Exporters', in V. Corbo, A. Krueger and F. Ossa eds. (1985) *Export-oriented Development Strategies: the Success of Five Newly Industrializing Countries*. Boulder: Westview Press.

—— (1992) *Economic Policy Reform in Developing Countries*. Oxford: Blackwell.

Krugman, P. (1994a) 'Competitiveness: A Dangerous Obsession', *Foreign Affairs*, vol. 73, no. 2, pp. 28–44.

—— (1994b) 'The Myth of Asia's Miracle', *Foreign Affairs*, vol. 73, no. 6, pp. 62–78.

Kueh, Y. Y. (1991) 'The State of the Economy and Economic Reform', in Hsin-chi Kuan and Maurice Brosseau (eds.) *China Review*. Hongkong: Chinese University Press.

Lall, Sanjaya (1992) 'Technological Capabilities and Industrialization', *World Development*, vol. 20, no. 2, pp. 165–86.

Landsberg, M. (1979) 'Export-led Industrialization in the Third World: Manufacturing Imperialism', *Review of Radical Political Economics*, 11. Reprinted in R. Peet (ed.) (1987) *International Capitalism and Industrial Restructuring*. Boston: Allen & Unwin.

Law, C. (ed.) (1991) *Restructuring the Global Automobile Industry: National and Regional Impacts*. London: Routledge.

Lazonick, W. (1991) *Business Organization and the Myth of the Market Economy*. Cambridge: Cambridge University Press.

Lee, K. (1991) *Chinese Firms and the State in Transition: Property Rights and Agency Problems in the Reform Era*. New York: M.E. Sharpe.

—— (1993) 'Property Rights and the Agency Problem in China's Enterprise Reform', *Cambridge Journal of Economics*, vol. 17, pp. 179–94.

Lewis, W.A. (1954) 'Economic Development with Unlimited Supplies of Labour', *Manchester School*, vol. 22.

Lichtenstein, P. (1991) *China at the Brink: the Political Economy of Reform and Retrenchment in the Post-Mao Era*, New York: Praeger.

Lipietz, A. (1986) 'New Tendencies in the International Division of Labor: Regimes of Accumulation and Modes of Regulation', in A. Scott and M. Storper (eds.) (1986) *Production, Work, Territory: The Geographical Anatomy of Industrial Capitalism*. Boston: Allen & Unwin.

—— (1987) *Mirages and Miracles: The Crises of Global Fordism*, London: Verso.

Lipton, D. and J. Sachs (1990a) 'Creating a Market Economy in Eastern Europe: the Case of Poland', *Brookings Papers on Economic Activity*, 1, pp. 75–147.

—— (1990b) 'Privatization in Eastern Europe: the Case of Poland', *Brookings Papers on Economic Activity*, 2, pp. 293–341.

—— (1992) 'Prospects for Russia's Economic Reforms', *Brookings Papers on Economic Activity*, 2, pp. 213–83.

Little, I.M.D. (1982) *Economic Development: Theory, Policy and International Relations*. New York: Basic Books.

Lo, D. (1995a) 'Economic Theory and Transformation of the Soviet-Type System', in H-J. Chang and P. Nolan (eds.) *The Transformation of the Communist Economies: Against the Mainstream*, London, Macmillan.

—— (1995b) 'Techno-Economic Paradigm versus the Market: On Recent Theories of Late Industrialization', *Economy and Society*, 24 (3): 443–70.

—— (1995c) *The Chinese Motor Industry: The Changing Strategy of the State, Firms and Transnational Corporations, and the Prospects for Future Development*, 2nd edition, Hong Kong: CERD Consultants Ltd.

Lo, D. and H. Radice (1995) 'Institutional Change and Economic Development in Central-Eastern Europe and China: Contrasts in the light of the "East Asian Model"', Paper presented at the European Science Foundation workshop: *Dynamics of Industrial Transformation—East-Central European and East Asian Comparisons*, Budapest University of Economic Sciences, Budapest, Hungary, 4–7 May 1995.

Lucas, R. (1988) 'On the Mechanics of Economic Growth', *Journal of Monetary Economics*, vol. 22, pp. 3–42.

McCombie, J.S.L. and A.P. Thirlwall (1994) *Economic Growth and the Balance-of-Payment Constraint*, London: Macmillan.

McMillan, J. and B. Naughton (1992) 'How to Reform a Planned Economy: Lessons From China', *Oxford Review of Economic Policy*, vol. 8, no. 1, pp. 130–43.

Mody, A. (1990) 'Institutions and Dynamic Comparative Advantage: the Electronics Industry in South Korea and Taiwan', *Cambridge Journal of Economics*, vol. 14, pp. 291–314.

Morgan, K. and A. Sayer (1988) *Microcircuits of Capital: 'Sunrise' Industry and Uneven Development*, Cambridge: Polity Press.

Murrell, P. (1991) 'Can Neoclassical Economics Underpin the Reform of Centrally Planned Economies?' *Journal of Economic Perspectives*, vol. 5, no. 4, pp. 59–76.

—— (1992a) 'Evolutionary and Radical Approaches to Economic Reform', *Economics of Planning*, vol. 25, pp. 79–95.

—— (1992b) 'Evolution in Economics and in the Economic Reform of the Centrally Planned Economies', in C. Clague and G. Rausser (eds.) (1992)

The Emergence of Market Economies in Eastern Europe. Cambridge, Mass: Blackwell.

—— (1993) 'What is Shock Therapy? What Did it Do in Poland and Russia?', *Post-Soviet Affairs*, vol. 9, no. 2, pp. 111–40.

Naughton, B. (1991) 'Why Has Economic Reform Led to Inflation?' *American Economic Review*, vol. 18, no. 2, pp. 207–11.

—— (1992) 'Implications of the State Monopoly over Industry and its Relaxation', *Modern China*, vol. 18, no. 1, pp. 14–41.

—— (1994) 'What is Distinctive about China's Economic Transition? State Enterprise Reform and Overall System Transformation', *Journal of Comparative Economics*, vol. 18, pp. 470–90.

—— (1995) *Growing out of the Plan: Chinese Economic Reform, 1978–1993*, Cambridge: Cambridge University Press.

Nelson, R. (1981) 'Research on Productivity Growth and Productivity Differences: Dead Ends and New Departures', *Journal of Economic Literature*, vol. 19, pp. 1029–64.

Odagiri, H. (1992) *Growth through Competition, Competition through Growth: Strategic Management and the Economy in Japan*. Oxford: Clarendon Press.

Pack, H. and L. Westphal (1986) 'Industrial Strategy and Technological Change', *Journal of Development Economics*, vol. 22, pp. 87–128.

Perkins, D. (1988) 'Reforming China's Economic System', *Journal of Economic Literature*, vol. 26, pp. 601–45.

—— (1992) 'China's "Gradual" Approach to Market Reforms', paper presented at the conference on *Comparative Experiences of Economic Reform and Post-Socialist Transformation*, July 1992, El Escorial, Spain.

Piore, M. (1992) 'Technological Trajectories and the Classical Revival in Economics', in M. Storper and A. Scott (eds.) *Pathways to Industrialization and Regional Development*, London: Routledge.

Piore, M. and C. Sabel (1984) *The Second Industrial Divide: Possibilities for Prosperity*. New York: Basic Books.

Putterman, L. (1984) 'On some Recent Explanations of Why Capital Hires Labor', *Economic Inquiry*, 22, pp. 171–87. Reprinted in Putterman ed. (1986).

—— (1992) 'Dualism and Reform in China', *Economic Development and Cultural Change*, vol. 40, no. 3, pp. 467–92.

Putterman, L. (ed.) (1986) *The Economic Nature of the Firm*. Cambridge: Cambridge University Press.

Qian, Y. and C. Xu (1993) 'Why China's Economic Reforms Differ: The M-form Hierarchy and Entry/Expansion of the Non-state Sector', Centre for Economic Performance Discussion Paper no. 154, London School of Economics.

Rawski, T. (1993) 'How Fast Has Chinese Industry Grown?', World Bank Policy Research Working Papers: Transition and Macro-Adjustment, no. 1194, Washington D.C., the World Bank.

—— (1994) 'Chinese Industrial Reform: Accomplishments, Prospects, and Implications', *American Economic Review*, vol. 84, no. 2, pp. 271–5.

Rodrik, D. (1992) 'Conceptual Issues in the Design of Trade Policy for Industrialization', *World Development*, vol. 20, no. 3, pp. 309–20.

Romer, P. (1986) 'Increasing Returns and Long-run Growth', *Journal of Political Economy*, vol. 94, no. 5, pp. 1002–37.

—— (1990) 'Endogenous Technological Change', *Journal of Political Economy*, vol. 98, pp. S71–S102.

—— (1992) 'Two Strategies for Economic Development: Using Ideas and Producing Ideas', *Proceedings of the World Bank Annual Conference on Development Economics 1992*, pp. 63–91.

—— (1994) 'The Origins of Endogeneous Growth', *Journal of Economic Perspectives*, vol. 8, no. 1, pp. 3–22.

Sachs, J. and W.T. Woo (1994a) 'Reform in China and Russia', *Economic Policy*, no. 18, pp. 101–45.

Sawyer, M.C. (1989) *The Challenge of Radical Political Economy*, Hemel Hempstead: Harvester Wheatsheaf.

—— (1991) 'The Nature and Role of the Market', *Social Concept*, vol. 6, no. 2, pp. 25–45.

Sayer, A. and R. Walker (1992) *The New Social Economy: Reworking the Division of Labor*. Cambridge (Mass.) and Oxford: Blackwell.

Schive, C. (1990) 'The Next Stage of Industrialization in Taiwan and South Korea', in G. Gereffi and D. Wyman (eds.) *Manufacturing Miracles: Paths of Industrialization in Latin America and East Asia*. Princeton: Princeton University Press.

Schmitz, H. (1984) 'Industrialisation Strategies in Less Developed Countries: Some Lessons of Historical Experience', *Journal of Development Studies*, vol. 21, no. 1, pp. 1–21.

Schmitz, H. and R. Carvalho (1989) 'Automation and Labour in the Brazilian Car Industry', *Journal of Development Studies*, vol. 26, no. 1, pp. 81–119.

Schmitz, H. and J. Cassiolato (eds.) (1992) *Hi-tech for Industrial Development: Lessons from the Brazilian Experience in Electronics and Automation*. London: Routledge.

Schoenberger, E. (1989) 'Multinational Corporations and the New International Division of Labour: a Critical Appraisal', in S. Wood (ed.) (1989) *The Transformation of Work? Skill, Flexibility and the Labour Process*, London: Unwin Hyman Ltd.

Shapiro, C. and J. Stiglitz (1984) 'Equilibrium Unemployment as a Worker Discipline Device', *American Economic Review*, vol. 74, no. 3, pp. 433–4.

Singh, A. (1992) 'The Actual Crisis of Economic Development in the 1980s: an Alternative Policy Perspective for the Future', in A. Dutt and K. Jameson (eds.) *New Directions in Development Economics*, Aldershot: Edward Elgar.

—— (1993) 'Asian Economic Success and Latin American Failure in the 1980s: New Analyses and Future Policy Implications', *International Review of Applied Economics*, vol. 7, no. 3, pp. 267–89.

Singh, I. (1992) 'China: Industrial Policy for an Economy in Transition', *World Bank Discussion Papers*, no. 143, Washington D.C., the World Bank.

Solow, R. (1994) 'Perspectives on Growth Theory', *Journal of Economic Perspectives*, vol. 8, no. 1, pp. 45–54.

Stephen, F. and S. Thompson (1988) 'Internal Organization and Investment', in Thompson and Wright ed. (1988).

Stiglitz, J. and A. Weiss (1981) 'Credit Rationing in Markets with Imperfect Information', *American Economic Review*, vol. 71, no. 3, pp. 393–410.

Stoneman, P. and Vickers, J. (1988) 'The Assessment: The Economics of Technology Policy', *Oxford Review of Economic Policy*, 4, i–xvi.

Storper, M. (1991) *Industrialization, Economic Development, and the Regional Question in the Third World: From Import Substitution to Flexible Production*. London: Pion Ltd.

Taylor, L. (1985) 'A Stagnationist Model of Economic Growth', *Cambridge Journal of Economics*, vol. 9, pp. 383–403.

—— (1992) 'Structuralist and Competing Approaches to Development Economics', in A.K. Dutt and K. Jameson (eds.) *New Directions in Development Economics*. Aldershot: Edward Elgar.

Taylor, L. and P. Arida (1988) 'Long-run Income Distribution and Growth', in H.B. Chenery and T.N. Srinivasan ed. *Handbook of Development Economics*, vol. 1, Elsevier Science Publishers B.V.

Teece, D. (1988) 'Technological Change and the Nature of the Firm', in Dosi *et al.* eds. (1988).

—— (1993) 'The Dynamics of Industrial Capitalism: Perspectives on Alfred Chandler's *Scale and Scope*', *Journal of Economic Literature*, 31, pp. 199–225.

Thompson, S. and M.Wright (eds) (1988) *Internal Organization, Efficiency and Profit*. Oxford: Philip Allan Publishers Ltd.

Tirole, J. (1988) *The Theory of Industrial Organization*, Cambridge, Mass: MIT Press.

Toye, J. (1987) *Dilemmas of Development: Reflections on the Counter-Revolution in Development Theory and Policy*. Oxford: Basil Blackwell.

Tsang, S.K. (1990) 'Controlling Money During Socialist Economic Reform: the Chinese Experience', *Economy and Society*, vol. 19, no. 2, pp. 217–41.

—— (1992) 'Against Big Bang: Theoretical and Practical Arguments', Working Paper Series no. ES91020, Business Research Centre, Hongkong Baptist College.

Tylecote, A. (1992) *The Long Wave in World Economy: The Present Crisis in Historical Perspective*. London: Routledge.

Tyson, L. (1993) *Who's Bashing Whom? Trade Conflict in High-Technology Industries*, Washington D.C.: Institute for International Economics.

Wade, R. (1990) *Governing the Market: Economic Theory and the Role of Government in East Asian Industrialization*. New Jersey: Princeton University Press.

Wang, X. (1993) 'Groping for Stones to Cross the River – Chinese Price Reform against Big Bang', Discussion Paper on Economic Transition no. 9305, Department of Applied Economics, University of Cambridge.

Watanabe, S. (1987) 'Introduction', in Watanabe (ed.) *Microelectronics, Automation and Employment in the Automobile Industry*, Chichester: John Wiley & Sons.

Weiss, J. (1988) *Industry in Developing Countries: Theory, Policy and Evidence*. London: Routledge.

Weitzman, M. (1993) 'Economic Transition: Can Theory Help?', *European Economic Review*, 37, pp. 549–55.

Weitzman, M. and C. Xu (1994) 'Chinese Township-Village Enterprises as Vaguely Defined Cooperatives', *Journal of Comparative Economics*, vol. 18, pp. 121–45.

Williamson, O.E. (1985) *The Economic Institutions of Capitalism: Firms, Markets, Relational Contracting*. New York: Free Press.

—— (1989) 'Transaction Cost Economics', in R. Schmalensee and R.D.Willig (eds.) *Handbook of Industrial Organization*. Elsevier Science Publishers B.V.

Williamson, O.E., M. Wachter and J. Harris (1975) 'Understanding the Employment Relation: the Analysis of Idiosyncratic Exchange', *The Bell Journal of Economics*, vol. 6, pp. 250–78. Reprinted in Putterman (ed.) (1986).

Womack, J., D. Jones and D. Roos (1990) *The Machine that Changed the World*. New York: Rawson Associates.

Wong, C. (1986) 'The Economics of Shortage and Problems of Reform in Chinese Industry', *Journal of Comparative Economics*, vol. 10, pp. 363–87.

Woo, W.T. (1994) 'The Art of Reforming Centrally Planned Economies: Comparing China, Poland, and Russia', *Journal of Comparative Economics*, vol. 18, no. 3, pp. 276–308.

Woo, W.T., W. Hai, Y. Jin and G. Fan (1994) 'How Successful Has Chinese Enterprise Reform Been? Pitfalls in Opposite Biases and Focus', *Journal of Comparative Economics*, vol. 18, no. 3, pp. 410–37.

World Bank (1987) *World Development Report 1987*. New York: Oxford University Press.

—— (1991) *World Development Report 1991*. New York: Oxford University Press.

Wulwick, N. (1993) 'What Remains of the Growth Controversy', *Review of Political Economy*, vol. 5, no. 3, pp. 321–43.

Yaghmaian, B. (1990) 'Development Theories and Development Strategies: an Alternative Theoretical Framework', *Review of Radical Political Economics*, vol. 22 (2–3), pp. 174–88.

Yenal, O. (1990) 'Chinese Reforms, Inflation and the Allocation of Investment in a Socialist Economy', *World Development*, vol. 18, no. 5, pp. 707–21.

Zhang, W. (1993) 'Decision Rights, Residual Claim and Performance: a Theory of How the Chinese Economy Works', paper presented at the international symposium on *Economic Transition in China*, Haikou, China, July 1993.

2. IN CHINESE

China Academy of Social Sciences, Institute of Japan Studies (CASS-IJS) (1988) *Riben Jingji de Huali* [The dynamism of the Japanese economy], Beijing: Hangkong Gongye Chubanshe.

China Academy of Social Sciences and State Statistical Bureau (CASS-SSB) (1992) 'Dui 1992 Nian Guomin Jingji Fazhan de Yuce ji Fengxi' [Forecast and analysis of national economic development in 1992], *Jingji Yanjiu* [Economic Research], June, pp. 3–10.

China Economic System Reform Research Institute (CESRRI) (1987a) 'Weiguan Gaigezhong de Shichan Jiegou yu Qiye Zhidu' [Market structure and enterprise system under microeconomic reforms], *Zhongguo Shehui Kexue* [Social Sciences in China], no. 4, pp. 63–80. English translation in *Social Sciences in China*, 1988, vol. 9, no. 3, pp. 42–66.

—— (1987b) *Jiannan de Tansuo: Xiongyali, Nanshilafu Gaige Kaocha* [Formidable exploration: investigation of reforms in Hungary and Yugoslavia]. Beijing: Jingji Guangli Chubanshe.

—— (1988a) *Riben Moshi de Qishi* [Revelation from the Japanese model]. Chengdu: Sichuan Renmin Chubanshe.

—— (1988b) *Gongye Zengzhang yu Jiegouxing Maodun* [Industrial growth and structural contradictions], Chengdu: Sichuan Renmin Chubanshe.

—— (1988c) 'Xinxing Chanye de Chengzhang yu Qiye Zuzhi Jiegou de Gaizao' [Growth of new industries and restructuring of enterprise organization], *Zhongguo: Fazhan yu Gaige* [China: Development and Reform], February, pp. 26–33.

—— (1988d) 'Fazhan Chenbaozhi, Shenfa Qiye Gaige' [Developing the contractual system, furthering enterprise reforms], *Zhongguo: Fazhan yu Gaige* [China: Development and Reform], no. 3, pp. 3–8.

Dangdai Zhongguo de Dianzi Gongye [The Electronics Industry of Contemporary China]. The Editorial Committee, 1987. Beijing: Zhongguo Shehui Kexue Chubanshe.

Dianzi Gongye Fazhan Zhanlie Yantao [Research on the Developing Strategy of Electronics Industry] (DGFZY). 1991. A joint MEI–World Bank project, Beijing: Dianzi Gongye Chubanshe.

Du, Haiyan (1992) 'Quanguo Gongye Qiye Lianlun Chenbao Bijiao Fengxi' [A comparative analysis of the two rounds of contracts of industrial enterprises], *Gaige* [Reform], no. 5, pp. 98–104.

Du, Haiyan *et al.* (1990) 'Guoyou Qiye de Zizhuquan, Shichan Jiegou he Jilizhidu' [The autonomy, market structure and incentive system of state-owned enterprises], *Jingji Yanjiu* [Economic Research], no. 1, pp. 3–14.

Du, Haiyan and Guo Jinggang (1993) 'Zhongguo Guoyou Qiye Gaige: Shidu, Xingwei yu Xiaolu' [China's State-owned enterprises reform: institutions, behaviours and efficiency], *Dongyu Luncong* [East Mountain Forum], no. 1, pp. 35–48.

Fang Xiangdong (1993) 'Xianshi Jingji Gejuexia de Qiye Gaige' [Enterprise reform under the existing economic arrangement], *Jingji Yanjiu* [Economic Research], no. 5, pp. 24–31.

Guo, Jinggang (1992) 'Guoyou Gongye Qiye Jilijizhi de Biange ji Xiaoguo Pingjie' [Effects of reforming the incentive mechanisms of the State-owned industrial enterprises: an appraisal], *Jingji Yanjiu* [Economic Research], no. 10, pp. 23–32.

Hong, Xiaoyuan (1988) 'Qiye Jituan de Chengzhan yu Shichan Jizhi de Fayue' [The development of enterprise groups and the formation of the market mechanism], *Jingji Yanjiu* [Economic Research], January, pp. 18–26.

Hua, Sheng, He Jiacheng, Zhang Xuejun, Luo Xiaopeng and Bian Yongzhuang (1986) 'Weiguan Jingji Jichu de Chongxin Gouzao' [Reconstruction of the microeconomic foundation], *Jingji Yanjiu* [Economic Research], no. 3, pp. 21–8.

Hua, Sheng, Luo Xiaopeng and Zhang Xuejun (1988) 'Zhongguo Gaige Shinian: Huigu, Fanshi he Qianjing' [China's ten-year economic reform: retrospect, reflection and prospects], *Jingji Yanjiu* [Economic Research], no. 9, pp. 13–37, no. 11, pp. 11–30 and no. 12, pp. 10–28.

Jiang, Xiaojuan (1993) *Zhongguo Gongye Fazhan yu Duiwai Jingji Maoyi Guangxi de Yanjiu* [Study on China's industrial development and foreign economic relations], Beijing: Jingji Guangli Chubanshe.

Jiang, Xiaojuan, Zhao Ying, Ren Jijun, Liu Hong and Xiong Yun (1993) 'Woguo Gongye Zengzhang yu Jiegou Biandong de Rugan Xintezhen' [Some new features of China's industrial growth and structural change], *Zhongguo Gongye Jingji Yanjiu* [Studies on Chinese Industrial Economy], no. 8, pp. 32–40.

Kang, Rongping (1992) 'Jishu Yinjin: Guoji Bijiao ji Zhongguo de Zhanlie' [Technology imports: international comparison and China's strategy], *Guangli Shijie* [Management World], May, pp. 161–70.

Liu, Guoguang and Zhou Guiying (eds.) (1992) *Zhongguo Gaige Chuanshu: Gongye Qiye Tizhi Gaige Juan* [Encyclopedia of Chinese reform: industrial enterprise system reform], Dalian: Dalian Chubanshe.

Liu, Shijin (1993) 'Guangyu Guoyou Qiye Laodong Tizhi Gaige de Jige Wenti' [Several issues concerning the reform of the labour employment system of SOEs], *Jingji Lilun yu Jingji Guangli* [Economic Theory and Economic Management], no. 5, pp. 30–3.

Liu, Wei and Yang Yunlong (1987) *Zhongguo Chanye Jingji Fenxi* [Analysis of China's industrial economy], Beijing: China International Broadcasting Press.

Lu, Feng, Luo Fanzheng and Huang Weiping (1987) *Woguo Jingji Tizhi Gaige de Huigu he Zhangwan* [Retrospect and prospects of China's economic system reform], Beijing: Zhongguo Fanzhen Daxue Chubanshe.

Ma, Hong (1992) 'Zhongguo Jingji Tizhi Gaige de Xingzhuang yu Zhanwan' [The present situation and prospects of China's economic system reform], in Wu Jiajun and Wang Haibo (eds.) *Jiushiniandai Zhongguo Jingji de Gaige yu Fazhan* [China's economic reform and development in the 1990s], Beijing: Jingji Guagnli Chubanshe.

Ma, Jiantang (1992) 'Woguo Guoyuo Qiye Xingwei Mupiao de Shizheng Fengxi' [An empirical study of the behavioural objectives of our country's State-owned enterprises], *Jingji Yanjiu* [Economic Research], July, pp. 20–6.

Ma, Xiliang (1993) 'Quanguo Dazhongxing Gongye Qiye Jishu Kaifa he Jishu Maoyi Zhuangkuang de Tongji Fengxi' [A statistical analysis of the situation of R & D activity and technology transactions by large-and-medium industrial enterprises], *Kexuexue yu Kexue Jishu Guangli* [Sciences and Scientific and Technical Management], no. 2, pp. 32–7.

State Commission for Economic System Reform (SCESR) (1992) 'Jiushiniandai: Zhouxiang Chengshuo de Zhongguo Jingji' [China's economy in the 1990s: towards maturity], *Guangli Shijie* [Management World], no. 5, pp. 11–20.

—— (1990) *Zhongguo Qiye Gaige Shinian* [Ten Years of Chinese Enterprise Reform], Beijing: Gaige Chubanshe.

State Council-Office of Industrial Census Leading Group (SC-ICO) (1990) *Zhongguo Gongye Xianzhuang* [Current Situation of Chinese Industry], Beijing: Renmin Chubanshe.

State Council-Enterprise Management Office (SC-MEO) (1991) 'Guanyu Zhengqiang Qiye Fazhan Houjing de Shikao' [Considerations on the enhancement of the developmental capability of the enterprises], in *Zhongguo Jingji Tizhi Gaiye Nianjian 1991* [China Economic System Reform Yearbook 1991], Beijing: Gaige Chubanshe.

State Council-Policy Research Unit (SC-PRU) (1992) 'Guoying Gongye Qiye Jingji Xiaoyi Kaocha' [Investigation of the economic efficiency of State-owned industrial enterprises], *Zhongguo Shihui Kexue* [Social Sciences in China], March, pp. 3–14. English translation in *Social Sciences in China* (English edition).

State Planning Commission-Enterprise Management Bureau (SPC-EMB) (1991) 'Gaohuo Dazhongxing Qiye' [Re-vitalising the large-and-medium scale enterprises], *in Zhongguo Qiye Guangli Nianjian 1991* [China Enterprise Management Yearbook 1991], Beijing: Qiye Guangli Chubanshe.

State Statistical Bureau of China (SSB) (1991) *Qiwu Shiqi Guomin Jingji he Shehui Fazhan Gaikuang* [General situations of economic and social development during the Seventh Five-Year-Plan period]. Beijing: Zhongguo Tongji Chubanshe.

Tang, Zongkun (1992) 'Guoyuo Qiye Lirun Zhuangyi he Qiye Zaishenchan Nenli' [Drain and redistribution of profits and reproduction capacity of State-owned enterprises], *Jingji Yanjiu* [Economic Research], no. 7, pp. 9–19.

Wang, Huijiong, Li Boxi and Zhou Lin (eds.) (1989) *Zhongguo Bumen Changye Zhengce Yanjiu* [Studies on China's Industrial Policy for Various Industrial Branches]. Beijing: China Finance and Economics Press.

Wang, Huijiong and Li Boxi (eds.) (1991) *Zhongguo Zhongchangqi Changye Zhence* [China's medium and long term industrial policy], Beijing: Zhongguo Caizhen Jingji Chubanshe.

Wang, Xiaoqiang (1988) 'Chaoyue Shiyouzhi Luoji' [Transcending the logics of private ownership], *Zhongguo: Fazhan yu Gaige* [China: Development and Reform], April, pp. 27–31.

Wu, Jinglian and Qian Yingyi (1993) 'Guangyu Gongsifa' [On corporatization], JJRB, 24 August 1993, p. 1.

Wu, Jinglian and Zhou Xiaochuan *et al.* (1988) *Zhongguo Jingji Gaige de Zhenti Sheji* [The comprehensive design of China's economic reform]. Beijing: Zhongguo Zhanwan Chubanshe.

Wu, Lianfang (1992) 'Taiwan Dianzi Gongye Xianzhuang yu Zhangwang' [Present situation and prospects of Taiwan's electronics industry], *Haixia Keji Jiaoliu Yanjiu* [Exchanges of Sciences and Technology Across the Strait], no. 2, pp. 1–11.

Yang, Mu (1989) *Chanye Zhengce Yanjiu* [A Study on Industrial Policy]. Shanghai: Joint Publishing Ltd.

Zhang, Shaojie (1987) *Jingji Yunxing yu Jingji Tiaojie* [Economic operation and economic regulation]. Hanzhou: Zhejiang Renmin Chubanshe.

—— (1988) 'Zhongguo Jingji Shenchen Jiegou de Biange' [The transformation in the deep structure of China's economy], paper presented at the international conference on *The New Stage of China's Economic Reform*, Hongkong, December 1988.

Zheng, Hongliang (1992) 'Gaige Guochengzhong de Guoyou Qiye Xingwei' [State-owned enterprises Behaviours under reform], *Jingji Yanjiu* [Economic Research], no. 5, pp. 22–9.

—— (1993) 'Xiangzheng Qiye Zhidu Gouzhao Tedian ji Qidui Guoyou Qiye Gaige de Qishi' [Characteristics of the institutional set-ups of TVEs and revalations for the reform of SOEs], *Jingji Lilun yu Jingji Guangli* [Economic Theory and Economic Management], no. 1, pp. 46–51.

Index